Competition Law in Brazil

Competition Law in Brazil

Third Edition

José Inácio Gonzaga Franceschini
Eduardo Molan Gaban
Marcos Paulo Amorim

This book was originally published as a monograph in the International Encyclopaedia of Laws/Competition Law.

Founding Editor: Roger Blanpain
General Editor: Frank Hendrickx
Volume Editors: Francesco Denozza & Alberto Toffoletto

Wolters Kluwer

Published by:
Kluwer Law International B.V.
PO Box 316
2400 AH Alphen aan den Rijn
The Netherlands
Website: www.wolterskluwerlr.com

Sold and distributed in North, Central and South America by:
Wolters Kluwer Legal & Regulatory U.S.
7201 McKinney Circle
Frederick, MD 21704
United States of America
Email: customer.service@wolterskluwer.com

Sold and distributed in all other countries by:
Quadrant
Rockwood House
Haywards Heath
West Sussex
RH16 3DH
United Kingdom
Email: international-customerservice@wolterskluwer.com

Printed on acid-free paper

ISBN 97890-411-8735-2

e-Book: ISBN 97890-411-8758-1
web-PDF: ISBN 97890-411-8788-8

This title is available on www.kluwerlawonline.com

Printed and Bound by CPI Group (UK) Ltd, Croydon, CR0 4YY.

The Authors

José Inácio Gonzaga Franceschini was born in São Paulo, the capital city of the State of São Paulo, in 1949 and has been a member of the Brazilian Bar Association – São Paulo Chapter since 1973. He is a graduate of the School of Law of the University of São Paulo (USP), Class of 1972 and holds post-graduate degrees in Penal Economic Law and International Law.
He has been actively engaged with Administrative Council for Economic Defense (CADE) (the Brazilian Antitrust Agency) since 1973 and is the author of: *Poder Econômico: Exercício e Abuso – Direito Antitruste Brasileiro* (Revista dos Tribunais, 1985), *Introdução ao Direito da Concorrência* (Malheiros, 1996), *Lei da Concorrência Conforme Interpretada pelo CADE* (Singular, 1998), *Direito da Concorrência – Case Law* (Singular, 2000), *Jurisprudência do CADE 2000–2001* (Singular, 2002), *Jurisprudência do CADE 1962–2003* (Singular, 2004), *Ensaios Reunidos* (Singular, 2004) and *Direito Concorrencial* (vol. VII of *Tratado de Direito Empresarial,* Revista dos Tribunais, 2016, co-author Vicente Bagnoli), as well as of miscellaneous articles, notably on business, international and commercial law issues, both from the substantive and procedural aspects, with an emphasis on competition law.
Franceschini has been invited to be a speaker at several international and national conferences on competition law and is a member of the committee appointed by the Brazilian Antitrust Agency (CADE) to draft the Brazilian Competition Law. He was awarded the prize '*most admired in* (Infrastructure and Regulatory) *Law*' by *Análise Advocacia 500* (2009 and 2012) and the laurels of recognition for contributing to the dissemination and development of Competition Law in Brazil, granted by the Brazilian Bar Association, São Paulo (2015).
He is a member of the Council of the Brazilian Institute of Studies on Competition, Consumer Affairs and International Trade (IBRAC), the São Paulo Attorneys Association (AASP), the International Relations and the Antitrust Committees of the São Paulo Attorneys Institute (IASP), the International Bar Association (IBA) and the Brazilian

The Authors

Bar Competition Committee – Federal Council and also the President of Pró-Terra – the Brazilian Technology, Environment and Agribusiness Association.
Languages known to him are Portuguese and English. His areas of Expertise are international, competition, international trade and administrative law.
franceschini@fm-advogados.com.br
OAB-SP No. 28.711

Eduardo Molan Gaban is a lawyer with sixteen years of experience and a consultant on antitrust & competition, economic law litigation and international trade matters. He graduated in Law at Pontifical Catholic University of São Paulo (PUC/SP), where he obtained his Master's in Economic Law. He holds a PhD from PUC/SP and New York University School of Law (as Visiting Fulbrighter). He is specialized in antitrust & competition as well as in international trade. Gaban has worked in various boutique law firms focused on economic law/antitrust as well as in the CADE in the city of Brasília. He has published several articles on antitrust & competition, economic law, economic regulation, as well as authored the following books: *Direito Antitruste: O Combate aos Cartéis*, published by Saraiva (winner of the Brazilian award *Troféu Cultura Econômica*, in the category 2008 best law book), *Estudos de Direito Econômico e Economia da Concorrência* (Juruá, 2009), *Antitrust Law in Brazil: fighting cartels* (Wolters Kluwer, 2011), *Regulação do Setor Postal* (Saraiva, 2012) and *Direito Antitruste* (4th Edition, Saraiva, 2016). He has been internationally acclaimed as a leading lawyer in competition/antitrust by the most important international publications of the sector, such as *Latin Lawyer 250, Chambers and Partners*, as well as *Euromoney*. He is currently a board member of the Higher Board of Legislative and Legal Matters of the Federation of Industries of the State of São Paulo (CONJUR/FIESP), leader and researcher of the Competition & Innovation Study Nucleus of the Pontifical University of São Paulo (NECI/PUC-SP). He is Vice-President of the Antitrust Committee of the IASP, Board member of the Fulbright Commission in Brazil, member of the Antitrust and Economic Regulation Study Committee of the Brazilian Bar Association (CECORE/OAB/SP), member of the Antitrust and Competition Committee of the International Chamber of Commerce (ICC), member of the Antitrust Committee and of the Trade Law and Customs Committee of the IBA, partner at Tauil & Chequer

Table of Contents

The Authors 3

List of Abbreviations 13

General Introduction 15

§1. General Background of the Country 15

§2. The Economic System 23

§3. The Legal System 24

§4. Historical Background of Antitrust Law 25

Part I. The Structure of Antitrust Law and Its Enforcement 29

Chapter 1. Sources of Antitrust Law 29

§1. National Sources 29

I. Laws 30
A. Law No. 7347, of 24 July 1985 30
B. Law No. 8137, of 27 December 1990 30
C. Law No. 8666, of 21 June 1993 31
D. Law No. 9784, of 29 January 1999 31
E. Law No. 9873, of 23 November 1999 32
F. Law No. 10149, of 21 December 2000 32
G. Law No. 11101, of 9 February 2005 32
H. Law No. 11482, of 31 May 2007 32
I. Law No. 12529, of 30 November 2011 33
II. Codes 33
A. Civil Procedures Code (Law No. 13105, of 16 March 2015) 33
B. Consumer Protection Code (Law No. 8078, of 11 September 1990) 33

§2. International Sources and Activities 33

§3. Secondary Sources 36

§4. Sources' Relation and Hierarchy 38

§5. Role and Authority of Precedents 38

Chapter 2. Scope of Application 40

§1. Territorial Reach 40

§2. Special Sectors 40

§3. State-Owned Enterprises and Public Utilities 41

§4. Sensible Effect and De Minimis 42

Chapter 3. Overview of Substantive Provisions 43

§1. Restrictive Agreements 43

§2. Dominant Undertakings 43

§3. Concentrations 43

§4. Other Prohibitions 44

§5. Tests of Illegality 46

I. Per Se Prohibition and Naked Restraints 46
II. Balancing Tests 47
III. Merger Tests 47

Chapter 4. Overview of Main Notions 50

§1. Undertaking 50

§2. Relevant Market 52

§3. Market Power/Dominant Position 54

§4. Agreements and Concerted Practices 58

§5. Restriction of Competition 59

§6. Monopolization and Abuse of Dominance 60

§7. Concentrations 63

§8. Joint Ventures 65

Chapter 5. Consequences of Violations and Enforcement Institutions 68

§1. Administrative Enforcement 68

I. The Antitrust Authorities 68
A. Formation, Composition 68
1. The CADE 68
a. The Administrative Tribunal 69
b. The General Superintendency (GS) 70
c. The Department of Economic Studies (DEE) 71
2. The Office of the Attorney General of the CADE (PFE) 72
3. The Office of the Federal Attorney General (MPF) 72
4. The SEAE 72
B. Investigating Powers 72
C. Adjudicating Powers (Ascertaining and Sanctioning) 73
1. Leniency Agreements 73
2. Settlement Agreements (*Compromisso de Cessação* – TCC) 75
3. Inspections 77
4. Dawn Raids 77
D. Other Institutional Tasks (Consultancy to Government) 78
II. Government Direct Enforcement Activities 78
III. Other Administrative Agencies Applying Antitrust Rules 79
IV. Administrative Fines 79
V. Administrative Injunctions and Other Restrictive Orders: Interim Measures 81

§2. Civil Enforcement 82

I. Competent Civil Courts 82
II. Sanctions 82
A. Nullity and Damages 82
B. Interim Measures 83

§3. Criminal Enforcement 84

I. Criminal Sanctions for Antitrust Violations 84
II. Other Application of Criminal Law to Relevant Conducts 84
III. Role of Prosecutors 85
IV. Competent Criminal Courts 85

Table of Contents

Part II. The Application of the Prohibitions 87

Chapter 1. Restrictive Agreements 87

§1. Horizontal Agreements 87

I. Cartels 87
A. Price Fixing 89
B. Market/Client Allocation 92
C. Production/Innovation Limitation 93
D. Group Boycott 93
E. Collusion on Others' Objects 94
II. Information Exchange Practices 95
III. Cooperation Agreements 99
A. Research and Development 101
B. Specialization and Standardization 101
C. Joint Production, Joint Purchasing and Joint Selling 102

§2. Vertical Agreements 103

I. Distribution 104
A. Exclusive Distributorship 105
B. Exclusive Dealing 106
C. Selective Distribution 107
D. Franchising 110
II. Technology Licensing, Know-How and Trade Secret Licensing 111
A. Patent Licensing, Trademark Licensing and Intellectual Property Licensing 113

Chapter 2. Dominant Undertakings' Prohibited Practices 117

§1. Exploitative Practices 117

I. Excessive/Unfair Pricing 117
II. Discrimination 118

§2. Exclusionary Practices 121

I. Predation 121
II. Tying 124
III. Rebates 125
IV. Refusal to Deal 126
V. Price Squeeze 128

Chapter 3. Concentrations 130

§1. Horizontal Mergers 131

§2. Vertical Mergers 140

§3. Market/Product Extension Mergers 142

§4. Pure Conglomerate Mergers 143

§5. Joint Ventures 147

Part III. Administrative Procedure 153

Chapter 1. Administrative Investigations Before the Antitrust Authority 153

§1. Initiative 153

I. General Sectors Enquiries and Ex Officio Investigations 153
II. Complaints 155

§2. Powers 156

I. Requests for Information 156
II. Investigating and Search Powers 157
III. Cooperation with Other State Institutions 158

§3. Right of Defence 159

I. Content and Notification of Opening Decisions 159
II. The Proceedings: Hearings, Access to File, Briefs 161
III. Final Hearing and Decision 162

Chapter 2. Voluntary Notifications and Clearance Decisions in Merger Control 163

§1. Preliminary Filing Obligations 163

I. Criteria and Thresholds 163
II. Turnover Calculation 166
III. Other Relevant Notions 166

§2. Structure of Proceeding 169

I. Preliminary Assessment and Full Investigation 169
II. Time Framework 171
III. Right of Defence 173

§3. Clearance and Conditional Clearance 173

I. Conditions and Undertakings 173
A. Content 173
B. Timing 176

§4. Relations with Other Merger Control Authorities 176

I. Other Authorities Within the Local Jurisdiction 176
II. International Coordination 177

Chapter 3. Challenging of the Administrative Decision 178

§1. Competent Courts 178

§2. Time Limits 179

§3. Scope of Judicial Review 179

Selected Bibliography 181

Index 195

List of Abbreviations

ABRANET	Brazilian Internet Association
ACC	Concentration Control Agreement
AGU	Federal Counsel General
AJUFE	Federal Judges' Association
ANATEL	National Telecommunication Agency
ANCINE	National Cinema Agency
ANEEL	National Electricity Regulatory Agency
ANP	National Petroleum Agency
ANS	National Supplementary Health Agency
ANTAQ	National Water Transportation Agency
ANTT	National Land Transport Agency
ANVISA	National Health Surveillance Agency
APRO	Agreement on the Reversibility of the Act of Concentration
BACEN	Central Bank of Brazil
CADE	Administrative Council for Economic Defence
CEDES	Economic and Social Law Studies Center
CGU	Office of the Comptroller General
CONAMA	Environment National Council
DEE	Department of Economic Studies
DNPM	National Department of Mineral Production
DPDC	Department of Consumer Protection and Defence
DPDE	Department of Economic Protection and Defence
EFTA	European Free Trade Association
EU	European Union
GS	General Superintendency
IASP	São Paulo Attorneys Institute
IBA	International Bar Association
ICN	International Competition Network
INPI	National Institute of Industrial Property

IPEA	Institute of Applied Economic Research
JV	Joint Venture
LDC	Antitrust Law
MERCOSUL	Common Market of the South
MPF	Office of the Federal Attorney General
OECD	Organisation for Economic Co-operation and Development
PFE	Federal Office of the CADE Attorney General
PROCON	Bureau of Consumer Protection
SANECON	Consumer National Secretariat of the Ministry of Justice
SBDC	Brazilian System of Competition Defence
SDE	Secretariat of Economic Law
SEAE	Secretariat for Economic Monitoring
SNDE	Economic Law National Secretariat
STF	Supreme Court
STJ	Superior Court of Justice
TCD	Performance Commitment Agreement
TRF	Federal Regional Court
UFIR	Fiscal Reference Unit
UNCTAD	United Nations Conference on Trade and Development
US	United States of America
WTO	World Trade Organization

General Introduction

§1. General Background of the Country

1. Brazil is a Federative Republic formed by the indissoluble union of States, Municipalities and the Federal District and is a democratic State governed by law.[1] The country fundamentals are its sovereignty, citizenship, and human dignity, social values of work, free initiative and political pluralism. The authority of the Federal Government is vested unto independent and harmonic Legislative, Executive and Judiciary powers.

2.

Figure 1 General Information, Indices and Data on Brazil Population Millions

1. All data included in this chapter is from the latest official records of the Brazilian Institute for Geography and Statistics – IBGE.

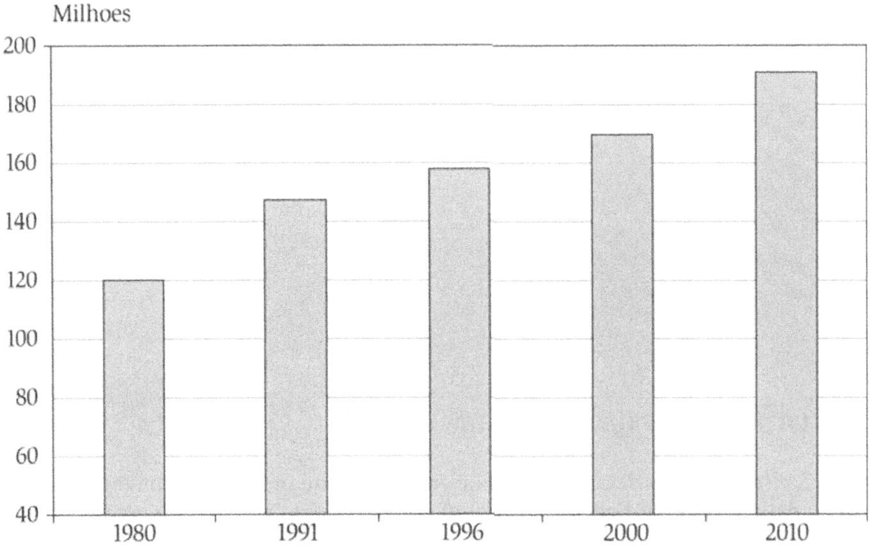

Source: IBGE, Demographic Census 1980, 1991, 2000, 2010 and population headcount 1996.

Table 1 Total Population and Populational Proportion by Sex, Large Age Groups and Location of Domicile

	1980	*1991*	*1996*	*2000*	*2010*
Total Population*					
By sex (%)					
Men	49.68	49.36	49.30	49.22	48.97
Women	50.31	50.63	50.69	50.78	51.03
By large age groups (%)					
0–14 years	38.20	34.72	31.54	29.60	24.08
15–64 years	57.68	60.45	62.85	64.55	68.54
65 or more	4.01	4.83	5.35	5.85	7.38
By location of domicile (%)					
Urban	67.59	75.59	78.36	81.25	84.36
Rural	32.41	24.41	21.64	18.75	15.64

* Including the population with unknown age in 1980 and 1996.

Figure 2 Education: Illiteracy Rates for Individuals Aging 10 Years or More 2007–2009

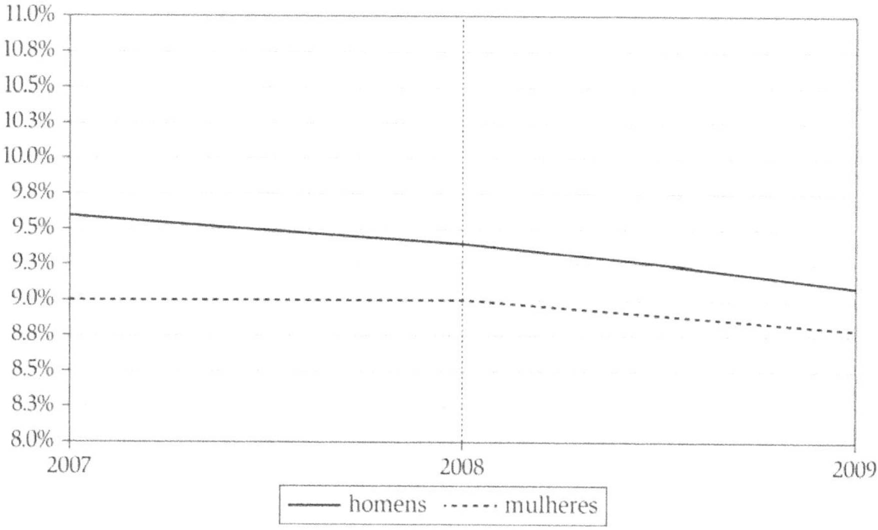

Source: IBGE, National Research by samples of domiciles.
Note: Translation: Homens (Men) / Mulheres (Women).

Figure 3 Unemployment Rates 2007–2011

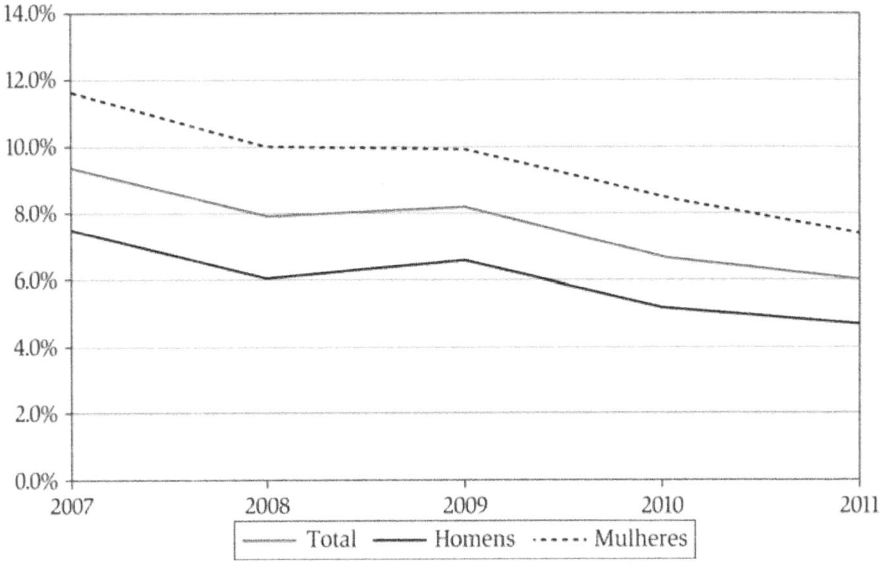

Note: Translation: Homens (Men) / Mulheres (Women).

Figure 4 Housing: Domiciles with Durable Goods 2007–2009

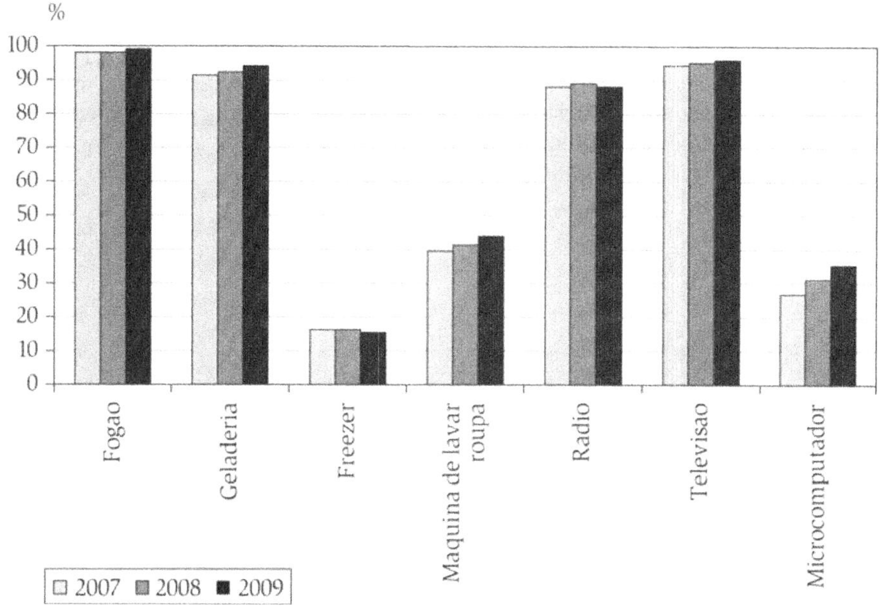

Note: Translations: Fogão (Stove)/ Geladeira (Ice Box)/ Máquina de lavar roupa (Washing Machine)/ Televisão (Television)/ Microcomputador (Personal Computer).

Figure 5 Agribusiness: Number of Establishments by Economic Field 2006

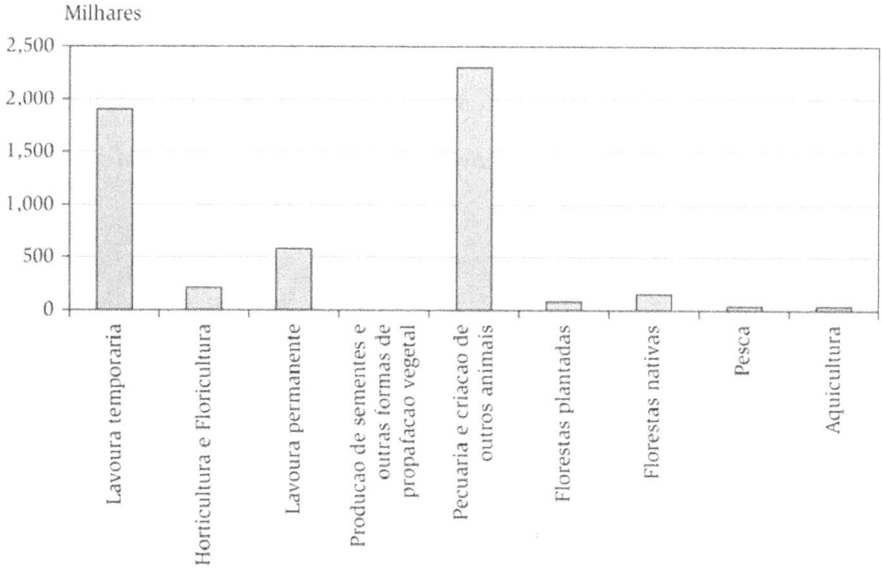

Note: Translation: Milhares (Thousands) / Lavoura Temporária (Temporary Crops) / Horticultura (Horticulture) / Lavoura Permanente (Standing Crops) / Pecuária (Livestock) / Produção Mista – Lavoura e Pecuária (Joint Production – Crops and Livestock) / Silvicultura (Forestry) / Pesca e aquicultura (Fishing and Aquaculture) / Produção de Carvão (Coal Production).

Figure 6 Industry: Annual Industrial Growth Rates

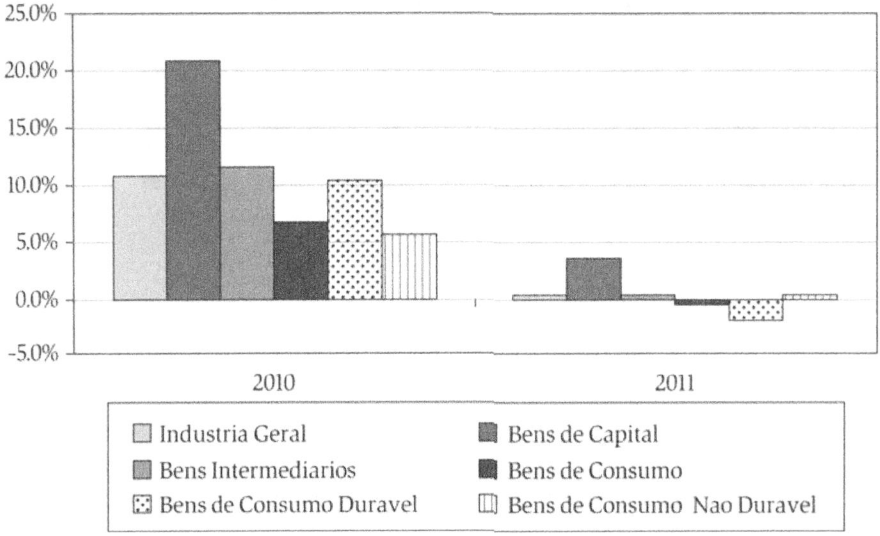

Note: Translation: Indústria Geral (General Industry) / Bens Intermediários (Intermediate Goods) / Bens de Consumo Durável (Durable Consumer Goods) / Bens de Capital (Capital Goods) / Bens de Consumo (Consumer Goods) / Bens de Consumo Não Durável (Non-durable Goods).

Figure 7 Trade: Employed Individuals by Trade Segments – 2006

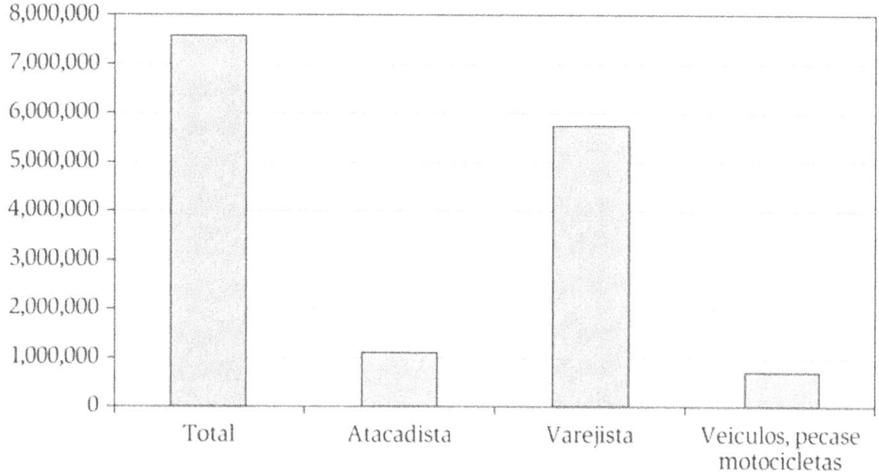

Note: Translation: Atacadista (Wholesaler) / Varejista (Retailer) / Veículos, peças e motocicletas (vehicles, Parts and Motorcycles).

Figure 8 Services: Number of Concerns by Type of Services – 2009

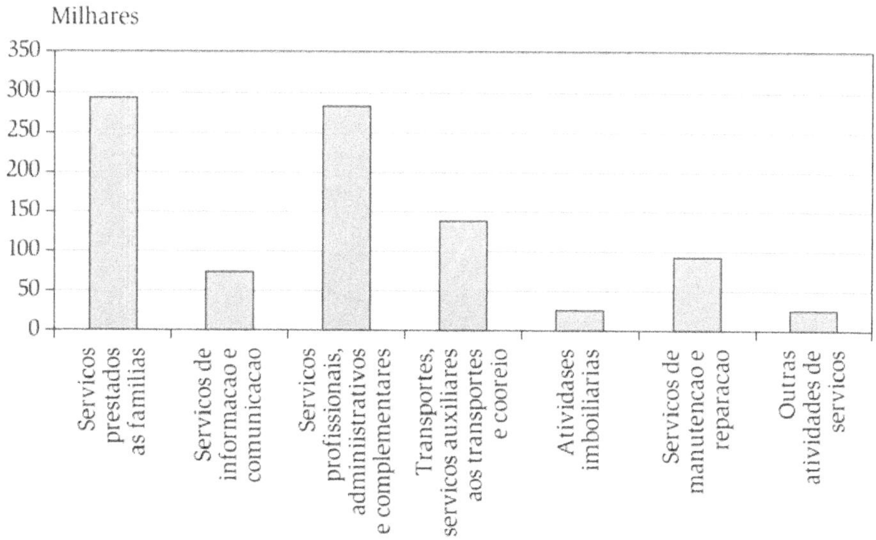

Note: Translation: Milhares (Thousands) / Serviços prestados às famílias (Services Rendered to Families) / Serviços de informações (Information Services) / Serviços prestados às empresas (Services Rendered to Corporations) / Transporte, serviços auxiliares aos transportes e correio (Transportation, Ancillary Services to Transportation and Mail) / Atividades imobiliárias e aluguel de bens móveis e imóveis (Realty and

Lease of Movable and Immovable Assets) / Serviços de manutenção e reparação (Maintenance and Repair Services) / Outras atividades de serviços (Other Kinds of Services).

Figure 9 National Accounts: Gross National Product – Value – 2006–2011

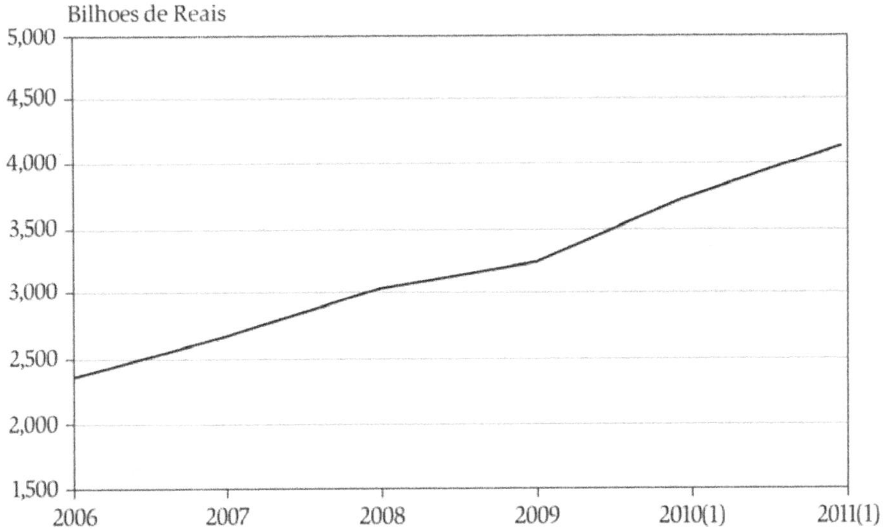

Figure 10 Gross National Product – Per Capita – 2006–2011

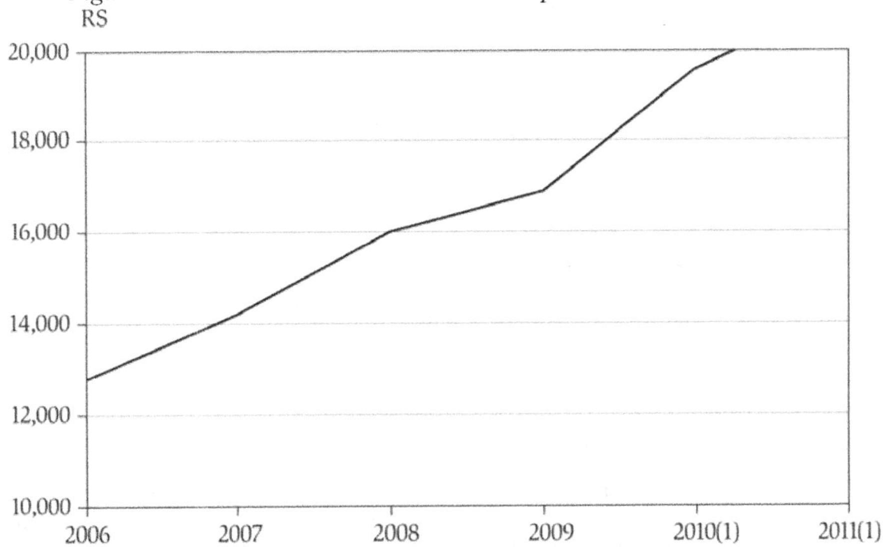

Note: Translation: Bilhões de Reais (billions of reais – BRL).

§2. The Economic System

3. The national economic order is based on capitalism, ensured by the principles of free initiative and private property.

4. Consistently with such principles, the direct exploitation of an economic activity by the State is only permitted whenever it is essential to meet national security requirements or to satisfy a relevant collective interest. As a normative authority and regulator, the State performs, under the law, the functions of monitoring, incentive and planning, provided that the latter is mandatory to the public sector and only indicative to the private sector.

5. Brazil is a large producer and exporter of mineral commodities and agricultural and manufactured products. Agriculture, industrial activities and services are currently expanding. Although considered an emerging economy, the Brazil's economy is one of the largest in the world.

6.

Table 2 Complementary Information, Data and Indices on the Brazilian Economy

Currency	*Real (Symbol BRL)*
GDP (Gross Domestic Product)	BRL 5.904 trillion (2015), approximately USD 1.77 trillion (nominal terms)
Per Capita Income (per capita GDP)	USD 8,670 (2015) (nominal terms)
GNP growth in recent years	5.7% (2004), 3.2% (2005), 4% (2006), 5.7% (2007), 5.1% (2008), 0.2% (2009), 7.6% (2010), 3.9% (2011), 1.8% (2012), 2.7% (2013), 0.1% (2014), - 3.8% (2015)
Inflation	10.67% IPCA (2015)
Unemployment rate	8.5% (2015)

Source: IBGE.

Table 3 Foreign Trade

Exports	USD 197.9 billion (2008)
Imports	USD 173.2 billion (2008)
Trade balance of payment	USD 24.7 billion
Principal trade partners	USA, China, Argentina and Germany
Main products exported from Brazil	iron ore, iron, steel, crude oil, soya and by-products, automobiles, planes, sugar cane, bovine meat, coffee and chicken meat

Main products imported into Brazil	crude petroleum, electronic chips, receivers/transmitters, auto parts, pharmaceutical products, automobiles, combustible oil, natural gas and aircraft engines
Main agricultural products	coffee, orange, sugar cane, soya, tobacco, corn and matte
Main livestock products	bovine meat, chicken meat and swine meat
Main mineral products	iron, aluminium, manganese, magnesite and tin
Main service activities	telecommunication, road transportation, technical and professional services rendered to corporations, cargo transportation, building and home cleaning services, computer services, air transportation and food services
Main industrial fields	food and beverages, chemical products, automobiles, fuel, basic metallurgic products, machinery and equipment, plastic and rubber products, electronic products and paper and pulp products

Source: IBGE.

From 2004 to 2013, the Brazilian economy experienced a significant growth. However, the economy was only stable in 2014 and decreased by 3.8% in 2015.

§3. The Legal System

7. Brazilian legal framework is a civil law system based on Roman-Germanic traditions. Contrary to the Anglo-Saxon system, statutory provisions are the primary source of law. Legal doctrine frequently is restricted to the dogmatic reading of the law, but, jointly with jurisprudence, are sources of interpretation and integration of legal statutes (de facto sources). Precedents are volatile and of restricted and temporary accountability, albeit of large interest in settling specific cases and legal debates.

8. Paying respect to its origins, the Brazilian legal framework is generally based on civil law, which largely influences principles of public law. In the past decade, the enforcement of Competition Laws, however, has to a certain extent deviated from such traditional civil law principles and, not infrequently, interpretation of economic-based statutes clashes with established legal principles of civil law. In so doing, public authorities often purportedly claim to best protect or diffuse collective interests by exercising greater discretionary powers. Such dispute has increasingly yielded parties adversely affected by administrative decisions to resort to the Judiciary seeking to obtain trials de novo, injunctive relieves or the annulment of administrative decisions.

9. The legal controversy and conflict between liberalism, civil rights and party autonomy, on the one side, and a regulatory State increasingly attempting to govern private activities, on the other, is still *in fieri*, and the Brazilian Judiciary has not yet shown any clear inclination as to which side it will eventually favour, if any.

§4. Historical Background of Antitrust Law

10. The first decision handed by the Brazilian Higher Courts in connection with competition issues (*Companhia Nacional de Tecidos de Juta*, represented by the jurist J.X. *Carvalho de Mendonça v. Count Álvares Penteado and Companhia Paulista de Aniagem*, represented by jurist Rui Barbosa) is dated 1913. The dispute concerned a non-compete obligation according to which the seller was prevented from re-establishing a new business at the same location or within the area of influence of the relevant business that was sold.

11. On 10 April 1913, the Brazilian Federal Supreme Court (STF), by majority vote, reversed a first instance decision rendered in favour of the defendants. The STF decided that, pursuant to Articles 209, 214 and 215 of the Brazilian Commercial Code of 1850, then in force, non-compete clauses were implicit in the sale of any business.

12. Subsequently, however, in ruling on a motion for clarification filed by the plaintiff, the STF amended its opinion by deciding that non-competition clauses were not an implicit obligation, since the waiver to the right of exercise of a commercial or industrial activity was not to be presumed. The opinion then established the standards for the validity of such restrictive provisions. The clause needed to be: (a) expressly agreed upon by the parties or undoubtedly result from the terms of the agreement, and (b) limited in time and object. The decision, thus, sought to ensure the effectiveness of the sovereign principle of free competition.

13. The Brazilian Federal Constitution of 1934, on its turn, was the first statute addressing competition issues. Article 115 of the Constitution stated: 'the economic order is to be organized consistently with the principles of justice and the needs of the national life, so as to ensure an existence with dignity. Within such standards, the economic freedom is ensured' (free translation).

14. Moreover, Article 116 of said Constitution established that certain economic activities could be monopolized 'for reasons of public interest' (free translation).

15. The Federal Constitution of 1934 was repealed by the Federal Constitution of 1937 that admitted direct and indirect State intervention in the economy, with the purpose of avoiding or settling market disputes (Article 135).

16. The first Brazilian Competition Law was then enacted in 1945 (Decree-Law No. 7666, of 22 June 1945), based on the bill drafted by the then Minister of Agriculture, Agamemnon Magalhães. Such statute was meant to govern and punish acts contrary to the moral and economic order and for this purpose it established the Administrative Commission for Economic Defence (CADE). Such law (known as Malaysian Law for imposing draconian penalties on anticompetitive offences), however, was short-lived and revoked a few months after its enactment.

17. The principle of free competition became an explicit constitutional principle under Brazilian Federal Constitution of 1946. Article 148 stated that:

> the law shall punish all and any form of abuse of economic power, including the union or grouping of individual and corporate concerns, regardless of their nature, that have the purpose of dominating the national markets, eliminating competition or arbitrarily increasing profits (free translation).

18. Despite the fact that the Brazilian Federal Constitution of 1946 was subsequently repealed (three times, in 1967, 1969 and 1988) by the Federal Constitutions, the principles established in the 1946 Constitution remained intact. The constitutional dignity of competition laws became a recognized standard throughout the country. In the period 1969–1983, all the States of the Brazilian Federative Republic included a similar constitutional provision in their respective State Constitutions, despite the fact that the Congress retains the power to enact competition laws and not the States.

19. Pursuant to the Brazilian legal system, such constitutional provisions, however, needed to be implemented to become effective and enforceable. For such purpose and originally, former Minister Agamemnon Magalhães, then a House Representative, drafted Bill No. 122 that was submitted to Congress on 15 April 1948. Such bill took fifteen years to be approved and resulted in the enactment of Law No. 4137, of 1962.

20. Law No. 4137/62 created the CADE, which still is the Brazilian administrative Competition Tribunal. The activities of the CADE, however, remained limited until 1991, when Law No. 4137/62 was repealed by Law No. 8151/91, which in turn was subsequently repealed by Law No. 8884/94. Law No. 4137/62 only governed market conducts and established no mechanism or procedure in connection with the review of mergers and acquisitions, save for a very broad reference to a requirement of 'contract registration' in connection with transactions that had the effect of: '(a) stabilizing production with consumption, (b) regulating the market, (c) standardizing production, (d) stabilizing prices, (e) specializing production and distribution, or (f) establishing a restriction in distribution to the detriment of other goods of the same kind or destined to meet related needs' (free translation of Article 74 of Law No. 4137/62). Such requirement was virtually ignored since the regulations governing the enforcement of Article 74 (Decree No. 52025, of 1963) provided that such requirement would not apply to 'regular commercial transactions' (no precise definition of such concept was supplied by the Decree), and no penalty was attached to failure in registering a deal.

21. In the meantime, in 1985, Law No. 7347 was enacted to govern class actions for the protection of consumer interests. Further, in 1990, anticompetitive conducts became criminal offences under Law No. 8137.

22. The effectiveness of Law No. 4137/62 was restrained by the political and economic environment in Brazil established with the Military Government regime resulting from the Military coup of 1964 that promoted strong State intervention in the economy. The enforcement of a Competition Law was explicitly considered secondary since the established general regime of price control and the vivid State participation in the economic activities of the country. Tax incentives and disincentives were then deemed to be more effective to the economic order than competition laws.

23. Market rules were finally re-established in the Brazilian economy when the price control mechanisms were largely abolished in the beginning of 1990 under the Federal Constitution enacted in 1988. Consequently, effective competition laws were deemed to be essential to a healthy economic environment, and a new law was enacted in 1991 (Law No. 8151).

24. Such law created the Economic Law National Secretariat (SNDE) within the Ministry of Justice. Its function was the review of legal issues relating to the enforcement of the competition law, whereas the review of economic issues became the attribution of the Secretariat of Economic Policy (SPE), of the Ministry of Finance.

25. The SNDE and the SPE were subsequently renamed as Secretariat of Economic Law (SDE) and Secretariat of Economic Monitoring (SEAE), which, together with the CADE, originally formed the Brazilian System for Economic Defence (SBDC) under Law No. 8884/94.

26. On 30 November 2011, Law No. 12529, the Brazilian Competition Law currently in force was enacted and restructured by the SBDC. Such law formally ratified the nature of the CADE as a federal authority and an administrative tribunal (Article 4), and was originally affirmed by Law No. 8884. Under the current law, the CADE was reorganized to comprise the Administrative Tribunal of Economic Defense, the General Superintendency (GS) and the Economic Studies Department (DEE) (Article 5). The SDE was extinguished and the SEAE was restricted to functions of competition advocacy by promoting competition among Government organs and before the Society (Article 19). The CADE together with the SEAE currently form the SBDC.

Part I. The Structure of Antitrust Law and Its Enforcement

Chapter 1. Sources of Antitrust Law

§1. National Sources

27. The principal sources of the Brazilian competition laws are set in the Federal Constitution of 1988.

28. The relevant constitutional provisions are Articles 1, item IV, 5, 170 and 173.

29. The principle of free initiative is consecrated as one of the fundamentals of the Federative Republic of Brazil by Article 1, item IV, of the Federal Constitution.

30. Article 5 ensures the constitutional right of the adversary proceedings, ample defence, presumption of innocence, due process of law and equal rights.

31. Title VII of the Federal Constitution governs the so-called Economic and Financial Order and rules (Article 170) that:

> the economic order, based on the valorization of human work and free initiative, seeks to ensure an existence with dignity to all, based on the rules of social justice, the following principles being observed, inter alia: (i) national sovereignty; (ii) private property; (iii) social function of property and (iv) free competition (free translation).

32. Punishment of anticompetitive conducts is governed by Article 173, §4, whereby 'the law shall punish the abuse of economic power that seeks the domination of the markets, the elimination of competition or the arbitrary increase of profits' (free translation).

33. As to the role of the State in the economy, Article 174 rules that:

> the State, as a normative and regulatory agent, shall exercise, in the manner established by law, the functions of monitoring, incentive and planning, provided that the latter is mandatory for the public sector and indicative to the private sector (free translation).

I. Laws

A. Law No. 7347, of 24 July 1985

34. It is a civil statute that governs class actions relating to the recovery of moral and patrimonial injuries caused, *inter alia,* to: (a) consumers (item II of Article 1), and (b) the economic order or the people's economy and has a subsidiary application to the administrative and judicial processes set forth by Law No. 12529 (Article 115 of the latter).

35. Pursuant to Article 1 (as amended by Article 117 of Law No. 12529):

> The actions for moral and patrimonial damage liability are governed by the provisions of this Law, whenever caused by:
>
> ....
>
> .... V – an offense to the economic order;
>
> .... (free translation).

36. A class action may be used to request the payment of a pecuniary compensation or the fulfilment of obligations to do or of refraining from doing something.

37. The following entities have legal standing to bring class actions: (i) the Office of the Public Attorney (*Ministério Público*), (ii) the Office of Public Defence (*Defensoria Pública*), (iii) the Federal and State Governments, the Government of the Federal District and Municipal Governments, (iv) public authorities, public concerns, foundations and mixed economy companies, (v) trade associations established from at least one year under applicable civil laws that have, among their institutional purposes, the protection of consumer, the economic order and the principle of free competition.

B. Law No. 8137, of 27 December 1990

38. It is a criminal statute that defines crimes against tax and economic order and against consumer relations. Article 4 (as amended by Article 116 of Law No. 12529) define the crimes against the economic order, as follows:

Article 4. Crimes against the economic order are:

> I – to abuse of the economic power, dominating the market or eliminating, totally or partially, competition through any form of arrangement or agreement between concerns.
>
> II – to enter into an agreement, protocol, arrangement or alliance among suppliers, seeking:

(a) the artificial fixing of prices or volumes sold or made;

(b) the regional control of the market by a company or group of companies;

(c) the control, to the detriment of competition, of a distribution or suppliers′ network.

Penalty – jail sentence (reclusion), of between 2 (two) and 5 (five) years, and fine.

C. Law No. 8666, of 21 June 1993

39. It governs public tender, binds and contracts with the Public Administration and defines the crimes for fraud at bids. Article 90 of the law deserves special attention:

> Article 90. To frustrate and fraud, through arrangements, combinations or any other way, the competitive nature of a bidding procedure, with the intent of obtaining, for himself or a third party, an advantage resulting from the adjudication of the bid.
>
> Penalty – jail sentence (detention), from 2 (two) to 4 (four) years, and fine (free translation).

40. Precedents indicate that such fine should be fixed in a value at least equal to 5% of the relevant contract value.

D. Law No. 9784, of 29 January 1999

41. This law governs administrative proceedings within the Federal Public Administration and has a subsidiary application to the administrative and judicial processes set forth by Law No. 12529 (Article 115 of the latter).

42. The statute requires, for example, the Public Administration to abide by the principles of legality, purpose, motivation, reasonability, proportionality, morality, ample defence, adversary proceedings, legal certainty, public interest and efficiency.

43. It also ensures that administrative proceedings will, *inter alia*, meet the standards of: (i) being enforced consistently with the law, (ii) meeting the general interest, (iii) being objective in meeting the public interest, (iv) meeting the ethical standards of probity, propriety and good faith, (v) indicating the circumstances of fact and of law that shall support the decision, (vi) observing the essential formalities to ensure the rights of the citizens, and (vii) guaranteeing the rights of communication, of submission of summations, of producing evidence and of appealing, in the procedures that may result in the imposition of penalties and in settling disputes.

44. However, the law sets forth the duties of the citizens *vis-à-vis* the Public Administration, *inter alia,* as follows: (i) to describe the facts pursuant to the truth, (ii) to act with loyalty, propriety and good faith, (iii) not to act in a vexatious manner and (iv) to supply the information that is required and to cooperate with the establishment of the facts.

E. *Law No. 9873, of 23 November 1999*

45. Such law contains the statutes of limitation governing the punitive action by the Federal Public Administration, as follows:

> Article 1. The punitive action of the direct and indirect Federal Public Administration, in its exercise of police authority and seeking to investigate offences to the law in force, shall be subject to prescription, counted as of the date the relevant action is committed, and, in the case of a permanent or continuous offence, as of the date such action shall cease.
>
> § 1. Prescription shall apply to administrative proceedings that remain suspended for more than three years, pending a final determination or the issue of any order, in which case the records will be ex officio dismissed, or at the request of the interested party, without prejudice to the investigation of the functional accountability resulting from the fact that the procedure is suspended, should it be the case.
>
> § 2. Whenever the facts that are the subject matter of the punitive action by the Administration constitute also a crime, the statute of limitation is governed by the term set forth in the applicable penal law (free translation).

F. *Law No. 10149, of 21 December 2000*

46. This statute governs Leniency Agreements and amends other provisions of Law No. 8884/94.

G. *Law No. 11101, of 9 February 2005*

47. This law governs judicial and extrajudicial recoveries and bankruptcy.

H. *Law No. 11482, of 31 May 2007*

48. It governs the standards to apply in the drafting and approval of settlements (Termo de Compromisso de Cessação – TCC) in connection with anticompetitive practices.

I. Law No. 12529, of 30 November 2011

49. This is the Competition Law that is currently in force in Brazil. It establishes specific rules governing and punishing anticompetitive conducts, and controlling mergers and acquisitions.

II. Codes

A. Civil Procedures Code (Law No. 13105, of 16 March 2015)

50. Pursuant to Article 115 of Law No. 12529, the Code is a secondary and supplementary statute to the Competition Law in connection with procedural rules.

B. Consumer Protection Code (Law No. 8078, of 11 September 1990)

51. Pursuant to Article 115 of Law No. 12529, the Code is a secondary and supplementary statute to the Competition Law and a guideline for the enforcement thereof (Article 1 of the Competition Law).

§2. International Sources and Activities

52. Brazil has an active participation in international cooperation fora and has entered into a series of international agreements concerning Competition Law studies and enforcement.

53. The SBDC is currently made by the Administrative Council for Economic Defense (*Conselho Administrativo de Defesa Econômica* (CADE)), and by the SEAE, a body of the Ministry of Finance. The SBDC is an active member of the International Competition Network (ICN) that was created in October 2001 by fourteen competition authorities around the world, with the purpose of promoting global convergence in connection with competition laws and of providing an independent and specialized forum to discuss such matters.

54. The CADE is the authority that represents Brazil at the ICN. Upon intensively acting at the ICN for two consecutive years as a coordinator of the Competition Policy Implementation Working Group – CPI – and as a coordinator of the working subgroup that drafted the project on relations between the competition authorities and the Judiciary, the CADE was elected member of the ICN Steering Group for the period of 2007–2009.

55. The principal goals of the ICN are: (i) to ensure an effective competitive process, (ii) to promote the consumer economic welfare, (iii) to maximize efficiency, (iv) to ensure economic freedom, (v) to ensure equilibrium among competitors in unequal conditions, (vi) to promote loyalty and equality, (vii) to promote consumer choice, (viii) to achieve market integration, (ix) to monitor privatizations and market liberation and (x) to promote competition in international markets.

56. Although Brazil is not a member of the Organisation for Economic Co-operation and Development (OECD), the SBDC is very active at the organization's Competition Committee (COMP) created in 1961. The main objectives of the COMP are: (a) to monitor and review the development of competition policies and laws in various countries and international organizations, (b) to review and analyse competition policies and laws, taking into account the interaction between competition laws and other public policies, (c) to promote cooperation among members in drafting and implementing competition policies and laws, (d) to cooperate with other committees of the organization in connection with competition issues, (e) to exchange information on competition matters that are developed in other fora and (f) to report and make recommendations to the OECD Director Council (made by representatives of member countries) on matters within the Committee jurisdiction.

57. The SBDC is also active at the OECD Trade and Competition Joint Group, created in 1996, at which it acts as an observer, jointly with Argentina, Chile, Hong Kong, the European Free Trade Association (EFTA), the World Bank, the World Trade Organization (WTO) and the United Nations Conference on Trade and Development (UNCTAD). The purposes of such groups are to review: (a) policies related to access to markets as scope and coverage, as well as in the implementation of competition laws, (b) international options to increase the coherence among the trade and competition policies, (c) impact of the competition measures and policies in trade and (d) impact of regulation of access to markets and the competitive process.

58. Brazil is also an active participant at international fora, such as at the BRICS international conferences on competition laws. On 21 September 2011, Brazil signed the Beijing Consensus of the Second BRICS International Competition Conference between competition authorities of Brazil, Russia, China, India and South Africa.

59. Brazil also imparts training to competition enforcement authorities of various countries.

60. Brazil is a party to the Mercosul Competition Defence Agreement (MERCOSUL/CMC/DEC. No. 43/10), dated 2010, which repealed the original Mercosul Competition Defence Protocol (also known as the Fortaleza Protocol), dated 17 December 1996, but is not yet effective, pending its ratification by the Mercosul Member States. Notwithstanding, Joint Ordinance CADE/SDE/SEAE No. 148, of 13 November 2009 has domesticated the 'Understanding on Cooperation among the Competition Authorities of the Member States of the Mercosul on the Applicability of their National Competition Laws' and the 'Understanding on Cooperation among the Competition Authorities of the Member States of the Mercosul on the Control of Economic Concentrations at the Regional Level' that were approved by the Mercosul Common Market Council on 7 July 2004 and 20 July 2006, respectively.

61. Brazil has also signed a series of international cooperation agreements with:

(a) Russia – Agreement between the Government of the Federative Republic of Brazil and the Government of the Russian Federation on cooperation in the Competition Policy Area, of December 2001 and programme on cooperation between the Federal Antimonopoly Service of the Russian Federation, CADE, SDE and SEAE, of 2009, 2011 (for 2012–2013) and 2014 (for 2014–2015).

(b) Argentina – Cooperation Agreement between the Federative Republic of Brazil and the Republic of Argentina on the cooperation between their competition authorities regarding the application of their competition laws, of 16 October 2003.
(c) United States – Agreement between the Government of the Federative Republic of Brazil and the Government of the United States of America (US) regarding cooperation between their competition authorities in the enforcement of their competition laws, of 26 October 1999, as promulgated in Brazil by Decree No. 4702, of 21 May 2003.
(d) Portugal – Technical Cooperation Protocol No. 1/2005 among the Competition Authority of Portugal, CADE, SDE and SEAE, and Technical Cooperation Protocol between the Competition Authority of Portugal and the SBDC, of 14 January 2010.
(e) Canada – Cooperation Agreement among the Commissioner of Competition, Competition Bureau of the Government of Canada, CADE, SDE and SEAE regarding the application of their competition laws (2008).
(f) Chile – Cooperation Arrangement between the *Fiscalia Nacional Económica* of Chile, CADE, SDE and SEAE regarding the application of their competition laws (2008).
(g) The European Commission – Memorandum of Understanding among the DG Competition, CADE, SDE and SEAE, of 8 October 2009.
(h) France – Technical Cooperation Agreement between the *Autorité de la Concurrence* and CADE, of 16 December 2011, as amended on 19 December 2014.
(i) Peru – Cooperation Agreement between the *Instituto Nacional de Defensa de la Competencia y de la Protección de la Propriedad Intelectual – INDECOPI*, of 29 July 2012.
(j) China – Memorandum of Understanding on cooperation in competition field between the State administration for industry and commerce of the People's Republic of China and CADE, of 13 September 2012.
(k) Ecuador – Cooperation Agreement between the *Superintendencia de Control del Poder de Mercado* – SCPM and CADE, of 19 November 2013.
(l) Colombia – Cooperation Agreement between CADE and the *Superintendencia de Industria y Commercio* – SIC, of 23 April 2014.
(m) Japan – Memorandum on Cooperation between CADE and the Fair Trade Commission of Japan, of 24 April 2014.
(n) Memorandum of Understanding on cooperation in the Competition Field between CADE and the Fair Trade Commission of the Republic of Korea, of 24 April 2014.
(o) World Bank – Memorandum of Understanding between the Integrity Vice-Presidency of the World Bank Group and CADE, of 22 December 2014.
(p) IDB – Agreement for the cooperation and sharing of information between CADE and the Interamerican Development Bank, of 6 January 2015.
(q) BRICS – Memorandum of Understanding between the competition authorities of the Federative Republic of Brazil, the Russian Federation, the Republic of India, the People's Republic of China and the Republic of South Africa, of 19 May 2016.

62. An interesting provision is found in the Cooperation Agreement entered by Brazil and Canada, authorizing the authorities of each country to contact citizens and individuals located in the other country to obtain information.

63. Such international activities and agreements have already resulted in a series of joint actions against international cartels. Examples of such actions have affected the international vitamin (1999), lysine (2000), aircraft fuel agents (2006), marine hoses (2007), compressors (2009) and freight forwarders markets. International cooperation has also been used in connection with merger review procedures, an example of which refers to the global merger of Owens Corning and Saint Gobain affecting the composites market and which resulted in the issue of a full divestiture order by CADE.

§3. Secondary Sources

64. Principal secondary sources of the Brazilian competition laws are made by multiple ordinances and resolutions issued by the SBDC, including, without limitation:

(1) Regulations:

- (a) CADE Ordinance No. 126, of 27 October 2011: Governs the creation of group of resolution analysis, which is responsible for the promotion of studies to evaluate the applicability of remedies assessed by CADE Resolutions.
- (b) BACEN Ordinance (Circular) No. 3590, of 26 April 2012: Governs the review of mergers and acquisitions notifications in the financial institution market by the Central Bank of Brazil (BACEN).
- (c) CADE Resolutions:
  - (1) Resolution No. 1, of 29 May 2012: CADE Internal Regulations.
  - (2) Resolution No. 2, of 29 May 2012: Regulates Article 88 of Law No. 12529, governing the notifications of mergers and acquisitions (acts of concentration).
  - (3) Resolution No. 3, of 29 May 2012: Regulates Article 37 of Law No. 12529, governing the fines on anticompetitive conducts and creates a List of Fields of Entrepreneurial Activities.
  - (4) Resolution No. 4, 29 May 2012: Establishes recommendations for experts' opinions.
  - (5) Resolution No. 5, of 6 March 2013: Amends the CADE Internal Regulations with respect to Settlement Agreements.
  - (6) Resolution No. 6, of 3 April 2013: Regulates Article 52 of Law No. 12529, governing the monitoring by the GS of compliance with CADE Resolutions, cease and desist orders and Settlement Agreements.
  - (7) Resolution No. 7, of 19 February 2014: Amends the CADE Internal Regulations.
  - (8) Resolution No. 8, of 1 October 2014: Amends the CADE Internal Regulations.
  - (9) Resolution No. 9, of 1 October 2014: Amends Resolution No. 2 that establishes criteria to notifications of acts of concentration.

(10) Resolution No. 10, of 4 November 2014: Governs the hypothesis of notification of associative contracts.
(11) Resolution No. 11, of 24 November 2014: Creates the Information Electronic System – SEI as the official CADE electronic document management system.
(12) Resolution No. 12, of 11 March 2015: Regulates the query procedure set forth in §4 of Article 9 of Law No. 12529.
(13) Resolution No. 13, of 23 June 2015: Regulates the procedure set forth in §§3 and 7 of Article 88 of Law No. 12529.
(14) Resolution No. 14, of 14 October 2015: Creates the CADE Electronic Filing Center.
(15) Resolution No. 15, of 25 May 2016: Amends the CADE Internal Regulations.

(2) Guidelines:

(a) Ordinance SEAE No. 70, of 12 December 2002: Guidelines for the Economic Analysis of Predatory Pricing.
(b) Ordinance SDE No. 51, of 3 July 2009: Guidelines for the Review of Charges on Eventual Anticompetitive Conducts in Public Procurements.
(c) Resolution CADE No. 4, of 29 May 2012: Guidelines for the issue of Technical Expert Opinions.
(d) Guidelines on Competition Compliance Programs.
(e) Guidelines on CADE's Antitrust Leniency Program.
(f) Guidelines on Cease and Desist Agreement for Cartel Cases.
(g) Guidelines on Gun Jumping.
(h) Guidelines for the Review of Horizontal Acts of Concentration (known as 'H Guidelines').

65. The CADE is not a regulatory agency, but rather an adjudicatory entity comprised of a Department of Economic Studies (DEE), a GS and an administrative tribunal enforcer of the Brazilian competition laws (Article 5 of Law No. 12529). In the exercise of its legal functions, the CADE shall be assisted by the Federal Office of the CADE Attorney General (PFE) and by the Federal Prosecution Office (MPF). It has no authority to address regulatory matters or to formulate economic policies, except in the exercise of advocacy of competition.

66. Special note is to be made in connection with the creation, in July 2008, of the Special Acting Group for the Repression of Cartel Formation, Money Laundering and Assets Recovery (GEDEC) at the Office of the State Attorney for the State of São Paulo, incumbent, *inter alia*, with the bringing of criminal and class actions in connection with anticompetitive conducts.

§4. Sources' Relation and Hierarchy

67. The Brazilian legal system is based on Federal Constitution. Other sources listed according to their hierarchical authority are: laws, decrees, ordinances, resolutions and normative instructions.

68. It should be noted, however, that the competition and other administrative authorities often make no hierarchic distinction among such statutes and administrative acts. The incentive for the citizens to resort to the judicial actions to ensure their rights is, therefore, adversely affected.

§5. Role and Authority of Precedents

69. Although Brazil is a civil law country, administrative jurisprudence (albeit volatile) and court precedents (more stable) may play a significant role before competition authorities and the Judiciary, as the case may be. Precedents do not enjoy the force of law, but are rather illustrative in supporting private claims before the Public Authority.

70. In addition, the CADE has issued nine Abstracts (*Súmulas*), which consolidate certain settled matters at the administrative level.

71. Most of the CADE Abstracts have been incorporated or repealed by Law No. 12529. The only CADE Abstracts, still in force, are the following:

(a) Abstract No. 4, published in the Federal Official Gazette of 9 December 2009:

72. 'A non-competition clause effective for the life of a joint venture (JV) is valid, provided that it shall keep a direct relation with its purpose and be restricted to the relevant market where the venture shall do business' (free translation).

(b) Abstract No. 5, published in the Federal Official Gazette of 9 December 2009:

73. 'A non-competition clause with a duration of five years starting from the sale of an establishment is valid, as long as such provision is related to the protection of the goodwill' (free translation).

(c) Abstract No. 6, published in the Federal Official Gazette of, 9 December 2009:

74. 'The fact that triggers the obligation to pay the notification fee set forth in Law No. 9.781/99 is the filing of the act of concentration application or of the request for clearance. The fee is due even if the interested parties subsequently withdraw the application' (free translation).

(d) Abstract No. 7, published in the Federal Official Gazette of 9 December 2009:

75. 'Restraining or creating difficulties, by any means, for medical doctors, members of a Cooperation to render services outside the Cooperative, is an anticompetitive conduct, provided that the latter shall enjoy a dominant position' (free translation).

76. The above-quoted Abstracts represent the consolidation of precedents affirmed by the Tribunal of the CADE.

77. Pursuant to Article 65, section 1, of the CADE Internal Regulations, the President of the CADE, any Councillor, the Superintendent General and CADE Attorney General have the authority to suggest to the Tribunal of the CADE the consolidation of settled matters into an Abstract. For such purposes, the final determinations to be consolidated into an Abstract must be made by the absolute majority of the Tribunal Panel members (Article 66 of the CADE Internal Regulations) in at least ten consenting precedent cases.

78. The CADE Abstracts are not binding either on CADE or on other administrative or judicial authorities. Notwithstanding, Abstracts are sound and strong guidelines that effectively advise and inform to the public and other authorities the understanding of the CADE on the relevant issues.

Chapter 2. Scope of Application

§1. Territorial Reach

79. Brazilian competition laws are extraterritorial and apply, without prejudice to conventions or treaties to which Brazil is signatory, to commercial practices made, totally or partially, within the Brazilian national territory or in foreign countries, provided that such practices shall have any effect in Brazil.

80. For this purpose, a foreign legal entity that does business in Brazil, or has a branch, agency, representative office, establishment, agent or representative in the country, shall be deemed to be a Brazilian resident.

81. As a consequence for an undertaking to fall within the scope of application of the Brazilian jurisdiction, it is sufficient to supply any product or to render any service within the Brazilian territory, regardless if such undertaking performs such activities directly, through a foreign legal entity or through a local subsidiary company.

82. The laws also provide that a foreign company may be served with a process and notified of any procedural action regardless of such company granting a power-of-attorney to a representative in the country, and of any contractual provision or corporate resolution to the contrary. Such service and notification may be made on the branch, agency, establishment or office located in Brazil.

83. Whenever the foreign legal entity or its Brazilian branch, agency, establishment or office is inaccessible for the service or notice, such actions may be perfected through notice or summons published in the Federal Official Gazette. All affected parties shall be presumed to be validly served or notified upon such publication.

§2. Special Sectors

84. Various laws governing regulatory agencies interface with the competition laws. Consulting and cooperating functions and competition promotion competences are vested into a number of such agencies, such as:

(a) National Cinema Agency (ANCINE) – Provisional Measure No. 2228-1, of 6 September 2001.
(b) National Electricity Regulatory Agency (ANEEL) – Law No. 9427, of 26 December 1996.
(c) National Petroleum Agency (ANP) – Law No. 9478, of 6 August 1997.
(d) Supplementary Health National Agency (ANS) – Law No. 9656, of 3 June 1998.
(e) Land Transportation National Agency (ANTT) and Water Transportation National Agency (ANTAQ) – Law No. 10233, of 5 June 2001.
(f) National Health Surveillance Agency (ANVISA) – Law No. 9782, of 26 January 1999.

(g) Insurance General Superintendency (SUSEP) – Decree No. 4270, of 10 December 1901.

(h) Central Bank of Brazil (BACEN) – Law No. 4595, of 31 December 1964.

85. None of such agencies, however, have legal authority to investigate and punish anticompetitive conducts, save as such conducts infringe applicable regulatory laws.

86. The CADE has no authority to address regulatory matters, except in the exercise of advocacy of competition. It may, for example, recommend the enacting of resolutions or the amendment of resolutions by competent regulatory agencies that are deemed to be anticompetitive. The CADE may also resort to the Office of the Attorney General to bring class actions or to obtain the enactment of the resolutions or amendment of those in force that are held anticompetitive from the competent regulatory agencies.

87. The only regulatory agency that has the authority to investigate anticompetitive conducts and to review mergers and acquisitions is the National Telecommunications Agency (ANATEL) – Law No. 9472, of 16 July 1997. In any event, the CADE is the only authority with exclusive jurisdiction to issue an administrative final determination on such cases.

§3. State-Owned Enterprises and Public Utilities

88. State-owned enterprises and public utilities are not immune from the Brazilian competition laws or from the authority of the CADE.

89. An interesting example refers to the charge brought by the Office of the Federal Attorney General (*Procuradoria Geral da República*) against the boards of Commerce of the Brazilian States and of the Federal District[2] in connection with the fixing of prices by the boards of Commerce for services rendered by public sworn translators.

90. Another example involved a complaint made by the State of Pernambuco Sugar Cane Cultivators' Union (*Sindicato dos Cultivadores de Cana-de-Açúcar do Estado de Pernambuco*) against the ANP, claiming that a certain regulatory regulation enacted by the agency (ANP Resolution No. 7, of 7 March 2007) was anticompetitive and tended to motivate the formation of a cartel by imposing a loyalty by the fuel dealer to the distributor company that displays the same 'flag', in the acquisition of hydrated alcohol.[3] The case was dismissed, but the CADE affirmed the jurisdiction in hearing charges against a governmental agency.

91. Article 31 of Law No. 12529/11 expressly reads that competition laws shall apply to all individuals, and public and private legal entities, as well as to all associations of legal entities and individuals, whether such associations are legally incorporated or not, and even to those entities that operate as legal monopolies.

2. Preliminary Investigation No. 08012.002856/2008-58, resolved on 27 Jul. 2011, in re. *Procuradoria Geral da República v. Juntas Comerciais dos Estados e do Distrito Federal.*

3. Preliminary Investigation No. 08012.012495/2007-77 (resolved on 30 Jan. 2013) in re. *Sindicato dos Cultivadores de Cana-de-Açúcar do Estado de Pernambuco v. ANP.*

§4. Sensible Effect and De Minimis

92. Sensible effect and *de minimis* immunities and exemptions are not available under Brazilian competition laws, neither in connection with anticompetitive conducts nor in relation to merger reviews.

93. On the contrary, Article 36 of Law No. 12529/11 expressly admits that potential anticompetitive effects are punishable conducts, and parties may generally be held accountable based on strict liability rules, with the sole exception of managers directly or indirectly responsible for the offence, in which case evidence of fault of wilful misconduct is required (Article 37, item III). Thus, save in the case of managers, penalties may be imposed regardless of intent and even if no actual anticompetitive effect is achieved by the relevant market conduct.

94. Lack of sensible effect issues may, however, be considered in mitigating the level of penalties imposed on anticompetitive conducts or in the granting of summary proceedings in merger reviews.

Chapter 3. Overview of Substantive Provisions

§1. Restrictive Agreements

95. In Brazil, restrictive or collaboration[4] agreements (both horizontal and vertical arrangements) that reduce information asymmetry among competitors and result in or induce into agreements on prices, output, input, clientele or other competitive variable are considered to be a cartel arrangement.

§2. Dominant Undertakings

96. Abuse of dominance is likewise an anticompetitive conduct punishable by the Brazilian Antitrust Law (LDC).

An undertaking is considered to be dominant whenever it, or the economic unit of which such undertaking is a member, shall control a significant portion of the relevant market, either as a supplier, a middleman, a purchaser or a financier of a product or service or of a technology related thereto.

97. The law (Law No. 12529/11, Article 36, §2) presumes that an undertaking is dominant whenever it, or the economic unit of which such undertaking is a member, shall control 20% of the relevant market, provided that such percentage may be altered by the CADE in connection with specific economic sectors (in practice, the CADE has, to date, never exercised such authority).

98. However, the law explicitly affirms that market dominance is not an illegal status and that, in fact, the conquer of the market as a result of a natural process based on the greater efficiency of the relevant player *vis-à-vis* its competitors shall not be considered an illegal market dominance.

99. The tests and impact of market dominance on merger reviews and on the investigation of anticompetitive conducts shall be further analysed in Part I, Chapter 4 Overview of Main Notions, §3, 'Market power / Dominant position'.

§3. Concentrations

100. Concentrations will be further analysed in Part II, Chapter 3 (Concentrations).

101. The concept of concentration under Brazilian law encompasses not only horizontal market concentrations but also vertical integrations. Further, under the law (Articles 88 and 90, of Law No. 12529/11), any act (including, without limitation, contracts, cooperative and other formal or informal arrangements), in any form, that may restrict or in any way injure free competition or result in the domination of a relevant market is considered an 'act of concentration' (as such transactions are known).

4. This topic will be further discussed on Part II – Restrictive Agreements.

§4. Other Prohibitions

102. Generally, anticompetitive conducts (known as 'offences to the economic order') are any acts, no matter how practised, that shall have the purpose of, or that may yield any of the following impacts, even if such impacts are not actually achieved (potential impact): (a) limitation or, misleading of, or any form of injury to, free competition or the free initiative, (b) market dominance, (c) arbitrary profit increase, or (d) exercise of abusive form of market dominance.

103. Anticompetitive conducts are twofold: (a) collective anticompetitive conducts, such as cartels, agreements between competitors, uniform conducts and concerted actions, and (b) individual anticompetitive conducts (including horizontal or vertical restrictive actions or arrangements).

104. The main prohibitions and administrative penalties relating to anticompetitive conducts in Brazil are stated in Law No. 12529/11, Article 36.

105. Except in the case of managers who are directly or indirectly responsible for the offence, in which case evidence of fault of wilful misconduct is required (Article 37, item III), determination of anticompetitive conduct does not require wilful misconduct or malicious intent. Strict liability is found in any action in any way intended or otherwise able to yield the following effects even if they are not achieved (Article 36):

(1) – to limit, restrain or in any way injure free competition or free initiative;
(2) – to dominate a relevant market of a certain product or service;
(3) – to arbitrarily increase profits; and
(4) – to abusively exercise a dominant position.

Seeking to act as a guideline, the law (Article 36, paragraph 3) shows a list of potentially anticompetitive conducts, which alone are not offensive, but only if the ultimate result of such actions will be one of the four prohibitions stated in Article 36, *caput*. Such potentially offensive actions are:

(1) – to agree, conjoin, manipulate or make adjustments with a competitor, in any way:

  (a) the prices of goods and services individually offered;
  (b) the production or the commercialization of a restricted or limited quantity of goods, or the offering of a restricted number, restricted or limited volume or frequency of a service;
  (c) the division of parts or segments of an actual or potential market of goods or services through, amongst other things, the distribution of clients, suppliers, regions or periods;
  (d) the prices, conditions, advantages or abstention in public bids;

(2) – to promote, obtain or influence the adoption of uniform or concerted business practices among competitors;
(3) – to limit or restrain market access by new companies;

(4) – to pose difficulties for the establishment, operation or development of a competing company or supplier, purchaser or financial provider of goods or services;
(5) – to restrain competitors' access to input, raw material, equipment or technology sources, as well as to their distribution channels;
(6) – to require or grant exclusivity in mass media advertisements;
(7) – to affect third-party prices by deceitful means;
(8) – to regulate markets of goods or services, establishing agreements to limit or control the research and technological development, production of goods or rendering of services, or to hamper investments aimed at the production of goods or services or at their distribution;
(9) – to impose on distributors, retailers and representatives of goods or services resale prices, discounts, payment conditions, minimum or maximum quantities, profit margins, or any other marketing conditions related to their business with third parties;
(10) – to discriminate against purchasers or suppliers of goods or services by establishing price differentials or discriminatory operating conditions for the sale or performance of services;
(11) – to refuse to sell goods or services under the payment conditions usually applied to regular business practices and policies;
(12) – to restrain or interrupt the continuance or development of business relationships for an indeterminate period, in view of the other party's refusal to comply with unreasonable or anticompetitive business conditions;
(13) – to destroy, render unfit for use or take possession of raw materials, intermediary or finished products, as well as to destroy, render unfit for use or hinder the operation of any equipment intended to manufacture, distribute or transport them;
(14) – to take possession of or restrain the use of industrial or intellectual property rights or technology;
(15) – to unreasonably sell goods or render services below cost;
(16) – to retain production or consumer goods, except for ensuring recovery of production costs;
(17) – to partially or fully discontinue company's activities, without a proven fair and acceptable cause;
(18) – to condition the sale of goods to the acquisition of another or to the contracting of a service, or to condition the performance of a service to the contracting of another or purchase of goods; and
(19) – to abusively exercise or exploit intellectual or industrial property rights, technology or trademark.

106. In repealing former Law No. 8884/94, Law 12529/11 deleted from the list of potentially anticompetitive individual conducts market-sharing, abusive pricing and exclusivity agreements. Nevertheless, market-sharing continues to be a classical offence, and currently more precisely pursued as a kind of cartel (Article 36, §3, item 'c').

107. Thus, for example, already under the aegis of the new law, in the Administrative Proceeding No. 08000.009354/97-82 (resolved on 20 August 2014), in re. *SDE, ex officio, v. AgipLiquigás do Brasil S.A. et alii*, Councillor Eduardo Pontual Ribeiro, condemned the principal distributors' firms of liquefied petroleum gas in the cities of Porto Alegre and Canoas, in the State of Rio Grande do Sul, for sharing the market by allocating on a monthly basis, to each participating firm, certain days in the month for the exclusive sale of cylinders to dealers.

108. On its turn, exclusivity arrangements have not been exempted, but only released from the presumption of illegality that vests the conducts listed in said §3, and are to be reviewed on a case-by-case basis under the rule of reason.

§5. Tests of Illegality

I. Per Se Prohibition and Naked Restraints

109. There are no per se offences under Brazilian law, and all anticompetitive conducts (including cartels and other conspiracies or collusive actions) are assessed based on the rule of reason. CADE's jurisprudence has, however, in the recent past adopted the European Union (EU) doctrine of anticompetitive conducts by object (such as cartels) and by effects, whereby, the former describes offences that are considered harmful to competition by their very nature, thus requiring no enquiry on the actual effects, and consequently on market power or other economic defences. Although not discussed in the Federal Courts so far, such jurisprudence seems to be supported neither by the Brazilian Federal Constitution (which adopts the principle of presumption of innocence) nor by Law No. 12529/2011 (Article 36, §3, which requires evidence of effects of the anticompetitive conduct).

110. Notwithstanding, in re. *SDE, ex officio, v. Peróxidos do Brasil Ltda. et alii* Administrative Process No. 08012.004702/2004-77, resolved on 9 May 2012, has accepted a quasi-per se offence in characterizing hard-core cartels by ruling that the mere evidence of existence of the conduct is sufficient to affirm the offence, and that the actual injure to competition yielding from a hard-core cartel is to be presumed.

111. The law expressly states a caveat: achieving a market control as a result of a natural process founded in greater efficiency does not constitute an offence. (Article 36, §1).

112. This topic will be further discussed.

113. The main prohibitions and penalties (in the criminal perspective) related to antitrust violations in Brazil are stated in the Law No. 8137/90, Article 4, and in terms of bid rigging, in the Law No. 8666/93, Article 90.

114. Interesting enough, while the actions are described as mere guidelines in Article 36, §3, item I of Law No. 12529/11, they may themselves characterize a criminal offence under Article 4 of Law No. 8137/90. Thus, the following shall constitute criminal offences:

(1) – abuse of economic power, dominating the market or eliminating, in full or in part, competition by means of any business arrangement or agreement;
(2) – sign contracts, agreement, alliance or adjustment between issuers, in order to:

(a) artificially fix prices or quantities sold or produced;
(b) achieve regional market control by a company or group of companies;
(c) control, in detriment of competition, distribution networks and suppliers:

Penalty - imprisonment from two (2) to five (5) years and fine.

115. Contrary to civil prohibitions, criminal offences require intent and only apply to individuals, not legal entities.

116. Ancillary to Law No. 8137/90, Article 90 of the Brazilian Public Tender Bids Law (Law No. 8666/93) states that it is also a criminal offence to defraud, through arrangements, agreements or any other means, the competitive nature of a bidding process, with the intent of securing for oneself or others, an advantage yielding from the adjudication of the bidding object. Such criminal actions are subject to jail sentence (detention) between two and four years, and fine.

II. Balancing Tests

117. Given that the Brazilian law does not entertain the concept of per se offences or naked restraints, balancing tests are governed by the rule of reason and by economic rationality tests, based on the concept that anticompetitive actions are those actions that result in negative net social results.

118. Article 1 of Law No. 12529/11 expressly states that the prevention of, and repression to, offences to the economic order are governed by the constitutional principles of free initiative, free competition, social purpose of property, consumer defence and repression to abusive exercise of economic power. Thus, Competition Law principles are constitutional by nature and the law explicitly rules that Society (and not any individual, or particular legal entity or organization or the Public Administration) is the rightful owner of the statutory assets. Consequently, the competition laws cannot be used to create or implement public, economic or other, policies, other than free competition policies. The improper use of competition laws to create or implement Government or political policies are considered to be 'social function deviations'.

119. Balancing tests will be further analysed.

III. Merger Tests

120. In the area of merger control, transactions or acts of concentration that impact Society negatively shall be illegal and, therefore, rejected by the authorities. Statutory tests are primarily efficiency and structural tests, and eventually, on national interest tests.

121. Such is the base ground of Article 88 of the Brazilian Competition Law that governs the clearance of market concentrations that in any way limit competition, as long as certain conditions that are listed in paragraphs 5 and 6 are met, as follows:

Paragraph 5. Concentration acts that implicate the elimination of competition in a substantial part of the relevant market, and which can create or reinforce a dominant position or can result in market domination of the relevant goods or services market will be prohibited, except the provision of paragraph 6 of this article.

Paragraph 6. The act that refer to paragraph 5 of this article could be authorised, as long as they observe the limits that are strictly necessary to achieve the following objective:

(1) cumulatively or alternatively:

(a) increase productivity or competitiveness;
(b) improve the quality of goods and services; or
(c) provide efficiency and technological or economic development; and

(2) the relevant benefits are shared with consumers.

122. In practice, efficiency tests have a limited actual use, except for price tests (whereby the transaction shall necessarily result in a price reduction). Reducing even further the role of efficiencies, the CADE ruled[5] that efficiencies are to be carefully reviewed and with suspicion, given that the calculation of efficiencies is a work of tentative estimation of future events, characterized by a high degree of uncertainties. Further, the CADE stated in such resolution that, in the purchase of a minority shareholding, there is no opportunity for the creation of efficiencies.

123. As to national interest tests, these are also of rare and only ancillary use.

124. Although not stated as such, Act of Concentration No. 08012.001205/2010-65 (resolved in February 2011), in re. *Braskem S.A., Petróleo Brasileiro S.A., Petrobras Química* and *Quattor Participações S.A.*, in creating a virtual monopoly in various sectors of the petrochemical industry, seems to be a clear, albeit rare, case of unconditional clearance (although not explicitly) based on national interest concepts. On the opposite side, while the *Braskem* case involved State-owned companies and strategic domestic areas, the opposite trend was seen in the case of Act of Concentration No. 08012.004423/2009-18 (resolved on 13 July 2011) in re. *Perdigão S.A. and Sadia S.A.*, relating to the private and commercial refrigerated food industry, in which clearance was granted conditional upon severe partial divestiture remedies.

125. National interest is occasionally considered, but only as a subsidy for the final determination. In Act of Concentration No. 08012.006121/2012-80 (resolved on 30 January 2013), in re. *Biolab Sanus Farmacêutica Ltda. et alii,* relating to the formation by competing domestic laboratories of a joint venture for the research, development, production, distribution and commercialization of biological, biopharmaco

5. *See* Acts of Concentration Nos 08012.001875/2010-81, 08012.001879/2010-60, 08012.002018/2010-07 and 08012.002259/2012-18 (resolved on 18 Jul. 2012), in re. *Votorantim Cimentos S.A., Camargo Corrêa S.A., Companhia Nacional de Cimento Portland, Cimpor – Cimentos de Portugal SGPS, S.A and CCB – Cimpor Cimentos do Brasil Ltda.*

and biotechnological products in general, the CADE stressed the interface between competition policies and industrial policies and pointed out that it would be possible to make a convergence between such public policies if the industrial policies are conceived as an instrument of pro-competitiveness, and if the latter expands its concept of the competitive process, by admitting that cooperation among competitors may be vital to the competitive vigour[6].

126. The foregoing notwithstanding, the CADE declared its concerns in the sense that such a collaboration JV should not be permitted '*to serve as a vehicle for a possible coordination among the already existing activities of the parties and of related parties*' and, notwithstanding the national interest in the venture, the transaction was not unconditionally approved, and only cleared upon the parties agreeing to enter into a Settlement Agreement containing governance clauses that sought to ensure the independence of the JV *vis-à-vis* the shareholders and the lack of coordination among related parties.

127. Somewhat in contradiction, the concept of national and consumers' interest has played a significant role in Act of Concentration No. 08012.012722/2010-60 (resolved on 11 April 2012), in re. *Copersucar S.A, Cosan S.A. Indústria e Comércio, Uniduto Logística S.A., Camargo Corrêa Óleo e Gás S.A., Odebrecht Transporte Participações S.A. and Petróleo Brasileiro S.A. – Petrobras*, in which the CADE, in discussing the Brazilian defective infrastructure in the field of liquid fuel multimodal transportation network, a matter of public interest, ruled that a transaction could be cleared even in those cases when it would not be possible to demonstrate that the efficiency gains yielded thereby, even in part, shall be passed over to the consumer, whenever it is demonstrated that the rejection of the deal would certainly cause a harm to the latter.

128. Additional comments on the criteria for the assessment of the impact of acts of concentration in the market and on free competition are found in Part III, Chapter 2 ('Voluntary Notifications and Clearance').

6. In a similar attitude, the Superintendency-General of the CADE decided that the operations carried out under the aegis of the National Program for the Promotion of Public Production and Innovation in the Health Industrial Complex, of the Ministry of Health, which culminated in the launch of the Productive Development Policy (PDP), whose guidelines are the strengthening of public laboratories, the promotion of public-private partnerships, the internalization of production and the strategic use of the State purchasing power, although a programme of public interest, requires its analysis from the point of view of their impact on potential competition. *See* the Opinion No. 262 of the Superintendency-General in the Act of Concentration No. 08700.003748/2014-92 (resolved on 20 Aug. 2014), in re. *Bionovis S.A. - Companhia Brasileira de Biotecnologia Farmacêutica, Ares Trading AS and Merck KGaA*, approved by the Superintendent-General of the CADE, Eduardo Frade Rodrigues (Dispatch No. 991).

Chapter 4. Overview of Main Notions

§1. Undertaking

129. The concept of undertaking is found in Article 31 of the Brazilian Competition Law, meaning any individual or private and public legal entity, as well as any association of legal entities or individuals, whether legally incorporated or existing de facto, regardless whether existing on a permanent or temporary basis, legally recognized or not, including those entities that operate under a legal monopoly. Such list contains only examples of undertakings and does not intend to be exclusive. The law acknowledges the impossibility of covering all possible forms of association in a dynamic market economy.

130. There is no requirement that a legal entity or individual be actually engaged in an economic activity to be considered an 'undertaking' and legal status or nature (civil or commercial) of the legal or de facto entity is irrelevant. Should such individual or legal entity be capable of causing or influencing a uniform conduct or an individual anticompetitive conduct, regardless of such individual or entity enjoying market power, it, he/she may be jointly held accountable for third-party antitrust offences.

131. Based on the foregoing, the CADE, in multiple cases, affirmed that the following may be responsible for anticompetitive conducts: (i) cooperatives,[7] (ii) federations and confederations,[8] (iii) trade, professional and other associations,[9] (iv)

7. For examples, *see* Administrative Process No. 08012.005459/02-42, resolved on 8 Dec. 2004, in re. *Procuradoria da República do Município de Bauru/SP v. Unimed de Jaú/SP – Cooperativa de Trabalho Médico* and Administrative Process No. 08012.001447/02-49, resolved on 20 Oct. 2004, in re. *Ministério Público do Estado de São Paulo v. Unimed de Franca – Cooperativa de Trabalho Médico*, concerning medical cooperatives that required exclusivity from medical doctors members of the organization.

8. *See* , for example, Preliminary Investigations Nos 08012.003380/1999-57, resolved on 16 Jan. 2008, in re. *Conselho Regional de Farmácia do Estado de São Paulo – CRF/SP v. UNIMED Intrafederativa – Federação do Nordeste Paulista et alii* and 08012.006637/05-03, resolved on 3 Sep. 2008, in re. *Conselho Regional de Farmácia de Minas Gerais v. Unimed Minas/ Federação Interfederativa das Cooperativas de Trabalho Médico do* Estado de Minas Gerais discussing medical services federations engaging in the drugstore business and the legality of tax benefits granted to cooperatives.

9. In Administrative Process No. 08000.024581/94-77, resolved on 3 Mar. 2004, in re. *Sindicato do Comércio Varejista de Derivados de Petróleo do DF, Rede Gasol (Grupo Cascão) and Grupo Igrejinha*, the CADE ruled that 'anticompetitive entrepreneurial practices may, finally, be carried out through associations and unions, such as industry federations or associations of a certain market segment or region. Such organizations used as vehicles of an offensive conduct, may also be accountable under the Competition Laws. The Brazilian Lawyers' Bar, the Medical Regional Council, the Engineers' Union and other professional organizations may be considered, likewise, active players, offenders of the Competition Laws' (free translation).

foundations,[10] (v) unions,[11] (vi) non-profit organizations[12] and (vii) autarkies and State-owned companies.[13]

132. Individuals that are neither stockholders nor managers of legal entities that have influenced in the adoption of anticompetitive conducts by a market player are also considered accountable for such behaviour.

133. By the same token, Brazilian subsidiary companies and their respective management that disseminate anticompetitive policies of their parent companies are jointly liable for the eventual illegal practices of the latter carried out abroad. Companies of a same economic unit are also responsible for the anticompetitive conduct of its affiliates. In Motion for Clarification No. 08700.003200/06-32, filed by Petrobras Distribuidora S/A and Agip do Brasil S/A, the CADE resolved that a controlling shareholder can be held responsible for the actions of its subsidiaries, even if not directly participating in the subsidiaries' actions.

134. The Public Administration itself may be an 'undertaking' for the purposes of the law. In the case *SDE, ex officio v. Sindicato dos Condutores de Veículos Rodoviários de Brasília – SINDICAVIR/DF and its members* (Administrative Process No. 08012.005769/98-92), the Government of the Federal District (Brasília) was found responsible for engaging in anticompetitive conduct in the exercise of its regulatory constitutional authority, through acts of State or executive acts. The CADE has admitted that it had no authority to act against the Public Authority, but had a residual competence in the exercise of competition advocacy by issuing recommendations or requesting the Public Authority to repeal the anticompetitive statute or regulation. In case of failure or refusal of such Public Authority to act accordingly, the CADE can resort to the Judiciary or request the Office of the Attorney General to act in court seeking to achieve compliance with its own recommendations and requests.

135. Another interesting resolution is found in Preliminary Investigation No. 08012.007704/2004-18, resolved on 7 July 2010, in re. *Antônio Luís Guimarães de Álvares Otero v. Qualix Serviços Ambientais Ltda. et alii*, concerning an allegation of collusive fraud in public tender bids. The CADE has resolved that, should there be circumstantial evidence that the public tender bid summons have been directed, the bidding authorities are to be included as defendants in the corresponding Administrative Process. In this case, the authorities would be the São Paulo City Secretariat of Services and Works *(Secretaria Municipal de Serviços e Obras)*, the Town Hall of the Municipality of São Paulo (*Prefeitura do Município de São Paulo*) and their respective Secretary and Mayor.

10. *See* , for example, Preliminary Investigation No. 08012.005052/01-34, of 24 Jul. 2008, in which *defendants Fundação Ruben Berta, Transbrasil S/A Linhas Aéreas, Amadeus Global Travel Distribution S/A and Amadeus Brasil Ltda.* were relieved of anticompetitive conduct charges based on prescription.
11. *See supra* n. 4.
12. *See supra* n. 4.
13. Article 31 of Law No. 12,529/11 explicitly rules that the competition law applies, *inter alia* to '(…) legal entities of public law (…), even if (they) are (engaged) in activities under the legal monopoly regimen' (free translation). *See* , for example, Preliminary Investigation No. 08012.007897/05-98, resolved on 23 Jul. 2008, in re. *Refinaria de Petróleo de Manguinhos S.A. and Refinaria de Petróleo Ipiranga S.A v. Petróleo Brasileiro S.A – Petrobras*, the Brazilian State-owned oil company concerning a charge of predatory pricing.

136. Also, an interesting case is in re. *Pneus Hauer Brasil Ltda. v. União Federal* (Preliminary Investigation No. 08012.009914/2006-11), in which claimant (*Pneus Hauer*) brought an antitrust action against the Federal Government (*União Federal*), claiming that the executive actions aimed at restraining the importation of used tyres was an anticompetitive conduct. Unfortunately, the debate on whether the Federal Government itself could be considered an 'undertaking' for purposes of the Brazilian Competition Law was stayed by a resolution of the Federal STF that affirmed the constitutionality of the Government actions.

§2. Relevant Market

137. The main standard in determining a relevant market in Brazil is usually the possibility of product substitutability from the demand-side (i.e., from the point of view of clients and consumers). Albeit it is possible to determine a relevant market from the supply-side (i.e., from the point of view of the manufacturer), the demand-side analysis is a primary standard whenever appropriate data is available for such purposes. Such circumstance clearly shows that the post-Chicago consumer protection doctrine has great influence in the Brazilian Competition Law. Pursuant to former CADE Resolution No. 20/99 (which in this respect is still effective as a guideline), '*a relevant market, in its product dimension, must include all products and services that are considered substitutes of one another by the consumer, given their characteristics, prices and applications*' (free translation).

138. The relevant market is the primary and determining factor in assessing the presence or the possibility of exercise of market power by the market player, in both anticompetitive conduct and merger cases. By defining the relevant market, the authorities are capable of identifying the boundaries of the market structure and of the level of competition among the incumbent players therein, both from a product and a geographic point of view.

139. As anticipated, the concept of relevant market is twofold: the product market and the geographic market. The underlying purpose of such concepts is to determine the geographic area where there is no product interchangeability, either because there is no viable equivalent substitute product available (meaning products that are homogeneous, that are sold at similar prices etc.) or because the distance separating the selling premises is such that the purchase of the relevant product is not possible (i.e., due to significant freight costs, physical-chemical specifications that make long-distance transportation impossible or, simply, the eventual unwillingness of clients and consumers to move to certain distances).

140. The CADE H Guidelines innovates by adding to the product and geographic markets the concept of a temporal/seasonal element, relating to the period of time during which a certain market operates, especially in connection with industries with service and production peaks versus natural idle periods (such as in the case of the transportation and electric power industries, or industries with seasonal variations (i.e., the food industry).

141. In short, a relevant market means a product or group of products in a given geographic area where such product or products are made or marketed, in which a monopolist firm would be able to impose a small but significant and non-transitory increase in price (SSNIP), without running the risk of consumers migrating to the consumption of another product or to another area for the purchase.

142. A relevant market is determined by the group of manufacturers and consumers, which is capable of reacting to the supracompetitive conduct of the undertaking resulting from the transaction and limiting its decisions with respect, *inter alia*, to price, volume and quality strategies.

143. The so-called hypothetical monopolist test is one of the tools used in Brazil to evaluate the level of substitutability among products and services, in order to determine a relevant market.

144. Pursuant to such test, the relevant market will be determined in terms of the product and/or service (product dimension) and of the geographic area where the sale of such product is economically feasible (geographic dimension). The relevant market is to be determined by the smallest group of products and by the smallest geographic area where a single hypothetical supplier (monopolist) is capable of imposing an SSNIP.

145. The hypothetical monopolist test considers the assessment of the reaction of the consumer to the hypothetical price increase, and thus of the degree of substitutability between goods and services for the purpose of determining the relevant market.

146. Initially, one is to consider the goods that are produced and marketed by the firms parties to the transaction and all of the territory where such firms operate. Subsequently, and in a sequence, a broader spectrum of products and geographic markets are to be considered up to the point in which it is possible to determine a market in which the imposition of an SSNIP would be possible to a hypothetical monopolist in such area. Should the result be such that the hypothetical monopolist shall consider that such price increase is not profitable, then the product that is the closest substitute and/or the region of origin of such substitute product shall be added to the relevant market.

147. The boundaries of the relevant market shall correspond to the first group of products and of locations found to be appropriate to a company, acting alone, or for a group of companies, acting in coordination, to impose a SSNIP and to consequently exercise market power. Thus, the relevant market will be determined within the limits of the smallest geographic radius and the smallest group of products where such standards will be met.

148. Parallelly, the test of the hypothetical monopsonist is applicable to investigate the unilateral impact of the purchasing power. Such test seeks to determine a geographic area, a product and a period of time, in which the formation of hypothetical monopsony in the intermediate market could generate an incentive and a significant and non-transitory possibility of causing a reduction in value of the purchase price of its inputs, in the upstream market. A competitive concern would then arise if, for example, such situation would generate an incentive for the monopsonist to restrict the supply and to increase prices to the downstream market.

149. The CADE is not limited to any particular methodology to determine the relevant market and, actually, is not bound to determine any and may leave such definition open. Whenever deciding to do so, however, it may consider, jointly or severally: (a) qualitative information, (b) information on prices, (c) flow of goods and consumers, (d) definition of radius, and (e) whenever necessary or possible, quantitative methods, such as the analysis of critical loss (or of critical elasticity).

150. The determination of the relevant market may also be affected by: (a) the possibility of firms discriminating consumers, in which case, the market may be limited to the group of consumers that may be affected by the discriminatory conduct, (b) the presence of anti-dumping duties affecting imports and (c) the nature of the market, such as in the case of a technology market, where patent rights may permit the creation of temporary monopolies restraining the creation of new technologies.

151. Once a relevant market is defined, the CADE may analyse the market shares. In those markets involving sale power, the data shall reflect the structure of supply, covering, *inter alia*, the production capacity, the unitary sales volume or value. In those involving purchasing power, the consumers' market share shall reflect the structure of demand, which may be calculated, *inter alia,* by the volume or value of purchase by each player. Such data may be considered jointly with the downstream structure of supply.

152. Once, and if, the relevant market and the market concentration levels are determined, and once the levels of barriers to entry and rivalry in the marketplace are assessed, the authorities will come to a conclusion as to the extent of market power in the case under review.

§3. Market Power/Dominant Position

153. Market power means the control of a significant part of the relevant market capable of provoking a variation in prices for a reasonable period of time through restriction in volumes. The exercise of market power created by an act of concentration requires that demand be or becomes inelastic to price as a result of the transaction.

154. On its turn, the Brazilian Competition Law provides that a dominant position shall occur whenever a given concern unilaterally, or a given group of firms, in coordination, are capable of exercising the control over a significant portion of the relevant market, and of altering its structural conditions, such as prices, volumes.

155. Thus, there shall be an exercise of market power whenever an undertaking (or group of firms) is capable of maintaining the prices for their products and/or services above the market average level, without incurring the risk of losing clients. In short, the market power allows the dominant undertaking to maintain prices at a level above market levels without causing consumers to migrate to competing products or services at more competitive prices.

156. In Brazil, it is assumed that a firm or group of firms will enjoy a dominant position if such firm or group shall control 20% or more of the relevant market. The CADE may, however, given special circumstances relating to the characteristics of the specific industry, consider other market shares in assessing market dominance.

157. The market share, however, is not, in itself, sufficient to determine market dominance and the possibility of exercise of market power. For example, brand or portfolio power may also permit dominance.

158. In a merger case, the probability of exercise of market power will be assessed not only if the market share of the entity resulting from the concentration is

20% or more of the relevant market, but also if the CR_4 level (meaning the sum of the market share of the four biggest incumbent players in such market) of concentration in such market shall be equal to or in excess of 75%.

159. The assessment of market power requires a complex analysis of multiple variables, such as the possibility of product substitutability by imported products, the actual level of competitiveness among the incumbent players (rivalry), the possibility of entry of newcomers, and the presence and level of barriers to entry and the bargaining power by the clients and consumers. The H Guidelines does not contemplate imports as a deterrent of market power, but such circumstance should not impair such consideration. Indeed, for example, the H Guidelines does consider the presence of anti-dumping duties as a factor that may affect the definition of the relevant market.

160. The presence of high barriers to entry and probability of exercise of market power, if found in the context of the review of a transaction may increase the impact of market foreclosure and, thus, result in a restraint of trade.

161. Barriers to entry are defined as any factor in a given market that may place a competitor in disadvantage *vis-à-vis* an incumbent player.

162. The higher the barrier to entry, the bigger will be the financial costs and the longer the time required for a newcomer to have its invested capital duly remunerated. Barriers to entry permit incumbent players to maintain prices at higher levels and make the entry of newcomers with productive capacity difficult.

163. Principal barriers to entry are: sunk costs, legal and regulatory barriers, the resources of the exclusive ownership of incumbent players, economies of scale and scope, the degree of integration of the production chain, the loyalty of consumers to established brands and the threat of reaction of incumbent players.

164. The history of entries in the market in the past five years is also considered in determining conditions for entry. In such analysis, the CADE may review the actual entry of a new competitor, as well as the failure of firms in attempting to enter the market, as well as any indicia of actual past entry.

165. In order to an act of concentration to be found harmless to competition, the entry of the newcomer must satisfy three statistical standards:

- First Standard: The time required by the entry cannot exceed the term of approximately two years or such term that is adequate to the competitive dynamics of the market under consideration, provided that such term is sufficient to permit the entrant to contest the eventual market power of the merged firms (*timeliness of entry*).
- Second Standard: The entry must be probable and effective, meaning that the result of the probability of entry analysis (APE) shall not be negative, upon considering the available sales opportunities (OV), the market idle capacity (CO), the residual sales opportunities (OVR) and the minimum viable scale (EMV); the greater the APE, the greater the probability of entry in the market (*likelihood of entry*).
- Third Standard: The entry must permit the newcomer the possibility of supplying products at such levels so as to permit it to discipline the market and prevent price increases (*sufficiency of entry*).

166. The merger review is carried out with due precautions in terms of assessing barriers to entry, based on which the assessment of exercise of market power will be made effectively and successfully.

167. The transactions that are entered into in markets characterized by low barriers to entry are usually of a lesser concern to the authorities. Indeed, the presence of high barriers to entry significantly contributes to the effectiveness of the exercise of market power, and the risks of injury to the market, such as those related to the imposition of conducts on rivals, the exclusion of efficient competitors and the restriction to the entry of newcomers.

168. Summing up, an entry will be considered possible if it meets the three standards, of: (i) timeliness, (ii) probability and (iii) sufficiency of the entry.

169. In such analysis, a frequently used methodology of determining the impact of a concentration and the need to investigate the possibility of exercise of market power is the Hirschmann-Herfindahl Index (HHI). Such index is the sum of the squares of the market shares of each firm, divided by 10,000. The figures, therefore, range between 0 (perfect competition) and 1 (monopoly). The HHI may also be expressed in percentages. Increases in the HHI correspond to a decrease in the level of competition and an increase of market power.

170. Based on the use of the HHI index, the markets are:

(a) not concentrated: with HHI lower than 1,500 points;
(b) moderately concentrated: with HHI between 1,500 and 2,500 points;
(c) highly concentrated: with HHI above 2,500 points.

171. Transactions that yield a HHI variation lower than 100 points ($\Delta HHI < 100$) and, in the case of a not concentrated market, if the market, as a result of the transaction shall remain with a HHI lower than 1,500 points, generally do not result in negative competitive effects, and thus, require no further analysis.

172. The criterion, although not tailored or fit to describe the characteristics of the Brazilian markets, is often used by the CADE (similar to the US Federal Trade Commission) to determine whether a transaction has an anticompetitive impact. In any event, the use of the HHI index is not determinant, but only indicative of a causal nexus and a starting point for the analysis of market power.

173. As a matter of fact, the HHI index is to be used with caution in markets with a large fringe and high market dispersion. It should also be flexibly used (a) should there be indicia of coordination among market players, (b) should one of the parties be a maverick or practice a disruptive market strategy, (c) whenever the merger shall refer to a newcomer, (d) should there be a significant cross shareholding between the parties and its competitors, (e) should the degree of market concentration not reflect the actual competitive dynamics of the market, and (f) should the merger increase a portfolio power.

174. In using the HHI index, the following parameters are taken into account in determining if a given transaction shall yield competitive concerns:

(a) in the case of moderately concentrated markets, if the transaction shall result in a market with HHI between 1,500 and 2,500 points and involve an index variation exceeding 100 points ($\Delta HHI > 100$);
(b) in the case of highly concentrated markets, if the transaction shall result in a market with HHI exceeding 2,500 points and involve an index variation between 100 and 200 points ($100 \leq \Delta HHI \leq 200$); and
(c) transactions resulting in a market with HHI in excess of 2,500 points and involve an index variation exceeding 200 points ($\Delta HHI > 200$).

175. The effectiveness of competition between the merged firms and their rivals, on its turn, may result in that the market power acquired through the transaction is less probable (rivalry).

176. An effective rivalry is probable in those environments in which an incumbent firm shall tend to adopt aggressive strategies seeking to increase its market share as a reaction to the exercise of market power by the merged firms.

177. Some variables may influence the analysis of rivalry, such as: (a) market concentration, (b) price dispersion, (c) profit margin, (d) market-share variations, (e) demand price elasticity, (f) crossed demand price, (g) supply price elasticity, (h) demand growth rates, (i) productive assets, (j) conduct monitoring, (k) vertical integration and portfolio, (l) pre and after sales services, (m) access to efficient distributors and logistic services, (n) access to credit, (o) committed clientele and points of sale, (p) economies of scale and scope and (q) use of idle capacity.

178. Act of Concentration No. 08700.003356/2014-84 (resolved on 4 July 2014), in re. *Copersucar S.A. and Cargill Agrícola S.A.*, the SG (Dispatch No. 746, published in the Federal Official Gazette of 7 July 2014, section 1, page 11) ruled that, from the point of view of effectiveness of competition analysis, the availability of idle capacity installed by the competitors is a crucial factor, though not unique. That is, if competitors do not have it, they will not be able to meet consumers' interests in diverting their purchases in the case of a price increase by the merged firm, unless it shall be economically viable for them to expand their existing production capacity in not more than two years.

179. Markets characterized by rivalry are expected to have effective rivals, that is, firms that are capable of competing with the merged firms, having equivalent technological capacity, competitive cost and price levels, similar scope and product quality and other factors that are decisive to the competitive potential needed to confront the merged firms after the consummation of the transaction.

180. Portfolio power may also make an entry difficult, as well as hinder the capacity of exercise rivalry in opposing incumbent players and facilitate anticompetitive conducts. In those markets characterized by economies of scope, firms that have a larger portfolio may be benefited by having lower average production costs *vis-à-vis* those having a small variety of products.

181. Extensive portfolios may reduce clients' transaction costs, thus inducing them to deal with a single firm that offers multiple types of products and brands, as opposed to competitors having a smaller variety. Also, from the clients' point of view, having a relationship with many suppliers shall cause them to face a significant transaction cost yielding from aspects such as negotiations of prices and purchase conditions for each product, preparation and control of contracts. From the suppliers' point of view, a portfolio power may maximize their brand exposure, whereupon its marketing efforts will be much more effective.

182. The firm enjoying portfolio power may take advantage of such circumstance to exercise market power by increasing prices and eventually gaining market share from smaller firms. It may conversely adopt an aggressive market foreclosure strategy by reducing prices in a target market segment, while subsidizing the loss in other markets (cross subsidies).

183. On the other hand, mergers may result in the creation of compensatory power capable of facing an existing market power. The analysis of efficiencies resulting from a transaction yielding compensatory power is to be made by using the rule of reason.

184. In short, market dominance is not expressed solely through market share, but further depends on the possibility of the unilateral behaviour not being contested.

§4. Agreements and Concerted Practices

185. An agreement is perfected whenever three elements are present: (a) parties, (b) object and (c) price or consideration, irrespective of its legality.

186. For the purpose of competition laws, agreements may be in writing (formal contract or deed, public or private, epistolary, by any other means, including electronic means) or tacit (including through conscious parallelism and uniform conducts), and, if in writing, need not to be signed by individuals empowered to represent the undertaking. Brazilian law adheres to the 'appearance doctrine', meaning that the contracting party need not investigate whether the other signatory is legally empowered to represent the undertaking if such individual is generally reputed or considered to be a representative.

187. Furthermore, the law (Article 32) rules that the liability for anticompetitive conduct shall be joint and severally vested into the offending legal entity and its managers and administrators in general, regardless of whether the latter shall be empowered to legally represent the former.[14]

14. Such understanding is not free from controversy. In the Public Civil Action No. 0029912-22.2001.403.6100 (2001.61.00.029912-6), in re. *Ministério Público Federal, v. Abbott Laboratórios do Brasil Ltda. et alii* the Judge of the fourteenth. Civil Trial Court in São Paulo, Alternate Judge, Cláudia Rinaldi Fernandes, on 16 Jun. 2010 resolved that the characterization of a cartel requires the direct participation of high level officers of the involved corporations, that enjoy control powers thereof, capable of resolving the adoption of such actions that are significant to the market and in production or in the rendering of services, thus directly affecting the collusive undertakings. Similarly, on, 9 Dec. 2011, the trial court decision of Judge Itagiba Catta Preta Neto, of the fourth. Federal Court of the Federal District, annulled the CADE Resolution based on lack of evidence of anticompetitive conduct, including the fact the participants had no powers to bind their respective employer undertakings (Ordinary Civil Actions Nos 2007.34.00.043978-7 and others). Such trial court resolution is under appeal to the higher courts.

188. In Brazil, concerted practices are tacit agreements, if not in writing, and concerted practices are a synonym of cartel. The CADE considers cartels and concerted practices alike.[15]

189. So, the main example of a restrictive agreement is the cartel (also more broadly known as 'concerted practice'). It consists of agreements entered into among firms that do business in the same relevant market, with the principal purpose of securing higher profits, *inter alia*, through price fixings, coordinated price adjustments or adjustments in commercial terms, reduction of volumes, changes or standardization of quality standards, market divisions or fraud at public tender bids.

190. Not all agreements among competitors are considered cartels. The authorities do consider and make a distinction of agreements that promote competition, development and efficiencies or that are at least neutral to competition, and those that harm competition. Although it is correct to say that allegedly 'good cartels' are not admissible, it is also true that, in Brazil, there is no per se offences, even in cartel cases, the review of which are, similar to other anticompetitive conducts, governed by the rule of reason.

191. Agreements among market players resulting in concerted actions may result in a detrimental impact on the competitive environment and result in an offence to the economic order. In such cases, the GS will commence an investigation on the anticompetitive behaviour, acting either ex officio or based on third-party complaints. The GS may start a preparatory procedure (if circumstantial evidence is insufficient to support the characterization of a possible cartel), an administrative investigation (if circumstantial evidence exists but is insufficient to support a formal charge) or an Administrative Process (if existing evidence is strong enough to support a charge and to identify the possible players). The CADE will reach its final determination upon reviewing the technical opinion (i.e., non-binding) of the GS.

192. Additional details of the procedures relating to the investigation of anticompetitive conducts are provided in Part III (Administrative Procedure).

§5. Restriction of Competition

193. Actions in restraint of trade may be found either in acts of concentrations as in market conduct; nevertheless, not every restrictive action is illegal under Brazilian law. To confirm an anticompetitive behaviour, it is necessary to demonstrate, under the rule of reason, if the harmful impact of the conduct shall supersede (i.e., overcome) the benefits. Only if the answer is in the affirmative, the conduct may be classified as an illegal restraint of trade.[16]

194. Restriction on competition need not to be an actual restriction, potentially (intentional or not) restrictive effects shall suffice for the underlying action to be held anticompetitive and punishable. Consequently, Brazil has adopted no *de minimis* rule

15. More details on cartels and concerted practices will be examined on Part II, Chapter 1 Restrictive Agreements.
16. Neither the Brazilian law nor the jurisprudence adopt the idea of *de minimis* rule for antitrust. If a given practice or a merger holds a restrictive object, it should be analysed under the rule of reason.

and the actual effect of an anticompetitive conduct on the market is irrelevant (Article 36, *caput*) to the entailment of liability.

195. An interesting example of such standard is found in re. *Conselho Regional de Farmácia do Distrito Federal – CRF/DF v. Abbott Laboratórios do Brasil Ltda. et alii*, Administrative Process No. 08012.009088/1999-48, resolved on 13 October 2005; the CADE affirmed that twenty-one pharmaceutical companies had engaged in cartel activities by merely permitting their employees (mostly sales managers having no powers to represent or bind their respective employers) to attend a social gathering promoted by an employee of a large distributor company. The CADE alleged that the purpose of the meeting was presumably to prevent or hinder the launching of generic medicine in Brazil, short of the enactment of the Generics Law, by reducing the credibility of such drugs. In its resolution, the CADE expressly recognized that the meeting had no actual impact in the market, but has ruled that the meeting was anticompetitive simply because it 'could' yield an anticompetitive impact.[17]

§6. Monopolization and Abuse of Dominance

196. A monopoly (of the Greek *monos*, one + *polein*, sell) occurs whenever there is, in a given market, only one supplier of a certain good or service. The market player, acting as a monopolist, can reduce production and alter the conditions of sale in the market, with the purpose of raising prices up to the level in which, by multiplying the volume that is produced by the price, the relevant firm will succeed in obtaining the maximum profit. The artificial nature of the price increase shall result in the expulsion of marginal clients and consumers from the market and the undue transfer of income from the current clients and consumers, thus yielding a loss of social welfare. Aside from high costs, the monopolized market also results in a loss of efficiency, since, lacking competition, the monopolist has no motivation to engage in technological innovations or to develop more efficient means to operate.

197. In such sense, monopoly power is defined by the capacity of an undertaking to fixing prices above the marginal cost, regardless of the competing firms demand elasticity, as determined by three factors:

(1) Market demand elasticity – the players' (firms) demand is to be as elastic as the market demand.
(2) Number of players – should there be many players, it is less probable that only one of them may significantly influence the market price.

17. It is worth noting that such administrative resolution was repealed and overruled on 9 Dec. 2011, by the trial court decision of Judge Itagiba Catta Preta Neto, of the fourth Federal Court of the Federal District, which annulled the CADE Resolution based on lack of evidence of anticompetitive conduct, including the fact the participants had no powers to bind their employer undertakings and ordered the CADE to pay the defendants legal fees in the amount of BRL 50,000 to each defendant (Ordinary Civil Actions Nos 2007.34.00.043978-7 and others). Such trial court resolution is under appeal to the higher courts.

(3) Firms interaction – even if the relations among the incumbent firms are easy, there can be a strong rivalry among them, so as to render coordination and collusion difficult in terms of price increases.

198. Economic inefficiency and the deterioration of the consumers' welfare resulting from a monopoly are characterized as challenges to the SBDC in their role of reducing monopoly power.

199. Monopolization, however, in itself, is not illegal in Brazil. On the contrary, Brazilian Competition Law expressly states that monopoly obtained through the player's own and valid efficiencies shall not be considered illegal market dominance.

200. Furthermore, there are cases when a monopoly is the most efficient means to produce a certain good or service. This is the case of natural monopolies that are found in markets with high economies of scale or scope requirements in comparison with the size of the demand. Such circumstances result in inefficiencies and even in an economic impracticability, should there be two or more players in the marketplace. In such cases, however, in order to avoid eventual abuses by the monopolist, such markets must be regulated, to confront the market failure. Such role is performed by the regulatory agencies (e.g., the ANATEL – for the telecommunications market, the ANEEL – for the electric power industry, the ANP – for the oil industry).

201. A monopsony is an inverse monopoly, meaning a monopoly from the client or purchaser-side, when there is only one purchaser and multiple suppliers of a certain good or service. In such cases, similar to monopoly cases, market power, or monopsony power, once exercised by the sole purchaser, may result in a loss of social welfare.

202. The monopsony power may reduce prices below the competitive level, thus squeezing suppliers and causing market unbalances in the upstream market, while yielding negative impacts in the downstream market and consumers.

203. The characterization of an abuse of a dominant position, although expressly stated in Law No. 12529/11, is not limited to the hypothesis set forth in its Article 36, paragraph 3. The illegal practice may result from other forms of action, in which case, although the burden of proof of the illegal conduct should be demonstrated by the CADE, in practice, the player enjoying market power often is required to show that it has not acted abusively and that its conduct is acceptable under the rule of reason. The de facto reversal of the burden of proof to the party charged with an anticompetitive conduct is improperly inspired on concepts of consumer law, and is a common practice of the competition authorities. An interesting example of such influence is found in Act of Concentration No. 08012.010109/2009-74, resolved on 17 March 2010, in re. *Cosan S.A. Indústria e Comércio, Crystalsev Comércio e Representação Ltda. et alii*, in which the CADE ruled that the precautionary principle, typical of consumer law, applies to competition laws.

Examples of abuse of dominant position may be found in:

(a) The conduct of physicians' cooperatives (cases primarily involving the cooperative Unimed) the Charter of which forced its members to accept an exclusive relationship with it. Doctors were required to abide by an exclusive dealing provision of the cooperative Charter and work solely within the Unimed network. The cooperative enjoyed a clear dominant position in the relevant market, and its conduct was considered by the CADE, in multiple occasions, to negatively affect the social welfare in the respective geographic areas of operations.

(b) In an infrastructure sharing case discussed in Administrative Process No. 08012.003048/2001-31 (involving *Associação NeoTV v. Globosat and others*) where exclusive dealings were entered in connection with the broadcasting (on pay TV) of national and State soccer championships. In such cases, the CADE resolved that the relevant broadcasting rights constituted an essential facility in the TV pay-per-view industry and held anticompetitive the underlying exclusivity dealing arrangement entered between Globosat and channel SporTV. As a result, it ordered the relevant television broadcasting contents, technical information, maintenance and other after-sale services to be sublicensed or subject to compulsory sales to third pay-per-view players on a non-discriminatory basis.

In a series of occasions, however, the CADE had set certain standards in which charges of abuse of dominant positions were dismissed. Examples are:

(a) In re. *Videolar S.A. v. Koninklijke Philips Electronics N.V*, (Preliminary Investigation No. 08012.005181/2006-37, resolved on 29 April 2009), there was a complaint made against *Philips Electronics* claiming that failure by the latter in enforcing its patent rights against the importation of non-licensed products constituted an abuse of a dominant position. The CADE dismissed the case.

(b) In re. *CADE v. Câmara do Livro do DF* (Preliminary Investigation No. 08012.006978/2005-71, resolved on 19 January 2011), the CADE decided that the granting of promotional discounts at book fairs, provided the latter are isolated events, both in terms of time and geographically, does not constitute an anticompetitive conduct, especially because, in such cases, the consumer has the possibility of purchasing books at any bookstore, even in the course of the fair, or through the Internet.

(c) In re. *Tribunal Regional do Trabalho da 1ª Região v. ThyssenKrup Elevadores S/A* (Preliminary Investigation No. 08700.004336/2007-41, resolved on 18 May 2011), the CADE affirmed that the eventual difficulties in the purchase of elevators' maintenance parts from the assembly company do not characterize an antitrust offence, given that competition in the marketplace is feasible, either through the purchase of original parts directly from their respective manufacturers, or through the use of aftermarket parts made by other manufacturers.

(d) In re. *Redisbel – Redenção Distribuidora de Bebidas Ltda. v. Companhia de Bebidas da América – AmBev* (Preliminary Investigation No. 08012.002417/2008-45, resolved on 13 July 2011), the CADE decided that the decision of a company to verticalize and increase its share in the direct distribution of its products is part of its legitimate trade strategy and may even result in the reduction of prices to the final consumer. Entrepreneurial decisions such as those relating to change in the distribution policies, refusal to deal certain products with distributors and even price discrimination among distributors are private matters, and the resulting controversies are to be settled by the Judiciary and not by the CADE.

204. In relation to the concept of abuse of a dominant position, the CADE has reviewed an interesting case debating the controversial issue of duty of competitors to cooperate. In the Administrative Process No. 08012.006439/2009-65 (resolved on 23 May 2012), in re. *Associação Brasileira de Bebidas – ABRABE* and *Cervejaria Kaiser S.A. v. Companhia de Bebidas das Américas – AmBev*, the CADE decoded that the artificial imposition by the competition authorities of a duty of competitors to cooperate should only occur when the incapacity of rivals reasonably competing in the market by its own products and commercial strategies becomes evident. Thus, pursuant to the CADE, any intervention that permits a rival to take possession, without its own efforts, entrepreneurship and differentiation, of the competitor's successful commercial strategies or of its efficiencies that benefit consumers through lower prices and a greater variety and quality of products, shall generate a negative impact on competition and, therefore, is contrary to the initiatives that yield benefits to consumers.

§7. CONCENTRATIONS

205. Paragraphs 5 and 6 of Article 88 of Law No. 12529/11 state that all acts of concentration that result in the elimination of competition of a significant part of the relevant market, or that may create or reinforce a dominant position, or that may result in the domination of a relevant market of goods and services are generally prohibited, except in such cases where the limits that are strictly necessary to achieve the following purposes are observed:

(1) – jointly or alternatively:

- (a) increase productivity or competitiveness;
- (b) improve the quality of goods or services;
- (c) enable efficiency and the technological or economic development; and

(2) – a relevant part of the yielding benefits is passed over to the consumers.

206. The *caput* (meaning the basic command of the statutory provision preceding its paragraphs) of Article 88 of Law No. 12529/11 states that: all acts of economic concentration which cumulatively meet the following criteria[18] are subject to the CADE notification requirement: (i) at least one of the groups involved in the operation registered, in the past financial year, a gross profit or total volume of business in the country, in the year prior to the operation, equivalent or superior to Brazilian Real (BRL) 750,000,000; and (ii) at least one other group involved in the operation has registered, in the past financial year, a gross profit or total volume of business in the country, in the year prior to the operation, equivalent or superior to BRL 75,000,000.

207. As opposed to former Law No. 8884/94, which adopted *a posterior* regime for the notification of mergers and acquisitions, the current Competition Law has a suspensory regime (Article 88, §2). Thus, as of the current law, in Brazil, all acts of

18. The statutory turnover threshold originally set by Article 88 of Law No. 12529/11 was adjusted by the Inter-ministerial Ordinance No. 992, of 30 May 2012.

concentration shall only be considered legally effective upon their final clearance by the CADE.

208. Pursuant to Article 88, §3, reportable transactions that are closed prior to their approval by the CADE are null and void, and the parties, thereto, are subject to a fine of no less than BRL 60,000 and not exceeding BRL 60,000,000 and to the commencement of an Administrative Process to investigate the facts.

209. Article 90 defines an act of concentration as being that transaction in which:

(1) Two or more previously independent companies are fused.
(2) One or more companies directly or indirectly acquire, by purchase or exchange of shares, quotas, bonds, or securities that are convertible into shares, or assets, tangible or intangible,[19] contractually or in any other way, the control or part of one or more companies.
(3) One or more companies merge into another company or companies.
(4) Two or more companies enter into an associative contract, or form a *consortium* or joint venture.

Resolution No. 10, of 4 November 2014, of the CADE regulates the hypothesis of mandatory notification of an associative contract, as required by item iv.

210. In connection with item iv above, the law has made a statutory exemption (Article 88, sole paragraph) exempting from notification transactions (and related contracts) that are directed to public tender bids held by the direct or the indirect Public Administration.

211. Further, CADE Resolution No. 2, of 29 May 2012 has created a *de minimis* rule, exempting certain stock purchases from the notification requirement. In general terms (Article 9), the following stock purchase agreements referred to in item ii above are subject to the CADE notification requirement, meaning the transactions that:

(1) – Result in the purchase of control.
(2) – Do not result in the purchase of control, but meet the *de minimis* rules of Article 10 (described below).
(3) – Are made by the controlling stockholder, whenever the acquired direct or indirect share purchased from at least one seller considered individually, shall be equal to, or exceed, 20% of the company or voting stock (Articles 9 and 11).

212. Further, Article 10 of the CADE Resolution No. 2/12 states that the following transactions are also subject to the CADE notification requirement:

(a) the purchase of a part of a firm, or of firms, that shall cause the purchaser to secure, thereby, the status of the largest individual investor;

19. In the Act of Concentration No. 08700.005924/2014-20, in re. *Paraná Equipamentos S.A. e Caterpillar Global Mining LLC.* (resolved on 25 Aug. 2014), the Superintendent-General of the CADE, Eduardo Frade Rodrigues (Dispatch No. 1005), approved Opinion No. 262 of the Superintendency-General, which considered that the transfer of intangible assets such as customer information, credit related to products and contracts, and liabilities, configures an Act of concentration.

(b) the purchase of a part of a firm, or of firms:

I. – Whenever the target company is neither a competitor of the purchaser, nor does it operates in a vertically related market:

(i) the purchase shall cause the purchaser to acquire a direct or indirect share equal to, or exceeding, 20% of the company or voting stock of the target company;

(ii) the purchase is made by a stockholder owner of 20% or more of the company or voting stock of the target company, whenever the direct or indirect share purchased from at least one seller considered individually, shall be equal to, or exceed, 20% of the company or voting stock.

II. – Whenever the target company is either a competitor of the purchaser, or operates in a vertically related market:

(i) the purchase shall cause the purchaser to acquire a direct or indirect share equal to, or exceeding, 5% of the company or voting stock of the target company;

(ii) the last purchase made by a purchaser that already controls 5% or more of the company or voting stock of the target company, which, either alone or in conjunction with other purchases, shall result in an increase of the purchaser's share equal to, or in excess of 5% of the company or voting stock.

§8. Joint Ventures

213. A JV consists of the formation of an association between two or more economic players for the creation of a new player, without the elimination of the original members, the purpose of which (usually seeking a profitable purpose) may be, *inter alia*, the research and development of new products, operation in a market other than that of the associated members or the participation in the same market of the associated members. JV may be evidenced by a mere contract arrangement or by the incorporation of a new firm.

214. In this line of thought, the JV may be considered as being a licit or an illicit horizontal arrangement, as the case may be, given that the venture may yield benefits or injury to competition. Generally, they are considered licit entities, since they constitute a collaboration agreement for the profit-making development of a new process, technology or entry in a new market.

215. The objective of a JV may be multiple and cover the production of goods, the rendering of services, the search for new markets and the mutual support in multiple levels of a product chain. The JV will operate for a limited period of time, which may be long or short, depending on the intended purposes.

216. The agreement entered between the participants of a JV shall have as its principal scope obtaining profit through the exploitation of a profitable economic activity. Each of the participants will contribute with a certain investment to achieve the common purpose. Such investment contribution may be made with the supply of raw materials, capital contributions, supply of technology, availability of distribution and sales networks, market know-how, trade secrets etc.

217. The JV does not require that the participants work together for its formation, and the alliance may be achieved through the execution of a collaboration agreement, the provision integration of companies or the incorporation of a new company have the participants as stockholders. As mentioned, as long as there shall be no fusion or merger, one of the characteristics of a JV is that the participants shall continue to operate independently, albeit preserving their mutual commitments for a long term.

218. The formation of a JV may yield many advantages to the associated concerns, such as the mitigation of the risks inherent to the business to be jointly explored, cost sharing with the budget and implantation of the project, the division of responsibilities or work and other goals that can be achieved by a single company. Another positive aspect of a JV concerns the business and enterprises for which there is a need of large initial investments for the launching of a project that will yield long-term benefits (the civil construction and the oil fields are examples of this kind, demanding large capital requirements).

219. For small- and medium-size enterprises (i.e., SMEs), a JV may represent a chance of jointly acting to overcome eventual barriers to entry and to gain effectiveness in competing in a more efficient manner in their original markets. An example is the strategy of using the creation of a JV as a step forward to reaching foreign markets that demand large investments or a specific know-how.

In short, JVs are characterized by:

- The conjunction of interests, cooperation and common efforts of the co-venturers, to achieve profit through a certain enterprise. The partners' contributions to the success of the deal may be made of goods, rights, expertise, know-how, cash, etc.
- The presence of profit subject to risk of loss is a factor that may make JV differ from partnerships.
- Joint control, resulting from the search for a common end.
- Obligation not to compete, or of loyalty, usually governed by applicable non-compete clauses, effective for the life of the enterprise and subsequently, so as to legally enable the very purpose of the transaction.
- Preservation of the individuality of the cooperating firms.

220. Currently, JVs are considered a kind of a collaboration agreement, as a result of the partnership that is formed by two or more firms seeking the creation of means to facilitate the union of interests or the exchange of resources for the achievement of a common goal. Such arrangements are usually restricted in time, and characterized by flexibility, non-compete undertakings and ease of incorporation.

221. Except only if the JV is formed with the special purpose of participating in public tender bids held by the direct or the indirect Public Administration (Article 88, sole paragraph), all JVs that meet the turnover thresholds set forth in Article 88 of

Law No. 12529/11 (meaning, if one of the firms or group of firms involved in the venture shall have recorded, a gross annual turnover in its last balance equivalent to BRL 750,000,000, and, any other firm or group of firms involved shall have recorded a gross annual turnover in its balance sheet equivalent to BRL 75,000,000), the transaction shall be subject to the CADE notification requirement, as an act of concentration.

Chapter 5. Consequences of Violations and Enforcement Institutions

§1. Administrative Enforcement

I. The Antitrust Authorities

A. Formation, Composition

222. The so-called SBDC is made of the following authorities: the CADE and the SEAE, of the Ministry of Finance.

223. Although not a member of the SBDC, the Brazilian ANATEL has legal authority and competence to hear anticompetitive conduct cases and to review mergers and acquisitions affecting the telecommunications market.

224. The BACEN, on its turn, is in dispute with the CADE at the Judiciary, claiming to have exclusive jurisdiction to review acts of concentration relating to financial institutions.

1. The CADE

225. The CADE is an adjudicatory entity having jurisdiction throughout the national territory, which is established as a federal autarky, linked (but not subordinated to) the Ministry of Justice, with head offices in the Federal District, and having the competences set forth in the Law No. 12, 529/11.

226. The CADE comprises of the following bodies:

(1) Administrative Tribunal of Economic Defense.
(2) General Superintendency.
(3) Department of Economic Studies.

227. The CADE is an adjudicatory entity with jurisdiction on all of the Brazilian national territory and was created by Law No. 4137, of 10 September 1962. Under Law No. 8884, of 11 June 1994, the CADE was recognized as a federal autarky. Autarkies are defined as public law, legal entities created by a special law, that are the rightful owners of their assets (thus, although a member of the Public Administration, its assets do not belong to the centralized Federal Government or Union) and that has administrative authority to take actions typical of a decentralized State.

228. The CADE, although an authority acting within the Ministry of Justice for budgetary purposes, does not act under the authority of the Minister of Justice. It is an independent authority, and its decisions are not subject to any administrative appeal, provided, however, that, under the Brazilian Federal Constitution, all administrative decisions issued by the CADE are subject to judicial control and enforcement.

229. The foregoing notwithstanding, there is a relationship of independence between the CADE and the Judiciary, save for such judicial control mechanism. Indeed, judicial resolutions in cases where the CADE is not a party are not considered a precedent for CADE and are not binding on it.[20]

230. The CADE through its bodies has the competence to advice, monitor and investigate abuses of economic power and shall ultimately rule, in the administrative level, on any anticompetitive conduct by individuals or legal entities. There are no individuals, legal entities or economic activities immune or exempted from the CADE's authority. The only unsettled matter refers to a possible exemption benefiting mergers and acquisitions in the banking area, since the BACEN claims to enjoy exclusive jurisdiction on such matters.

231. The issue is currently being debated at the Judiciary.[21]

a. The Administrative Tribunal

232. The Panel of the CADE administrative tribunal is composed of a President and six Councillors chosen from among citizens over 30 years old, with a notorious legal knowledge and unblemished reputation and nominated by the President of the Republic. The nominations are examined and approved by the Federal Senate, for a term of office of four years, being prohibited reappointments of office.

233. The principal functions of the Panel of the administrative tribunal include: ruling on the scrutiny of an illegal anticompetitive conduct and to impose penalties thereon; definitive hearing, at the administrative level, all procedures commenced by the GS; to issue cease and desist orders; approving Settlement Agreements and agreements of undertakings; hearing on appeal the precautionary measures imposed by the Superintendent General or by the Councillor Examiner; requiring information

20. In Administrative Proceeding No. 08000.009354/97-82 (resolved on 20 Aug. 2014), in re. *SDE, ex officio, v. AgipLiquigás do Brasil S/A et alii*, Councillor Eduardo Pontual Ribeiro ruled that decisions made by the Judiciary in class actions are not binding on the CADE, given the independence of the civil, administrative and criminal proceedings from one another. He went further to state that such understanding is to prevail even if the Council has joined the judicial procedure as an assistant, given that the pleading in the civil action is distinguished from the merits of the Administrative Process judged by CADE. While the former seeks, civil damages yielding from the antitrust offence, the latter aims the imposition of a penalty of an administrative nature.
21. S.A. Bradesco & Banco de Crédito Nacional (BCN) filed a *writ of mandamus* (Mandado de Segurança No. 2002.34.00.033475-0/DF) against the decision of the CADE that affirmed having jurisdiction to review mergers and acquisitions involving banking institutions and imposed a fine on such parties for extemporaneous notification. The banks succeeded in obtaining a favourable decision annulling the fine at the trial level. Such resolution was reversed under appeal, by majority vote, at the fifth Group (Turma) of the Regional Federal Court for the first Region (Tribunal Regional Federal da 1ª Região). On 30 Aug. 2010, the first Session of the Superior Court of Justice (Superior Tribunal de Justiça), reversed once again the resolution to cancel the fine but there was no final resolution as to whether the CADE or the BACEN has jurisdiction on such matters. The issue is still unsettled and appeals are pending.

from any individual, body, authority or public and private legal entities; ruling on acts and conducts that are subject to its approval or clearance under the law and seeking for enforcement of its decisions before the Judiciary.

234. The CADE Councillors have the authority to cast their votes on all cases heard by the Panel, to issue orders (like subpoenas in the US) and opinions on matters addressed by the Panel and to adopt precautionary measures and fix daily fines for breach thereof.

235. Although the administrative tribunal of the CADE is the final adjudicatory authority, at the administrative level, the investigation of anticompetitive conducts and the review of mergers and acquisitions are primarily made by the GS, with the non-mandatory participation of the DEE. Although investigative authority and review of mergers and acquisitions are vested into, and made by, the GS, the Tribunal has full authority to ultimately perform all such tasks, whenever it deems appropriate, especially given the fact that the technical statements of both GS and DEE are non-binding opinions.

236. The current Brazilian Competition Law became effective on 29 May 2012. In the course of its first anniversary under Law No. 12529/11, the CADE has reviewed 262 mergers and acquisitions, of which 250 were unconditionally cleared by the GS and 1 by the administrative tribunal in the exercise of its call-back authority, while in 2 cases the administrative tribunal issued a partial divestiture order and in 2, the transaction was approved subject to changes in their respective non-compete clauses and the remaining 7 were not cognized.[22]

237. Under the former Law No. 8884/94, the average time for the review of acts of concentration was of 154 days. Under the current Brazilian Competition Law, such average time was reduced to twenty days in fast-track cases and to sixty-nine days in more complex transactions.[23]

b. The General Superintendency (GS)

238. The GS is a body of the CADE, composed of a Superintendent General and two Deputy Superintendents, appointed by the former. The Superintendent General shall be selected from among citizens over 30 years old, with notorious judicial or economic knowledge and unblemished reputation, appointed by the President of the Republic, once approved by the Federal Senate.

239. The Superintendent General shall hold office for two years, and reappointment for a single subsequent term is permitted.

240. The specific functions of the GS in connection with the enforcement of competition laws are, *inter alia*: permanently monitor commercial activities and practices by individuals and legal entities enjoying a dominant position in the relevant

22. *See* http://www.cade.gov.br/Default.aspx?b0839365bc52a66cbe8bdd74c387.
23. Ditto as in the immediately preceding footnote.

market; commencing preparatory proceedings[24] and administrative investigations[25] in light of circumstantial evidence of anticompetitive conduct and Administrative Processes;[26] dismiss circumstantial evidence by closing preparatory proceedings and administrative investigations; requesting information from any individual or legal entity, bodies, public authorities, and public or private legal entities; to engage into *in loco* inspections of inventories, objects, papers, commercial books, computers and electronic files; seeking dawn raids through the Judiciary; proposing Settlement Agreements; adopting precautionary measures and entering into Leniency Agreements.

241. Whenever there is a charge of an anticompetitive conduct brought by an individual or legal entity (provided that the GS may also act ex officio), the Superintendent may, depending on the kind and strength of circumstantial or other evidence available to it, commence: (i) a preparatory procedure (whenever the evidence available is feeble), (ii) administrative investigations (whenever the evidence is not robust, but is not negligible), or (iii) Administrative Process (whenever the evidence of an anticompetitive conduct is robust).

242. Article 48 and following of Law No. 12529/11 govern such procedures. Law No. 9784/99 (which governs administrative procedures at the Federal Public Administration Level) and by the Brazilian Code of Civil Procedures also apply to those procedures in a subsidiary fashion. The secondary applicability of the Brazilian Code of Penal Procedures is occasionally admitted.

c. The Department of Economic Studies (DEE)

243. The DEE, headed by a Chief Economist, is responsible for the preparation of economic studies and opinions, ex officio or at the request of the Panel of the administrative tribunal, the CADE President, the Councillor Examiner or the Superintendent General, ensuring the accuracy and technical and scientific update of the CADE Resolutions.

244. The Chief Economist will be appointed jointly by the Superintendent General and the CADE President, from among Brazilian citizens of unblemished reputation and outstanding economic knowledge.

24. The full name of such proceedings is 'Preparatory Proceedings for an administrative investigation of an Offence to the Economic Order' (*Procedimento Preparatório de Inquérito Administrativo para Apuração de Infrações à Ordem Econômica*). Under the former Law No. 8884/94, such procedure was simply called Administrative Proceeding (*Procedimento Administrativo*).

25. The full name of such proceedings is 'Administrative Process of Investigation of an Offence to the Economic Order' (*Processo Administrativo para Apuração de Infrações à Ordem Econômica*). Under the former Law No. 8884/94, such procedure was simply called Preliminary Investigation (*Averiguação Preliminar*).

26. The full name of such process is 'Administrative Process for the Assessment of Administrative Sanctions for Offences to the Economic Order' (*Processo Administrativo para Imposição de Sanções Administrativas por Infrações à Ordem Econômica*). Under the former Law No. 8884/94, such procedure was simply called Administrative Process (*Processo Administrativo*).

2. The Office of the Attorney General of the CADE (PFE)

245. The Council has an Office of the Attorney General of the CADE incumbent with, *inter alia*: advise the CADE on legal issues and to represent it before the courts; bring judicial actions to enforce the decisions and opinions of the CADE; to file motions, under the authority of the administrative tribunal of the CADE, seeking the judicial enforcement of cease and desist orders; judicially settle disputes concerning anticompetitive conducts, under the authority of the Tribunal and the prior opinion of the Federal Attorney General; issue non-binding opinions on matters within the competence and jurisdiction of the CADE; ensure the enforcement of the Brazilian Competition Laws and perform such other tasks provided for by the CADE Internal Regulations.

246. The Attorney General is nominated by the President of the Republic from among Brazilian citizens older than 30 years of unblemished reputation and outstanding legal knowledge and examined and approved by the Senate of the Republic for a term of office of two years, renewable once for an additional two-year term. The Office is also made by federal attorney members of the Office of the Federal General Counsel (AGU).

3. The Office of the Federal Attorney General (MPF)

247. The Federal Attorney General for the Republic has the authority to designate a member of his Office to participate in all cases heard or reviewed by the CADE.

248. The representative of Office of the Federal Attorney General at the CADE has the authority to issue non-binding opinions, either ex officio or at the request of the Councillor Examiner. Its primary function is to overview the proper enforcement of the law by public authorities.

4. The SEAE

249. The SEAE is a special body of the Ministry of Finance and was created by Provisional Measure No. 813, of 1 January 1995. This body shall advocate competition before Government bodies and the Society.

250. The SEAE functions are currently related to the promotion and defence of competition, proposing economic legislation and regulation, monitoring markets and engaging into economic studies, either ex officio or at the request of the CADE, the international trade authorities and the Consumer Law authorities. In exercising its functions, the SEAE may request information and documents from any individual or firm, authority or legal entity.

B. Investigating Powers

251. The GS has the authority of, *inter alia*, permanently monitoring commercial activities and practices by players enjoying a dominant position in any relevant market, seeking to prevent anticompetitive conducts and, for such purposes, it may require information and documents as needed, with due observance of legally ensured confidential treatment thereto. It may also engage *in loco* inspections and seek judicial dawn raid orders.

252. As mentioned above, whenever a charge is placed or there is a suspicion of an anticompetitive conduct, the GS may, depending on the consistency of the available evidence, order the commencement of any of the following investigating procedures: (i) preparatory proceeding (weak evidence), (ii) administrative investigation (reasonable but insufficient evidence) or (iii) Administrative Process (robust evidence of an anticompetitive conduct). It has the authority to close cases (subject to the call-back right of any CADE Councillor) or to propose the assessment of fines and other penalties on firms by the CADE administrative tribunal for anticompetitive conducts.

253. In the case of mergers and acquisitions (acts of concentration), the GS reviews the notification documents and has the adjudicatory authority to clear the underlying transactions (subject to the call-back right of any CADE Councillor) or to propose divestiture remedies to the CADE administrative tribunal.

254. As noted above, Article 13, item VI (c) of Law No. 12529 conferred to the GS, additional authority, such as the right of inspecting companies *in loco*, and their inventory, books, computers and magnetic files, and of obtaining copies of documents, and of entering into Leniency Agreements with parties pleading guilty, as long as they fully cooperate with the investigations.

C. *Adjudicating Powers (Ascertaining and Sanctioning)*

1. Leniency Agreements

255. The Leniency Programme was established in Brazil in 2000 and enables not only a cartel member but also a party to any anticompetitive conduct to reveal its actions and cooperate with the competition authorities in exchange of civil and criminal immunities in relation to its illegal practices, or of the mitigation of applicable penalties.

256. Indeed, the GS may enter into Leniency Agreements that may result either in the exemption of fines or its reduction to one to two-thirds of the otherwise applicable penalty. In Administrative Process No. 08012.001826/2003-10, resolved on 19 December 2007, in re. Department of Economic Protection and Defence *(DPDE), ex officio, v. Associação das Empresas de Vigilância do Rio Grande do Sul – ASSEVIRGS*, et al., relating to the security surveillance cartel in the State of Rio Grande do Sul, a Leniency Agreement was entered by Vigilância Antares Ltda. and his principal officer Mr Rubem Isnar Baz Orleri. The legal entity was found guilty and a fine equal to 15% of the company's after tax gross turnover, in 2002, was imposed, but the penalty was reduced to zero in favour of the lenient. The same applied to Mr Orleri (penalty reduced to zero).

257. Article 87 of Law No. 12529/11 also provides for immunity of the parties' signatory to Leniency Agreement from criminal procedures. The granting of criminal immunities is usually expressed in the relevant Leniency Agreement, provided that such statutory and contractual provisions are questionable to the extent that the GS (nor does have any other authority, including the Public Prosecutor) has no constitutional right to exempt a party pleading guilty of a criminal action from a criminal prosecution.

258. Entering into a Leniency Agreement, furthermore, does not exempt the applicants from civil damages actions (including class actions). Currently, very few individual or class actions seeking indemnity for anticompetitive actions have been brought. For no other reason, in Administrative Process No. 08012.009888/2003-70, resolved on 1 September 2010, in re. *AGA S.A* et al., Councillor Examiner Luiz Fernando Furlan complained that:

> in Brazil, however, there is almost no news on private actions brought in connection with damages caused by cartels. Thus, an important factor to deter the practice of collusion is lost. The injured parties also fail to be indemnified for damages caused (free translation).

259. As a consequence, the Councillor ordered various organizations[27] to be notified of the CADE Resolution in motivation of their bringing class or private actions against the cartel members.

260. The following are the requirements for the execution of a Leniency Agreement.

261. The immunity is granted in case of the effective cooperation of the applicant with the investigations in order to enable: (i) the identification of the other co-participants in the offence, and (ii) the obtaining of information and documents that may prove the characterization of the offence.

262. Additional requirements (to be met on a cumulative basis) are: (i) that the signatory party be the first to apply in connection with the anticompetitive conduct under investigation; (ii) that such party shall completely cease its participation in the offensive conduct as of the date of application; (iii) that the GS is not in the possession of sufficient evidence to ensure the characterization of the offensive conduct and the identification of the offenders; (iv) that such party shall plead guilty and fully and permanently cooperate with the investigations and the Administrative Process until a final determination is made thereon.

263. The CADE is incumbent with determining if the agreement has being thoroughly complied with, at the time the case is ultimately heard. If the GS had no knowledge of the offence at the time of application, the lenient may be benefited with the dismissal of the case in his/its favour; otherwise, the CADE may reduce the fine imposed on the offensive conduct by one to two-thirds, as the case may be. The decision as to grant immunity or reduce the fine is purely discretionary.

264. A party interested in joining the Leniency Programme may ensure its position as 'Marker' in the line of interested parties, as long as it shall supply the information and documents requested by the GS within no later than thirty days. To ensure access to its passcode, such party must immediately inform the GS on the facts

27. The following Government entities and organizations were notified by the CADE: Federal Medicine Council (Conselho Federal de Medicina), Industry National Confederation (Confederação Nacional da Indústria), Private Hospital National Association (Associação Nacional de Hospitais Privados), Brazilian Hospital Federation (Federação Brasileira de Hospitais), Ministry of Health (Ministério da Saúde), Ministry of the cities (Ministério das Cidades) and Companhia de Saneamento Básico do Estado de São Paulo – SABESP (the State of São Paulo sanitation company).

(what), on the offenders (who), on the location (where) and on the time (when) of the relevant anticompetitive conduct.

265. The proposal may be orally presented, whereupon it shall be put in written form by the GS.

266. Negotiations on the leniency arrangement may vary at the GS discretion, provided that there is no other cartel member interested in the leniency. Should no agreement be reached, all documents supplied to the GS shall be returned. Thus, by law, such returned information shall not be taken by the authorities as a confession as to the facts, nor a pleading of guilt, and shall be kept confidential by the GS.

267. The law also provides for a 'Leniency Plus' arrangement, whereby any party that is not eligible to enter into a Leniency Agreement may supply information to the authorities on any cartel activity unknown to the GS, other than that under investigation, whereupon such party shall benefit from all advantages of leniency with respect to such other cartel and the mitigation of the fine to be eventually imposed on it on the first case, by one-third. To date, however, there is no known Leniency Plus case.

268. The implications of the Leniency Agreement entered by a legal entity may be extended to managers and administrators of the lenient party, participants of the offence.

269. Finally, the law permits the entering of a Leniency Agreement by legal entities or individuals that are leaders of a cartel.

2. Settlement Agreements (*Compromisso de Cessação* – TCC)

270. The defendants in any administrative procedures investigating anticompetitive conducts may seek to enter into a Settlement Agreement with the CADE, proposing to cease the practice under investigation or its effects. The Settlement Agreement may also be proposed to the defendant by the Superintendent General (Article 190 of the CADE Resolution No. 1/12, as amended by Amendment No. 1/13 to the CADE Internal Regulations, as approved by CADE Resolution No. 5, of 6 March 2013). The CADE has the discretionary authority (but not the obligation) to enter into such arrangement (Article 85 of Law No. 12529/11).

271. The motion for a Settlement Agreement is to be made by the filing of an application with the Councillor Examiner, if the case is already under the review of the administrative tribunal, or with the Superintendent General of the GS, if the case is under his review (Article 179 of CADE Internal Regulations, as amended). Such motion can be filed only once and may be placed on a confidential basis (Article 85, §§5 and 6, of the Brazilian Competition Law), provided that the Settlement Term, once signed, will become of public domain (Article 85, §7).

272. The filing of the motion by the defendant or the proposal made by the Superintendent General shall not suspend the underlying Administrative Process (Article 85, §6, of the Brazilian Competition Law and Articles 179, §1 and 190, §5 of the CADE Internal Regulations, as amended), provided that such suspension will be granted upon the execution of the respective Settlement Term (*Termo de Compromisso*), which suspension will remain effective for the life of the term, whereupon, assuming full compliance thereof, the Administrative Process will be definitively closed (Article

85, §9), but only with respect to the party that has signed the term. It shall not benefit other non-signatory parties to the investigation.

273. Except for cartel cases derived from Leniency Agreements (Article 185, of CADE Internal Regulation), which expressly require the lenient to, necessarily, admit its participation in the investigated conduct, the filing by the defendant of a motion, or the acceptance by the defendant of negotiating the proposal of the Superintendent General, for a Settlement Agreement shall not be construed as a confession as to the facts, nor as an admission of illegality of the conduct under investigation (Articles 179, §5, and 190, §7, of the CADE Internal Regulations, as amended).[28]

274. The Settlement Term will permit a summary court action for its enforcement (*título executivo extrajudicial*) (Article 85, §8) and shall mandatorily contain (Article 85, §1):

(a) *inter alia*, the specification of the obligations undertook by the defendant ensuring the cessation of the practice under investigation or of its effects;
(b) the *amount* of the fine in case of breach of Settlement Term;
(c) the amount of a pecuniary contribution, if any, by the defendant to the Fund for the *Defense* of Diffuse Rights, provided that such contribution is mandatory in case of a cartel investigation (Article 184 of the CADE Regulations, as amended);
(d) if *the* underlying investigation shall refer to a cartel charge, the undertaking by the defendant of its obligation to cooperate with the investigations (Article 186 of the CADE Internal Regulations, as amended).

275. The pecuniary contribution shall be negotiated between the applicant and the CADE, by taking into account the amplitude and the usefulness of the collaboration of the applicant with the investigations, the moment when the motion for a Settlement Agreement is filed and the following parameters (Article 187 of the CADE Internal Regulations), as amended:

(1) – in the case of the first applicant, a percentage reduction of 30–50% of the expected fine in case of an adverse final determination in the underlying Administrative Process;
(2) – in the case of the second applicant, a percentage reduction of 25–40% of the expected fine in case of an adverse final determination in the underlying Administrative Process;
(3) – in the case of other applicants, a percentage reduction of not exceeding 25% of the expected fine in case of an adverse final determination in the underlying Administrative Process; and

28. In Motion No. 08700.006078/2014-66 (resolved on 6 Aug. 2014) applied by *Hipercard Banco Múltiplo S.A.* and *Bompreço Bahia Supermercados Ltda.*, Councillor Alessandro Octaviani Luis argued that the non-recognition of unlawfulness of the conduct by the party to the Settlement Agreement or by the CADE, or even the absence of payment of a financial contribution by the firm, is not sufficient in itself to eliminate the interest of the Public Administration in entering into a TCC, to the extent that such factors do not affect the effective enforcement of the antitrust policy.

(4) IV. – in case of cartel investigations, the percentage reduction should not exceed 15% (Article 188 of the CADE Internal Regulations).

276. Once an agreement is reached in connection with the terms of the Settlement Agreement, it shall be submitted to the CADE administrative tribunal for approval, provided that the Tribunal shall not have the authority to amend it, but only to either accept or reject it in its entirety (Article 191, §2, of the CADE Internal Regulations, as amended).

277. Similar to a Leniency Agreement, the Settlement Agreement shall not exempt the defendant from civil liability and from third-party indemnity actions, but unlike Leniency Agreements, it shall further not exempt the defendant from criminal liability.

3. Inspections

278. The GS may order inspections *in loco* at a company's headquarters, premise, office or branch, if such company is under investigation.

279. In such cases, the company to be inspected must be notified in advance, and the inspection cannot be initiated prior to 6 a.m. or later than 8 p.m.

280. The need of prior notice has caused inspection actions to be rare. The competition authorities have given preference to dawn raid/search and seize actions, since the element of surprise is considered to be crucial to securing the evidence.

4. Dawn Raids

281. The Office of the CADE Attorney General (PFE) at the request of the GS has legal standing to judicially apply for search and seizure procedures to collect objects, papers of any nature, such as commercial and accounting books, computers and magnetic files from any individual or legal entity in the interest of an investigation.

282. Alternatively, to the civil action by the AGU, the competition authorities not infrequently resort to the cooperation of the Office of the State or Federal Attorney General, or the Federal or State Police, to promote dawn raiding with criminal impact. Indeed, the competition authorities may also resort to criminal dawn raiding given that many anticompetitive conducts are simultaneously criminal offences. In Administrative Process No. 08012.009888/2003-70, resolved on 1 September 2010, in re. *AGA S.A et alii.*, the legality of the competition authorities (then the SDE) resorting to and using information collected in criminal dawn raiding has been questioned, but the motion was overruled by the CADE, under the argument that, although Article 35-A of Law No. 8884/94, then in force, only provided for civil dawn raiding by the SDE, there is no statutory prohibition to the authorities to resort to criminal investigation actions.

283. Dawn raiding has been a recurrent practice of the competition authorities, especially in fighting cartels. During the first year of effectiveness of the current Brazilian Competition Law (2012-July 2013), the SG engaged itself in five dawn raidings, affecting the following industries: fuel (in the city of Mossoró, State of Rio Grande do Norte), uniform, school materials and backpacks public tender bids (in the city of São Paulo, State of São Paulo), salt (cities of Rio de Janeiro, State of Rio de

Janeiro, and Natal and Mossoró, State of Rio Grande do Norte), silicates (cities of Mogi das Cruzes, Cajamar and Rio Claro, State of São Paulo, Rio de Janeiro, State of Rio de Janeiro, Jaboatão dos Guararapes, State of Pernambuco and Criciúma, State of Santa Catarina) (all in 2012) and wheat flour (cities of Maceió, State of Alagoas, Fortaleza, State of Ceará, Natal, State of Rio Grande do Norte, and Recife, State of Pernambuco) (2013).[29] In 2011, still under the former Law No. 8884/94, only two dawn raids occurred.

284. Both in the case of inspections and of dawn raiding, the authority in charge is required to show a search warrant, but is permitted to enter the premises without further permission and usually using police force, regardless of whether the investigated party is represented by an onsite lawyer or not.

285. The authorities are usually granted full powers to carry the raid, including, without limitation, the authority to inspect or seize inventory, objects, papers of any nature, commercial books, computers and magnetic files, and to require copies of any documents or electronic data.

D. Other Institutional Tasks (Consultancy to Government)

286. Brazilian Competition Law does not provide for other institutional tasks, such as consultancy to Parliament/Government, except that the general public may consult the CADE on ongoing market conducts (Article 9, §4). Responses given by the CADE in the exercise of such general consultancy task, however, are non-binding on it, reason why such function is rarely exercised.

287. The CADE, however, in many instances has engaged itself in competition advocacy by recommending regulatory agencies and other public authorities to repeal administrative acts (ordinances, protocols, normative instructions, etc.) that are held anticompetitive. The SEAE is explicitly incumbent with such actions of competition advocacy under Article 19, item VI, of Law No. 12529. The CADE may further resort to the cooperation of the Office of the Federal or State Attorney General to bring applicable class actions to achieve such purposes.

II. Government Direct Enforcement Activities

288. Save for requests for information and documents in the course of proceedings and inspections *in loco*, administrative authorities, including the CADE, have no authority to engage in direct enforcement activities.

289. Dawn raiding orders and the enforcement of the CADE Resolutions must be applied for and obtained through the courts.

29. http://www.cade.gov.br/upload/Balanço%201%20ano%20nova%20lei%20%28consolidado%29.pdf.

III. Other Administrative Agencies Applying Antitrust Rules

290. Although regulatory agencies may have an interface with the competition authorities, on a consulting and cooperation basis, no administrative agency has the authority to apply antitrust rules.

The only exceptions are:

(a) ANATEL, created by the General Telecommunications Law of 1997 that has jurisdiction to investigate anticompetitive conduct and review mergers and acquisitions in the telecommunications market.

291. In any event, the ANATEL has the authority to issue non-binding opinions on antitrust matters related to the telecommunications market, but not to make a final determination thereon. Such is of the exclusive competence of the CADE:

(b) BACEN claims to have exclusive jurisdiction to applying antitrust rules in connection with financial institutions. In 2001, the AGU issued the Opinion No. GM-20 AGU/LA 01/2001 (ratified by Opinion No. 02/2009/MP/CGU/AGU). That opinion is legally binding on the Federal Public Administration level (Articles 40 and 41 of Complementary Law No. 73/93). Such opinion is rejected by the CADE, which insists in being competent to rule on such matters and claims that BACEN has the authority to address the issue on regulatory matters only. The issue is yet unsettled and currently being disputed in the courts.

IV. Administrative Fines

292. Anticompetitive conducts are subject to the following fines.

In case of legal entity offenders, a fine between 0.1% and 20% of the offender's gross turnover in Brazil in its last fiscal year before the commencement of the relevant Administrative Process, in the field of the business activity in which the violation occurred, is imposed. The level of the fine is measured proportionately to the actual participation and accountability of each offender, individually. Thus, cartel leaders are bound to pay higher fines. Fines imposed by Brazilian authorities are rapidly increasing, as proven in recently resolved Administrative Process No. 08012.009888/2003-70, resolved on 1 September 2010, involving *AGA S.A et alii.* In such cases, the following fines were imposed.[30]

Table 4 *Chart of Fines*

Defendant	*Fine*
IBG	BRL 8,464,063.31
Air Products	BRL 226,094,021.74
Air Liquid	BRL 249,257,134.59

30. The amounts are to be adjusted by applicable indexation rates until the date of actual payment.

AGA/LINDE	BRL 237,687,956.72
White Martins	BRL 2,218,699,838.45
Mr Oliveira	BRL 84,640.63
Mr Perez	BRL 452,188.04
Mr Cerezine	BRL 452,188.04
Mr Gallo	BRL 452,188.04
Mr Pilão	BRL 498,514.27
Mr Netto	BRL 475,375.91
Mr Campos	BRL 4,437,399.68

Source: Item 6.4 of the CADE Examiner's leading Vote casted in Administrative Process No. 08012.009888/2003-70.

293. The actual payment of the fines, however, is frequently suspended through a court injunction, provided that such judicial temporary relief is in most cases granted conditional upon the placement of a bond with the court in the amount of the fine.

294. In case of managers directly or indirectly involved in the offence practised by the legal entity to which he is related to, fines are imposed between 1% and 20% of the fine imposed on the legal entity offender.

295. In case of other individuals and public and private legal entities, including associations, whether incorporated or not, that do not exercise a commercial activity, the fine is between BRL 50,000 and BRL 2,000,000,000. Similar to legal entities leaders of a cartel, individuals, leaders of trade associations held responsible for cartel activities also pay higher fines.[31]

296. In case of recidivism, the fines will be doubled. Such was the case of *White Martins Gases Industriais Ltda.* in the above-mentioned Administrative Process No. 08012.009888/2003-70, resolved on 1 September 2010 (*AGA S.A et alii*). In case the offence fails to cease subsequent to a final determination of an anticompetitive conduct or should a precautionary measure of a Settlement Agreement fail to be complied in accordance with its terms, the offender will be subject to the payment of a daily fine not lower than BRL 5,000, provided that such amount may be multiplied up to fifty should the economic status or the gravity of the offence shall so recommend.

297. Should a party without cause refuse to supply an information or document legally requested by the CADE or the SEAE, or should he/it omit such information or supply it in a misleading or retarded manner, such party shall be subject to the payment of a daily fine of BRL 5,000. Such fine may be multiplied up to twenty should it be necessary to ensure effectiveness to the request, given the economic status of the offender. Such fine is to be calculated on a daily basis. The branch, office or establishment

31. In Administrative Process No. 001826/2003-10, resolved in 2007, relating to the cartel of security surveillance companies in the State of Rio Grande do Sul, a penalty was imposed on individuals equal to 15% of the fine imposed on the legal entities found to be cartel members. The fine imposed on the Executive Secretary of the industry trade association was aggravated by an additional 5%.

of a foreign legal entity located in Brazil shall be joint and severally liable for the payment of the fine.

298. Should a defendant or a third interested party, upon being legally summoned to make oral depositions, fail to do so, such defendant or party shall be subject to a fine between BRL 500 and BRL 15,000.

299. Impeding, obstructing or in any hindering a legally authorized inspection shall be subject to the payment of a fine between BRL 20,000 and BRL 400,000.

300. Pecuniary fines are not the only penalty yielding from the ascertainment of an anticompetitive conduct by the CADE. Other accessory administrative penalties are:

(a) publication of a notice in the press informing the public of the CADE adverse decision and containing an Abstract thereof, for two subsequent days, during one to three consecutive weeks;
(b) prohibition to enter into agreements with an official financial institution and to participate at public tender bids relating to the purchase, sale, public works and services, public concessions at the federal, State and municipal levels, and with indirect Public Administration entities, for five years;
(c) registration of the offender with the Consumer Defence National Registry;
(d) recommendation to the competent public authorities: (i) to grant compulsory licensing of industrial property rights owned by the offender, and (ii) not to grant the offender the right to pay federal taxes in instalments and to terminate tax incentives or public subsidies eventually granted to him/it;
(e) the spin-off of legal entities, the transfer of stock control, the sale of assets, the partial cessation of an activity; and
(f) prohibition of doing business in one's own name or as representative of a legal entity, for a term not exceeding five years or any other action necessary to eliminate the negative impact of the anticompetitive conduct.

V. Administrative Injunctions and Other Restrictive Orders: Interim Measures

301. In connection with investigations related to anticompetitive conducts, both the Councillor Examiner and the GS have authority to adopt precautionary measures whenever there is a founded fear that the defendant may directly or indirectly cause or be in the position of causing an irreparable harm to the market or an injury that is difficult to remedy, or make ineffective the final determination on the case.

302. The precautionary measure shall order the immediate cessation of the practice and, whenever possible, the reversal to the *status quo ante*, and shall fix a daily fine on the eventual breach.

303. Precautionary measures are subject to voluntary appeal to the Panel of the administrative tribunal within five days from its adoption. Such appeals shall not enjoy a suspensive effect.

§2. Civil Enforcement

I. Competent Civil Courts

304. Individual private actions are to be brought before the Brazilian State Courts. Appeals of State trial court resolutions are heard by the State Court of Justice (State Appellate Courts). Appeals of State Appellate Courts, on their turn, are heard by the Superior Court of Justice (STJ – Superior Tribunal de Justiça) and/or by the Federal STF – *Supremo* Tribunal Federal, as the case may be. Cases heard by the STJ relate to alleged violations of federal law, while cases heard by the STF relate to alleged violations of constitutional law.

305. Collective actions seeking the protection of diffuse or collective interests may also be brought by consumer protection bodies, by the Office of the Attorney General (both Federal and State) and other bodies of the Public Administration. Such actions may likewise seek the cessation of anticompetitive conducts or agreements or the payment of damages.

306. In the case of actions brought by the Office of the Federal Attorney General or by federal bodies of the Public Administration, such actions are to be brought before the Federal Courts. Appeals of Federal trial court resolutions are heard by the Federal Regional Tribunal (TRF– Tribunal Regional Federal) (Federal Appellate Courts). Appeals of Federal Appellate Courts, on their turn, are likewise heard by the STJ and/or by the STF, as the case may be.

II. Sanctions

A. Nullity and Damages

307. Private parties that are individually adversely affected by anticompetitive actions may seek relief through judicial cease and desist orders in connection with illegal (null and void) agreements, or recovery of losses and lost profits.

308. Pursuant to Article 47 of Law No. 12529/11, all parties having legal standing that are harmed by an anticompetitive conduct are permitted to bring judicial actions, either individually or collectively (in the case of homogeneous interests), to seek the cessation of the illegal practice, and the payment of indemnity for losses and damages, regardless of a pending administrative investigation, which investigation will not be suspended by such court action.

309. Although such statutory provision permits a judicial action to be brought in the course of an administrative action, the admissibility of such a judicial action is questionable, since it is a general understanding that only the CADE has jurisdiction to declare that a given conduct is anticompetitive, at a first level.

310. An example of such understanding may be found in Class Action No. 00.24 09709934-5 involving *Associação de Hospitais de Minas Gerais – AHMG v. White Martins Gases Industriais Ltda., Air Liquide Brasil Ltda., AGA S.A., Air Products*

Brasil Ltda. and Indústria Brasileira de Gases Ltda. – IBG, pending before the 28th Civil Court of Belo Horizonte, State of Minas Gerais.

311. In such action, plaintiff filed a motion for an anticipated provisional trial court resolution ordering defendants (which were then being investigated for cartel activities in the medical and industrial gas market) to cease charging supracompetitive prices. The court found initially that it was unable to grant the motion, pending CADE's final determination. Immediately after such determination, affirming the practice of conspiracy by defendants, the motion was granted on 5 November 2010, and the firms were ordered to supply medical gases (oxygen, carbon dioxide, nitrogen and medical compressed air) only at competitive prices (oddly, however, the court did not explain what it meant by 'competitive prices').

312. Thus, indemnity actions are more safely brought after the final CADE determination and based on the general principles of Article 402 of the Brazilian Civil Code (Law No. 10406/2002), which reads: 'Except for the cases expressly (otherwise) provided by Law, losses and damages due to a creditor shall include, in addition to what he/she has actually lost, what he/she has failed to profit' (free translation).

B. Interim Measures

313. The CADE Resolutions are extrajudicial instruments and, as such, enjoy the statutory benefit of being enforceable under summary proceedings. Administrative enforcement, however, is not permitted, and the CADE must resort to the courts for such purposes, including seeking for interim measures.

314. The judicial enforcement of resolutions imposing a pecuniary penalty may commence with the imposition of a pledge on assets or funds of the defendant party adversely affected. Conversely, the defendant may suspend the effects of the enforcement action, but only with the placement of a bond, ensuring the payment of the fine.

315. Cease and desist orders may also enjoy the benefit of judicial interim measures ordering specific performance or other affirmative actions ensuring the final practical result of a possible granting of the CADE's pleadings. Conversion of a cease and desist order into an obligation to pay for losses and damages only in such cases where specific performance or a similar practical action is impossible. The appointment of a judicial trustee is permitted to ensure specific performance of cease and desist orders, provided that no trustee has been appointed to date.

316. The law (Article 47) permits private parties injured by anticompetitive conducts and authorities and organizations having legal standing to bring public civil actions (a concept similar to class actions), to bring court action against undertakings that offend the economic order, seeking the cessation of the illegal practice and indemnity. Such civil actions shall not stay or suspend the corresponding administrative action before the CADE and may be brought at any time, before, concomitantly or subsequently to the administrative action. Such actions, however, are to date rare.

317. Virtually all interim measures granted by the civil courts relate to the requirement of parties seeking to annul a CADE Resolution to place a bond in the amount of the fine or other obligations imposed by the CADE. Interim measures in favour of the enforcement of a CADE Resolution in any legal actions between private parties are scarce. One of the very few cases relate to the interim order issued by the

28th Civil Court of Belo Horizonte, State of Minas Gerais, mentioned above, in Class Action No. 00.24 09709934-5 involving *Associação de Hospitais de Minas Gerais – AHMG v. White Martins Gases Industriais Ltda., Air Liquide Brasil Ltda., AGA S.A., Air Products Brasil Ltda. and Indústria Brasileira de Gases Ltda. – IBG*, where the court unclearly ordered the defendants to charge only 'competitive prices' in the sale of their products.

§3. Criminal Enforcement

I. Criminal Sanctions for Antitrust Violations

318. Information on criminal actions is scarce, since such cases are usually handled and resolved *in camera*.

319. Cartel is the only civil-administrative offence that is also characterized as a criminal offence under Law No. 8137, of 27 December 1990, as noted in Part I, Chapter 1 'Sources of Antitrust Law – National Sources'. Criminal liability is naturally attributable to individuals, but it is questionable that criminal actions may be brought against legal entities.

320. The SDE, for example, in issuing Ordinance No. 51/2009, containing the 'Guidelines for the Review of Complaints on Possible Competition Offences in Public Bids and the Standard Draft Statement of Independent Preparation of a Bid Quote' clearly stated in its item 17 that criminal liability can only attach to individuals, not legal entities.

II. Other Application of Criminal Law to Relevant Conducts

321. Article 111 of the Brazilian Competition Law (Law No. 12529/11) provides that in case a trustee is judicially appointed to enforce a cease and desist order, and performance of his duties is obstructed by the actions of a manager, officer or any other individual, or should any of such individuals take any action that directly or indirectly annul the effects (in total or partially) of the trustee's actions, or disobey any order legally issued by the trustee, such actions are punishable as a criminal resistance, disobedience or coercion in the course of the procedures (Articles 329, 330 and 344 of the Brazilian Penal Code).

322. Preventive imprisonment is also permitted by Article 312 of the Brazilian Penal Procedures Code, while Law No. 7960/89 provides for temporary arrest orders against those individuals who impede or hinder compliance with search and seize warrants in dawn raiding actions.

323. Temporary arrest warrants may be issued by the competent criminal judge at the motion of a criminal prosecutor and shall be valid for five days, extendable for an additional five-day period, in case of extreme need.

III. Role of Prosecutors

324. Criminal prosecution of antitrust offences is conducted by both the Federal and State Offices of the Attorney General, as the case may be. Such Offices frequently act in close cooperation with the competition authorities. The GS is an administrative authority and hence has no authority to enforce Criminal Law.

325. Administrative cartel investigations are most commonly and simultaneously the subject matter of criminal investigations carried out by the competent criminal prosecutor.

326. The GS also has close cooperative relations with the Brazilian Federal and State Polices, in the performance of criminal investigations and the enforcement of search and seizure warrants.

IV. Competent Criminal Courts

327. Criminal antitrust offences may be heard by the State criminal courts or by the Federal criminal courts, as the case may be. Generally, the State courts are the competent judicial authorities to hear cases involving anticompetitive conduct, including cartel arrangements, provided that Federal courts have the authority to cognize and hear criminal actions whenever the underlying case shall involve the direct interest of the Federal Government, such as in the case of crimes committed to the detriment of goods, services or interests of the latter (Article 109, item IV, of the Brazilian Federal Constitution), including those crimes that adversely impact strategic national economic sectors or the supply of essential services. Moreover, anticompetitive conducts with interstate impact shall likely (but not necessarily) be heard by the Federal courts.

328. Determining whether a State criminal court or a Federal criminal court is the competent authority to hear criminal antitrust offences is currently and frequently a non-trivial task and subject to large controversy.

Part II. The Application of the Prohibitions

Chapter 1. Restrictive Agreements

329. As discussed in Part I, Chapter 3 (Overview of Substantive Provisions), in Brazil, restrictive agreements (either horizontal or vertical) can be classified as cartels if they result in market domination and the reduction of consumer welfare.

330. The terms 'cartel', 'collusion' and 'concerted practice' are used by CADE as synonyms, simply and generally meaning any action or arrangement between competitors capable of artificially altering the competitive environment in any economic variable, such as prices, output, input, market-sharing.

331. Restrictive agreements, however, are to be reviewed, in all cases, including in the case of a cartel, under the rule of reason, and not all collaboration among competitors are necessarily illegal.

§1. Horizontal Agreements

332. Horizontal agreements are those arrangements involving incumbent or potential players within a same relevant market, that is, undertakings that are at the same level of the industrial chain and the products of which compete with each other.[32] Cartels and cooperation agreements among competitors are samples within the universe of horizontal agreements.

333. Horizontal agreements and non-horizontal practices (such as vertical agreements) are treated similarly by the CADE. Although the methodology for the review may differ, given the nature of each, horizontal and non-horizontal practices raise the same level of concern to the authorities.

I. Cartels

334. Cartels are formal or de facto arrangements among competitors whereby the parties thereto eliminate rivalry and information asymmetry, and standardize their commercial behaviour seeking to artificially practice prices close to monopoly levels and artificially absorb consumers' revenues.[33] To the extent, cartels are capable of

32. Opinion No. 291/2007
33. Although cartels are discussed under this section (Horizontal Agreements), it should be highlighted that, in Brazil, they can also involve vertical relations.

concentrating market shares and of acting collusively, their actions come close to monopolies and, *inter alia*, negatively impact motivation to innovate, result in the control of supply and adversely affect quality standards. Their purpose is to achieve the highest mark-up level and consequently expand the social dead weight loss.

335. Not all arrangements among competitors constitute a cartel. Certain joint activities involving competing concerns may, on the contrary, enhance competition, such as arrangements that increase productive efficiency, reduce risks, improve product quality or motivate research and development. Price-fixing arrangements, public tender bid frauds and output restrictions, however, clearly limit competition to the benefit of a few companies to the detriment of others and to the consumers.

336. Certain characteristics facilitate the identification of markets tending to the formation of a cartel, such as: (a) the presence of few players active in the market; (b) similarity of costs, processes, economic objectives, level of vertical integration and production among such players; (c) homogeneous products or services; (d) unavailability of substitute products; (e) high barriers to entry; (f) market-share stability; (g) easiness in securing price and volume information on other competitive companies; and (h) presence of a trade union. Obviously, none of such characteristics, alone, is sufficient to evidence the presence of a cartel.

337. Under Brazilian law, a cartel can only be formed if the relevant undertakings shall, jointly or separately, enjoy a market share equal to or in excess of 20% in the relevant market. Although cartels are held to be the most aggressive form of anticompetitive conducts, penalties imposed thereon are to be measured by the same general standards applicable to all other offences, that is, based on the actual or potential adverse impact on the market and consumers and the advantage secured by the cartel members thereby.

338. The characterization of a cartel, however, requires the presence of an action or omission displaying a causal nexus between such action or omission and the actual or potential injurious result. In demonstrating the presence of a cartel, it is necessary to determine whether there is a direct evidence of an agreement among economic players versed on some economic variable affecting their business activities, provided that the mere uniformity of prices without prior agreement among the relevant parties is insufficient to that effect. Cartels may be proven through reliable witness depositions, minutes of meetings, taping of telephone conversations, exchange of correspondence, physical or moral threats by cartel members on dissenting parties, etc.

339. Although considered the most severe anticompetitive conduct, cartels are not per se offences under Brazilian law that admit defences under the rule of reason. However, accountability may be found based on strict liability, and no proof of intent or of actual damage is required. CADE's jurisprudence has, in the recent past, adopted the EU doctrine of anticompetitive conducts by object (such as cartels) and by effects, whereby the former describes offences that are considered harmful to competition by their very nature, thus requiring no enquiry on the actual effects, and consequently on market power or other economic defences. Such jurisprudence has not been tested in the courts yet.

340. Cartels may be explicit or tacit, and evidenced through institutionalized arrangements operated through verbal mechanisms and recorded e-mails, correspondence, minutes of meetings, etc.) or parallel conduct resulting from tacit communication (price adjustments, boycotts, etc.). Conscious parallelism, however, is deemed to be insufficient evidence of cartel arrangements in homogeneous product (commodities) oligopolies, whereupon a *plus factor* (evidence of collusion) must be attached to the parallel conduct. A mere parallelism may simply reflect certain market structures or dynamics.

341. The CADE precedents make a distinction between a hard-core cartel and a diffuse cartel.[34] In the first case, the arrangement is the result of a secret agreement among competitors, with some kind of organization, and not resulting from an eventual coordination, but rather in the creation of permanent mechanisms to achieve its illegal goals, while in the second case the arrangement is characterized by coordination among competitors, with the same purpose of a hard-core cartel, but without the characteristics of permanence and organization.

342. The CADE's case law (further analysed) considers horizontal conspiracies and vertical restraints entailing a voluntary adherence of the parties to anticompetitive arrangements affecting prices, output, input, inventory and other economic variables and reducing asymmetry of market information alike as cartels.

343. Thus, cartels may be horizontal (of undertakings participating of the same industrial chain) or vertical (of undertakings participating in different levels of the industrial chain), and may be classified as classic or hard-core cartels (naked cartels made of competitors aligned to fix prices, share geographic markets and clients, to restrict supply or standardize technology) and ancillary restraints (when the standardization of commercial behaviour is not the primary goal of the cartel members, but a consequence of a larger purpose, such as the establishing of self-regulation rules for the industry or of gentlemen agreements, etc.).

344. Horizontal cartels should disclose a content that makes the cartel members' business policies predictable and result in certain stability as to the cartel duration and effectiveness.

345. Price-fixing, market/client allocation, production/innovation limitations are perhaps the clearer examples of cartel arrangements.

A. Price Fixing

346. Price-fixing is perhaps the best example of a horizontal collusive agreement, but may likewise be a unilateral anticompetitive conduct (vertical arrangements).

347. A good example of a price-fixing cartel is the international vitamin cartel (Administrative Process No. 08012.004599/1999-18) that involved a large number of global pharmaceutical companies that, between 1990 and 1999, agreed to fix prices. In 2007, the CADE imposed severe penalties on the cartel members, based on their respective gross turnover.

348. The case started in Brazil when the competition authorities (SDE) learned from news published in the press on penalties being imposed in the US on vitamin producers that pled guilty to a charge of collusion through an international cartel formed to manipulate prices between 1990 and 1999, and on similar investigations being carried out by the European Commission. The SDE then concluded that there

34. *See* Administrative Process No. 08012.004702/2004-77 (resolved on 9 May 2012), in re. *SDE, ex officio. v. Peróxidos do Brasil Ltda. et alii.*

was such cartel formed by F. Hoffman – La Roche Ltd., Basf Aktiengesellschaft and Rhône-Poulenc (formerly Aventis Animal Nutrition), having its intelligence centre:

> located in the parent companies of the involved groups, abroad, and (where) their worldwide branches were in charge of implementation and monitoring of the agreement on prices and volumes of vitamins marketed in each location, pursuant to the agreed budget.

As stated by the SDE, and pursuant to the investigations carried in the US, the cartel consisted of a continuing arrangement among the companies to establish, raise and maintain prices for the vitamins, as well as to share the volume of sales and market shares.

349. To affirm jurisdiction, the SDE concluded that there was strong evidence that the cartel yielded anticompetitive impacts in Brazil likewise, due to the strong interface and dependence of the Brazilian subsidiaries with their parent companies, cartel members. At the time, the vitamins were all virtually made using imported compounds. Thus, any restrain in the volume of sales and all price adjustments made by the parent companies, as a result of the conspiracy, would necessarily restrict competition in Brazil, since all such actions were capable of artificially limiting the volume made available for sale to the Brazilian domestic market and raising prices, if compared to prices applicable to a competitive market.

350. At the end of the case, the CADE, by majority vote, resolved that the three European companies were guilty (their respective Brazilian subsidiaries were released from the charges) and penalties were imposed on them as follows:

(a) F. Hoffman- La Roche Ltd.: fine of BRL 12,112,558.32, equal to 20% of the turnover on the exports of vitamins to Brazil on the year preceding the start of the Administrative Process, adjusted by applicable indexation rates.
(b) Basf Aktiengesellschaft: fine of BRL 4,726,362.37, equal to 15% of the turnover on the exports of vitamins to Brazil on the year preceding the start of the Administrative Process, adjusted by applicable indexation rates.
(c) Aventis Animal Nutrition: fine of BRL 847,125.19, equal to 10% of the turnover on the exports of vitamins to Brazil on the year preceding the start of the Administrative Process, adjusted by applicable indexation rates.

Note: Councillor Luiz Fernando Schuartz dissented, arguing that the case was solely based on evidence collected abroad and that there was no sufficient evidence of cartel activities in Brazil.

351. On its turn, price charts prepared by trade or professional associations were the most common cases of debate. Discussions on horizontal price-fixing arrangements had begun in the 1990, given that, prior to such period, the Brazilian Government adopted a price-control policy that actually required companies to jointly discuss prices through their respective trade associations in preparation of industry discussions with Government price-control authorities.

352. One of the first cases involving horizontal price-fixing was Administrative Process No. 53/1992 (resolved in June 1993), at the request of the Office of the Public Attorney in the State of Sergipe, against the State of Sergipe Hospital Association.

353. Thereafter, a large number of price-fixing cases were brought to the attention of the CADE. In a nutshell, the CADE Resolutions created a few a priori standards of legitimacy of price charts issued by trade or class associations: (i) the chart must be published as a market research and constitute a mere suggestion to the members of the association and are to be subject to no retaliation for non-compliance; (ii) the association must have no powers or conditions to influence in or induce the adoption of the price chart by competitors, to the detriment of the market and consumers; and (iii) the market must have a low level of concentration and be competitive, displaying rivalry among incumbent players and low entry barriers. No quality level standard is required by the CADE.

354. In Preliminary Investigation No. 08012.006307/1999-73 (resolved on 23 February) in re. *CADE v. Sindicato de Produtores de Castanha de Caju – SINCAJU*, price-fixing arrangements discussed between a producers' union and a consumer industry union were reviewed. The conclusion was that there is no anticompetitive conduct in a minimum price arrangement entered into between such unions, provided that the consumer industry union lacked market power, and that the price charts would not be binding on the associated purchasers. Similarly, price charts prepared by trade associations displaying costs and containing formulas for the calculation of resale margins are also, in principle, not illegal.

355. Professional associations are also subject to competitive scrutiny in issuing professional fee charts, except for labour unions and organizations that represent the interests of workers before their respective employers in collective bargaining. As opposed to the latter, professional associations seek to increase the bargaining power of their members, thus eventually creating anticompetitive concerns. The CADE, for example, has multiple cases ruling anticompetitive the adoption of a professional fee chart by a physicians' cooperative, provided that the characterization of the anticompetitive offence was in such cases affirmed merely by the demonstration of potential detriment to competition.

356. Price charts published by official entities in connection with the exercise of public functions are, however, permitted. In Preliminary Investigation No. 08012.002856/2008-58 (resolved on 27 July 2011), in re. *Procuradoria Geral da República v. the Boards of Commerce of the Brazilian States and of the Federal District* (*Juntas Comerciais dos Estados e do Distrito Federal*) in connection with the publication of price charts by the boards of Commerce regarding the services rendered by public sworn translators, the CADE ruled that, given that such professionals exercise a public function, as opposed to the work performed by the free translators, who do not enjoy public faith and whose activities can be performed by any professional, on a competitive environment, the adoption of price charts by the boards of Commerce is a statutory action and not offensive to competition laws.

357. Immunity was also granted to publishers in fixing maximum book prices, given that Law No. 9610/98 expressly permits the fixing of the cover price for the purpose of calculating the rights of authorship to be paid to the work author.[35]

358. Price-fixing may occur in the fixing of maximum prices, of minimum prices or of fixed prices and in neither case is a per se offence in Brazil.

359. Price-fixing is at all times governed by the rule of reason, enabling efficiency defences. Indeed, the impact of resale price maintenance may be negative (such as: (i) restraint to intrabrand competition, (ii) incentive to the formation of upstream cartels, (iii) incentive to the formation of downstream cartels, (iv) increase of unilateral market power, (v) raising of barriers to entry, or (vi) price discrimination seeking the exercise of monopoly power), or positive (such as: (i) elimination of the double marginalization problem, (ii) elimination of free riding, (iii) preservation of the product image, (iv) strengthening of inter-brand competition, (v) incentive to the entry of newcomers, (vi) enhancement of distributors' loyalty and cooperation with suppliers, and (vii) increase of the capacity of suppliers to face the purchasing power of large retailers that market multiple brands, including their own).

360. Mere price suggestions should be insufficient to the determination of an anticompetitive conduct, especially in markets that are not characterized by collusion and if based on plausible economic rationale, provided that no mechanisms are established to ensure the adoption of the suggested price (indirect coercion).

B. Market/Client Allocation

361. Similar to price-fixing, market/client allocation is a classic example of cartel activities.

362. Perhaps the benchmark case of market/client allocation in Brazil is that of the international vitamin cartel (Administrative Process No. 08012.004599/1999-18), mentioned above, involving global pharmaceutical companies that, between 1990 and 1999, agreed to, in addition to fix prices, share the global vitamin market. For details, *see* the above Price-Fixing section.

363. Market/client allocation is an efficient mechanism adopted by cartels to face the complex task of maintaining the stability and cohesion of a cartel. Indeed, lacking such a mechanism, clients can react to the cartel by migrating from one supplier to another. Furthermore, an eventual market expansion may create new business opportunities, requiring the coordination of the cartel members through market and profit-sharing.

364. The characterization of a market/client allocation cartel does not actually require an effective sharing of markets or clients. Similarly, the mere sharing of sensitive information on market conditions and clients by competitors may lead or induce to market/client allocation and may be treated similarly.

365. Given the sensitiveness of conflict of interest management and, the complexity of the administration of a market/client allocation (and of price-fixing agreements), cartel members, not infrequently, either assign to a third party, the leadership or management of the cartel activities or seek advice from outside consultants.

---

35. Preliminary Investigation No. 08012.001743/2002-40 (resolved on 27 Jul. 2011) in re. *João Carlos Ferreira da Silva v. Editora Globo et alii.*

In re. *SDE, ex officio v. Aro Mineração Ltda., Sociedade Mineradora Arroio dos Ratos – SOMAR and Comprove – Consultoria e Perícia Contábil Cível S/C* (Administrative Process No. 08012.000283/2006-66, resolved on 17 April 2008), related to the civil construction sand cartel, the parties engaged the consulting services of the accounting firm *Comprove*, whereupon the CADE ruled that the outside consultant, the services of whom will enable or facilitate the implementation of a cartel, shall be held liable, therefore, pursuant to Article 21, item II, of Law No. 8884/94 (corresponding to Article 36, paragraph 3(ii) of Law No. 12529/11). Such statutory provision considers punishable the party that obtains or influences the adoption of uniform commercial conduct or of a concerted action among competitors. Strict liability standards were applied.

C. *Production/Innovation Limitation*

366. Production/innovation limitation agreements among competitors are also considered hard-core cartels.

367. Pursuant to Article 36, §3, item viii, of Law No. 12529/11, parties that engage in market regulation arrangements by agreeing in limiting or controlling technological research and development or the production of goods or the rendering of services may be held liable for anticompetitive conducts. Further, if the limitation is caused by the abusive exercise of industrial property, intellectual, technology or trademark rights, the conduct shall represent an offence under §3, item XIX of the Brazilian Competition Law.

368. The law also contemplates and similarly deals with the hypothesis of agreements that hinder investments destined to be used in production of goods and services, or in distribution.

369. Perhaps one of the principal cases dealing with market regulation through agreements that sought to limit production and consequently impose abusive prices is the so-called international vitamin cartel case (Administrative Process No. 08012.004599/99-18, resolved on 14 February 2007, in re. *SDE and SEAE v. F. Hoffmann – La Roche Ltd. et alii*). For more details on this case, please *see* the Price-Fixing section above.

D. *Group Boycott*

370. Group boycotts seeking to bar the entry of newcomers in the relevant market or to exclude suppliers or clients from the market are anticompetitive conducts.

371. The CADE landmark case was Administrative Process No. 08012.009088/1999-48, in re. *Conselho Regional de Farmácias do Distrito Federal – CRF-DF v. Abbott Laboratórios do Brasil Ltda. et alii*, relating to an alleged cartel activity through the pharmaceutical industry trade association (*Associação Brasileira da Indústria Farmacêutica - ABIFARMA*) purportedly seeking to boycott the entry of generics in the market through: (i) the fixing of common sale conditions to medicine distributors, (ii) the adoption of a uniform trade conduct concerning the distribution of medicine, (iii) restrictions affecting the access of newcomers to the market, (iv) creation of difficulties to the operations of distributors in the market and their development, and (v) refusal to sell certain medicines to the non-complying distributors.

372. The case began in October 1999, based on apocryphal minutes of a meeting held by sales managers working for the defendant pharmaceutical companies where the alleged boycott would have been discussed. Although CADE was unable to find any actual damage to the market resulting from the discussions, on 13 April 2005, it issued a decision declaring the meeting illegal and imposing a minimum statutory fine on the companies, based on the argument of 'potential' injury to competition. The adverse administrative decision was based on indirect circumstantial evidence supported by CADE's experience and on arguments of strict liability that would not require the individualization of the conduct of each party to the meeting and permit a collective condemnation.

373. The CADE's decision was challenged by each of the defendants before the judiciary[36] and was overruled at the trial court level on 9 December 2011, and such decision was upheld under appeal brought by the CADE by the 6th Panel of the TRF – 1st Region, on 30 March 2015, when Justice Kássio Nunes Marques affirmed that the administrative decision was '*an undue condemnation by the CADE, whether because of the lack of evidence of the formation of an "agreement" to render the entry of generic medicine in the domestic market difficult, whether due to the lack of identification of the conducts of the condemned parties permitting the characterization* (of each party's conduct) *and the graduation of the penalty*' (free translation). The TRF decision is currently under appeal by the CADE at the STJ and STF.

374. Such a TRF decision has set new standards for the review of cartel cases by requiring minimum evidence for the determination of a collusive act, such as: (a) the mere presence of a company officer, and the mere participation of such an officer, in a meeting with competitors is insufficient to characterize a cartel, specially whenever that officer shall lack authority to bind his firm to an illegal agreement, (b) the mere receipt, as addressee, of a suspect message is insufficient evidence of a collusive conduct, there being no obligation of the recipient to repudiate such message, (c) adverse decisions are strictly required to individualize the conduct of, and the penalties assessed on, each of the parties, (d) it is not permissible to the CADE to fail to bring charge against all parties involved in the allegedly illegal conduct (in the case, the CADE failed to include the trade association, ABIFARMA, as a defendant) (principle of indivisibility of the action), and (e) a condemnatory decision requires the presence of causal nexus between the conduct and the anticompetitive effects on the market.

E. Collusion on Others' Objects

375. Most of the cartel cases heard by the CADE relate to price-fixing and market-sharing, which are classical examples of hard-core cartels. Most of such cases relate to charges brought against physicians' cooperatives and retail fuel dealers.

376. More recently, the competition authorities have become increasingly concerned in connection with possible cartel arrangements defrauding public tender bids, and multiple cases (still unresolved) have been brought, notably in connection with bids relating to port, data processing, security and transportation services.

36. In total nineteen Annulment Actions (Ordinary Annulment Action Nos 2007.34.00.043979-0 and others) that were ultimately unified and judged by Judge Itagiba Catta Preta, of the fourth Federal Court in Brasília.

377. Attempting to prevent these collusive behaviours, the SDE enacted Ordinance No. 51, of 3 July 2009, containing Guidelines for the Analysis of Charges in connection with possible anticompetitive offences in public tender bids. The principal forms of anticompetitive conduct identified by the SDE are:

(a) fictitious bids or coverage bids (courtesy, figurative or symbolic biddings);
(b) suppression of bids (companies that agree not to bid and withdraw from the bidding process);
(c) bid-ridding; and
(d) market-sharing.

378. The GS is paying close attention to blockades of presence biddings (collusive action between a producer of a good or service object of the bid, and at least two other legal entities (usually distributors of the latter), seeking to prevent other bidders from being qualified at the present bid process. Also, the GS is cautious in connection with *consortia* formed to participate in public tender bids, whenever the latter is formed by companies that are capable of participating in the bid individually using their own financial, technical and/or human resources. The legality of such *consortia* is to be reviewed by the GS under the rule of reason.

379. Facilitating cartel activities related to public tender bids by trade associations is also a major concern of the authorities. [Administrative Process No. 08012.008507/2004-16, resolved on 16 December 2014, in re. *Instituto Nacional do Seguro Social em Bauru (SP) e Procuradoria Federal Especializada do Instituto Nacional do Seguro Social em Osasco (SP).v. Associação Brasileira de Ortopedia Técnica — ABOTEC, Estar Bem Aparelhos Ortopédicos e Podologia Ltda. EPP, Casa Ortopédica Philadélfia Ltda., Ortopedia Belo Horizonte Ltda., Ortolab Órtese e Prótese Ltda., Ortoservice Comércio e Serviços Ortopédicos Ltda., Ortopedia A Especialista Ltda., Ortopedia Americana Ltda., Ortopedia Fubelle Ltda., Ortopedia Germânia Ltda., Ortopedia Kamia Ltda. ME, Ortopedia Lapa Ltda. e Ortopedia Mathias Ltda. EPP.*]

II. Information Exchange Practices

380. The Brazilian competition authorities are concerned with both direct information exchange practices, specially found at trade association meetings, and potential illegal exchange of information, through acts of concentration, notably JVs.

381. Information exchange practices may characterize cartel activities (and not merely a restriction by effect), especially if the group of parties exchanging information jointly have a market share in excess of 20%. Trade associations, although organizations, the existence of which is protected by applicable provisions of the Brazilian Federal Constitution that ensure the right of individuals to associate[37], are a major source of

37. Article 8. *Professional or union association is free, with regard for the following: Constitution of the Federative Republic of Brazil: constitutional text of 5 October 1988, with the alterations introduced by Constitutional Amendments No. 1/1992 through 64/2010 and by Revision Constitutional Amendments No. 1/1994 through 6/1994. – 3rd ed. – Brasília: Chamber of Deputies, Documentation and Information Center, 2010.*

concern to the authorities, given the possibility of members discussing sensitive commercial issues in the course of meetings.

382. For such purposes, the SDE has published a small brochure named '*Combate a Cartéis em Sindicatos e Associações*' ('Fighting Cartels at Unions and Associations', Collection SDE/DPDE No. 03/2009), which briefly sets guidelines as to what issues are permitted, and which are void in trade association discussions. The publication recognizes that one of the principal functions of a trade association or union is to inform its members on important industry issues and that such exchange of information may yield pro-competitive impacts, such as gains in efficiency, cost reductions and increased labour safety. Summarizing, the following are main features of such guidelines:

> Exchange of information and discussions on the following issues are likely not to constitute an anticompetitive conduct:

(a) Discussion of new legislation, amendment of existing laws and draft laws.
(b) Reduction of taxes and issues related to barriers to the importation or exportation of goods or services.
(c) Research on security equipment or accessories, or other matters of interest to the industry, generally including environmental issues, the results of which must be made available on reasonable terms to the entire industry (with mandatory adoption of these results by members being prohibited).
(d) Institutional information on the industry in general.
(e) Economic and public opinion trends.
(f) Public policies associated with the industry and labour matters.
(g) Trade protection actions (anti-dumping or safeguards cases).

383. However, the exchange of information on the following matters is generally prohibited:

(a) Matters relating to costs, purchase or sale prices, price trends, price changes and their implementation, methodology of calculating discounts or rebates or profit margins.
(b) Issues relating to credit or terms and conditions of purchase, sale or resale, whether or not standardized.
(c) Issues relating to the sharing of territories, customers, or activities related to the purchase of parts or raw materials (procurement or sourcing).
(d) Matters pertaining to production levels, inventory or supplies, production processes or methods, parts, pieces and raw materials and technological developments.
(e) Issues related to proposals for controlling, regulating or limiting the business, operations or trade practices, such as the so-called rules of business 'fairness' or 'ethics'.
(f) Matters that relate to joint research agreements among firms (except concrete cases to be considered case-by-case).
(g) Proposals to prohibit participation of any company in the industry association.

384. Commercially sensitive issues, such as current and future prices, market shares, costs, production levels, marketing plans, growth plans, discount policies and others are matters of high competitive concerns.

385. In order to mitigate the risks of anticompetitive conduct, the trade association or union, in collecting information on such sensitive issues is recommended to follow certain safety guidelines:

(a) to collect only 'historical' data (the SDE recommended that the data should be at least one year old to be safe, but experience has shown that, depending on the market, three months old data may be acceptable);
(b) to disseminate the information only in an aggregated form, so as not to permit the identification, the source of the information;
(c) to adopt a mechanism of confidential collection of sensible information under the responsibility of an external and independent auditor (black box), and ensure under contract that the identification of the members participating in the programme and of the data supplied by each of them be kept confidential;
(d) to ensure that the supply of information is strictly voluntary;
(e) to make statistic information yielding from the programme available to the public, and not only to members, at a reasonable cost.

386. The same concerns, *mutatis mutandis*, apply to the exchange of information through the creation of third-party agents or organizations created by competitors for industry-wide market or credit analysis or statistics.

387. However, exchange of information, or the possibility thereof, among competitors may constitute an act of concentration subject to the CADE review and approval, even if no formal agreement is entered into by the relevant parties. Such is, for example, the case of joint purchase and sale agencies, including B2B[38] and B2C[39] organizations, cooperative JV arrangements etc. Such transactions are held by the Brazilian authorities as deals that may potentially result in the creation of a cartel forum and, whenever cleared are customarily approved conditional to the creation of firewall or Chinese wall precautions, and to strict governance rules.

388. Indeed, cross shareholdings, cooperative joint ventures and minority shareholdings in competitor's ventures are prime concerns of the CADE in reviewing mergers and acquisitions in the context of preventing illegal information exchange practices. Structural remedies and, less often, behavioural or governance remedies are frequently adopted by the CADE in such occasions. Such issues are discussed in Brazil in the context of exchange of information, more precisely in the context that such acts of concentration are vehicles to potential illegal exchange of information.

389. Indeed, the CADE is generally suspicious of JVs. In Act of Concentration No. 08012.004907/2010-09, cleared on 15 December 2010, involving *CPLPAR Holding*

38. B2B's are business-to-business exchanges, meaning tools in the electronic trade that use the Internet as a means to achieve business transaction. They permit the participants to engage in a large variety of trade activities (e.g., purchase and sale transactions).
39. B2C or business-to-customer is the direct e-commerce between the manufacturer, seller or service renderer and the final consumer, through the Internet.

S.A., CPA Trading S.A e *Cattalini Terminais Marítimos Ltda.*, for example, it was stated that:

> such (JV) structure may increase the risk of collusion, especially with respect to price fixing, to matters concerning commercial policies (sale terms and conditions, costs, client and/or supplier definition and on which market to do business – products and territories, among others) and to other competitive variables (free translation).

390. And further:

> Such potential risk may be increased should such structure (JV) permits – or fails to prevent – a reduction in the cost of internal communication – and coordination, facilitating the exchange of information that is competitively sensitive. Thus, it is important to assess if the arrangement prevents, motivates or is neutral in connection to exchange of such information in the intimacy of the joint venture (free translation).

391. A benchmark case discussing joint production agreements relates to Acts of Concentration Nos 08012.010192/2004-97 (involving *Suzano Sul Papel e Celulose and Ripasa S/A Papel e Celulose*) and 08012.010195/2004-19 (involving *Votorantim Celulose e Papel and Ripasa S/A Papel e Celulose*), resolved on 8 August 2007, whereby the two leading integrated pulp and paper manufacturers, Suzano and Votorantim, acquired Ripasa, thus reducing the market structure to only three competitors. In such transaction, Suzano and Votorantim formed a *consortium* (Conpacel – Consórcio Paulista de Papel e Celulose) to acquire the stock control (on a 50%–50% basis) and plant of Ripasa, which ceased to be an independent producer and changed into a joint captive producer to the purchasers. The parties were required to enter into a Settlement Agreement (Agreement of Undertaking) whereby the plant would be managed by an independent manager subject to strict governance rules granting management full and independent managing authority *vis-à-vis* Suzano and Votorantim and preserving the exchange of sensitive information to the parties.

392. Subsequently, another important case, then addressing the issue of cooperative joint ventures, was Act of Concentration No. 08012.01196/2005-53 (resolved on 17 December 2008), involving the JV *between Air Liquide Brasil Ltda. and White Martins Gases Industriais Ltda.*, relating to the joint supply by the two competing concerns of industrial gases to a new steel mill. First, in determining the industrial gas market structure, the CADE has decided that, in the case of a cooperative JV, incorporated with the purpose of constructing a new productive capacity to supply a single consumer, even if the partners, thereto, shall continue to operate as independent players in the market, their respective shares are to be added to one another in determining the market structure, whenever the transaction shall facilitate the exchange of sensitive competitive information between them.

393. Further, the CADE has considered, in the merger review, that the reduction of transaction risks yielding from the JV is not an efficiency capable of off-setting competitive risks of a deal, provided that scale gains and increase of installed capacity are, provided that such efficiencies are specific to the transaction, whereupon the exchange of information risks were circumvented with behavioural remedies, replacing the active participation of one of the parties to the venture in the management, thereof, by a third-party independent manager. The interests of such party were protected as a capital investment, but avoiding the risks of undue exchange of information.

394. Similar concerns with exchange of information were raised in a wave of acquisitions by cement producers of minority shareholding in concrete-disposal firms. The discussion, in such cases, related to the consequences of the resulting vertical integration and of the access of the minority shareholder to sensitive information pertaining to the target company. In such cases, the CADE, in clearing the relevant transactions, has required the adoption of governance rules rendering impossible the participation of the minority competing shareholder in management decisions of the target company. Examples of such cases are to be found in Acts of Concentration Nos 08012.008939/2008-51 (resolved on 3 March 2009), involving *Votorantim Cimentos Brasil Ltda. and Pavimentadora e Construtora Vicente Matheus Ltda.* and 08012.000637/2009-15 (resolved on 17 June 2009), involving *Companhia de Cimento Ribeirão Grande and CJ Mineração.*

III. Cooperation Agreements

395. Cooperation among competitors is not to be deemed anticompetitive in essence; however, it receives rigorous treatment by the CADE in order to avoid anticompetitive effects. Since 2014, this type of arrangement between players has been assessed under the control of structures as a type of merger – named by CADE's Resolution 10/2014 as associative agreements.

396. Brazilian experience with cooperation agreements is primarily related to B2B ventures (i.e., ventures, or translations, comprising only players, not involving customers and/or consumers). Primary concerns relate to the facilitation of price coordination and other competitive variables to the detriment of the market.

397. In Act of Concentration No. 08012.003632/01-97, resolved on 29 September 2004, involving *Sadia S/A, Cargill Agrícola S/A* and *Danone S/A*, for example, the CADE expressed that, despite the efficiencies and possible pro-competitive impacts resulting from B2B exchanges due to their cooperative nature, such cooperation may conversely facilitate anticompetitive conducts, such as: (i) the possibility that joint purchases may lead to a monopsony power; (ii) the facilitation of collusion and coordination among competitors, due to the ease of sharing information; and (iii) the possibility of implementing exclusionary actions that may increase rivals' costs. In said case, the CADE has cleared the formation of the B2B *consortium,* subject only to the parties not being required to exclusive use of the exchange in outsourcing.

398. Similar to the US FTC Guidelines (of 1992), in Act of Concentration No. 08012.00001/01-16, resolved on 16 June 2004, involving General Motors Corporation, Ford Motor Company, Renault S/A, Nissan Motor Co. Ltd., Oracle do Brasil Sistemas Ltda., DaimlerChrysler AG and Commerce One Inc., the CADE raised five questions in order to determine whether a cooperation agreement involving exchange of sensitive information may suggest collusion among competitors:

(a) to which market structure B2B serves? The highest the market concentration of those sharing the information, the greatest shall be the possibility of an anticompetitive impact;
(b) who shares the information? The exchange of information among competitors, although not in all cases, is generally capable of injuring competition;
(c) what kind of information is shared? Information relating to competitive variables may injure competition;
(d) what is the 'age' of the information? Current or future information shall have greater probabilities of resulting in anticompetitive impacts than past information; and
(e) the shared information is accessible through other channels? The supply of information that is only shared through a portal or that is shared, with difficulties, through other channels, increases the probability of an anticompetitive impact.

399. In order to avoid the risks of coordination among competitors, certain mechanisms are to be considered to minimize the risk of anticompetitive impacts relating to B2B, as follows:

- to restrict the access to certain information, specially through firewall and intrusion detection systems;
- to enter into confidentiality arrangements;
- to adopt rules that impede that members of the board of the portal to have access to sensible information on other competitors;
- to use auditing mechanisms that may ensure that the relevant operational rules are being followed; and
- to impose fines on non-compliance of operational rules.

400. Other cooperation agreements under the scrutiny of the authorities are co-marketing agreements which, being capable of restraining competition, are subject to the CADE notification requirements. Currently, there is a large debate in connection as to which kinds of cooperation agreements in general are reportable as 'acts of concentration', given that the Brazilian Competition Law currently in force expressly listed 'associative contracts' (Article 90, item IV) as a transaction subject to notification, provided, however, that the CADE has, to date, failed to define what an 'associative contract' means or to regulate which of such contracts are reportable.

401. Considering the general assessment that collaboration agreements are not to be considered prima facie anticompetitive, a non-competition clause entered in a collaboration agreement effective for the life of the contract is, in principle, acceptable, since such provisions usually spell out the very essence of the purpose of the relevant contract.

402. In confirmation of such understanding, in Act of Concentration No. 08012.012129/2011-02 (resolved on 14 March 2012), in re. *Astic ED Participações S.A.* and *Instituição Educacional São Miguel Paulista S/S Ltda.*, the CADE reaffirmed its settled jurisprudence that a non-compete clause effective for the life of a JV between two undertakings is valid, even if such a term shall exceed five years.

A. Research and Development

403. Research and development have consistently been considered pro-competitive activities by the CADE. The relevant geographic market has been defined as global in scope and the market characterized by low barriers to entry.

404. The CADE, nevertheless, has in the recent past changed its prior, more liberal approach in connection with the notification requirements of research and development collaboration agreements. This approach represented a major setback in terms of policies motivating innovation.

405. Indeed, while in prior cases, the CADE requested the notification only of those R&D agreements that lead to the execution of commercial arrangements by the parties for the marketing of new products. Such requirement was based on the assumption that the R&D agreement had an impact on the market structure of the final product. In the Act of Concentration No. 08012.007963/2009-53 involving *Monsanto do Brasil Ltda. and Basf S/A*, resolved on 11 November 2009, the CADE has adopted a most conservative approach, by requiring notification of research and development agreements in their early stages, even if no market structure would be modified thereby, or even if entered abroad by parties not using assets located in Brazil, simply because such arrangements would entail the sharing of equipment and know-how by the contracting players.

406. Such a conservative approach was explicitly stated in Act of Concentration No. 08012.006735/2011-81 (resolved on 10 August 2011), in re. *Bayer S.A. and Soytech Seeds Pesquisa em Soja Ltda.*, when CADE ruled that research and development agreements in general, whenever entered between firms of the same field of economic activity constitute acts of concentration subject to CADE's scrutiny.

407. In short, the CADE concluded that: (i) the transaction resulted in a horizontal concentration in the activities of research and development by Monsanto and Basf, and (ii) a vertical integration between: (a) the development of technology, and (b) the activities of production and marketing of the final products that would eventually be developed through the use of the technology developed by the partners.

B. Specialization and Standardization

408. Specialization and standardization are phenomena generally accepted as prima facie favourable to consumers' interests.

409. Unification and standardization of productive processes are held to be positive externalities in both contractual arrangements or in agreements contemplated in acts of concentration (it should be noted that, under the concept of Article 90, item IV, of the Brazilian Competition Law, contractual arrangements and agreements may also be classified as 'acts of concentrations' should they constitute an 'associative contract', a term yet undefined and not regulated), to the extent that they may promote a greater efficiency in the use of raw materials.

410. The CADE benchmark case relating to standardization is debated in Preliminary Investigation Nos 08012.006835/2003-05 and 08012.004062/2005-86, in which the main manufacturers of powder detergents and members of the Brazilian category trade association (*Abipla*) had agreed to standardize the product packaging, seeking to enable the consumer to have greater information transparency.

411. Such initiative was supported by the consumer defence authorities (Procon and INMETRO). They considered the initiative an action favouring the prevention of consumer misleading (i.e., indirect price increase through reduction in volume not transparently informed in the packaging). Standardization, in this case, was assessed as a practice that, by reducing consumer information costs, could motivate inter-brand competition by the greater possibility of consumers monitoring and comparing prices and product quality.

412. Notwithstanding the fact that the CADE had found that standardization as pro-competitive, it also determined that non-compliance by a market player with such industry-wide agreement would not constitute any anticompetitive offence, but rather a legitimate exercise of the constitutional principle of free initiative.

C. Joint Production, Joint Purchasing and Joint Selling

413. In Brazil, cooperative JV and concentrative JV are both considered and treated as concentrations, and subject to CADE notification requirements under Article 90, item IV, of the Brazilian Competition Law.

414. There is no case law treating cooperative JV differently than concentrations. On the contrary, an interesting example of such understanding is the CADE Resolution of 11 November 2009, in Act of Concentration No. 08012.007963/2009-53, between *Monsanto do Brasil Ltda. and Basf S/A*, dealing with a cooperative JV arrangement for the research and development in connection with new forms of applications or new presentations combining the herbicides Roundup Ultra and Roundup Ready (Monsanto) and Comet (Basf). In such a resolution, CADE concluded that research and development collaboration agreements, even when they do not change any market structure or not prima facie anticompetitive, are subject to the CADE notification requirement as an Act of concentration under Article 88 of Law No. 12529/11.

415. Joint production (and toll arrangements between competitors), joint purchasing and joint selling arrangements are presumed to be legal actions, but regular acts of concentration subject to the CADE notification requirements.

416. In such category are B2B JVs, swap agreements, production capacity lease arrangements and toll manufacturing agreements.

417. Purchase or selling electronic exchange arrangements, whereby competing or complementary industries unite to achieve sharing synergies relating to administrative infrastructure and personnel, as well as economies of scale and scope before suppliers with the purpose of increasing their individual bargaining power and achieving more favourable transactional terms, are presumed to be economically rational and legal, albeit subject to the CADE scrutiny.

418. Joint purchasing or selling arrangements are, furthermore, favourably considered whenever representing countervailing mechanisms to monopoly power in the industrial upstream or downstream chain.

419. Nevertheless, the CADE has, likewise, experienced negative approaches to joint production and selling arrangements. In Acts Concentrations Nos 08012.002315/99-50 and 08012.004117/99-67, concerning the incorporation of *Brasil-Álcool S.A. and*

Bolsa Brasileira do Álcool Ltda. by major Brazilian sugar and alcohol producers, in May 1999. As an integral part of such an arrangement, the parties have agreed to certain loyalty and exclusivity arrangements relating to the marketing of sugar and alcohol, including certain price-fixing clauses, uniform conduct and market-sharing seeking to face circumstantial crisis affecting the relevant market. The CADE ruled that such arrangement represented an illegal crisis cartel and ordered full divestiture.

420. Failing company defences were similarly argued before the CADE and dismissed by it in Act of Concentration No. 08012.000002/01-61 (resolved on 12 May 2004), whereby *Amorim Pinto e Cia. Ltda., Aro S.A. Exportação, Importação, Indústria e Comércio, Indústrias Reunidas Renda S.A., Metalgráfica Cearense S.A. and Tapon Corona Metal Plástico Ltda.*, the principal metal-stopper producers in Brazil, entered into a Commercial Association Agreement seeking to reorganize the production and marketing of such product, claiming that the decreasing demand and the existing overcapacity of the industry required greater efficiency and rapid restructuring of the product manufacturers. For such purpose, the applicants incorporated a joint production company (*Cia. de Rolhas Metálicas das Américas S.A. – CROMA*), merging all of their respective production activities into a single exclusive legal entity. Once again, the CADE decided that cartel crisis is not acceptable and ordered full divestiture, aside from ordering the commencement of a cartel investigation against the parties' members of CROMA.

421. Unwritten collaboration agreements, on their turn, are likely to be considered cartel arrangements subject to prosecution.

§2. Vertical Agreements

422. Vertical agreements describe arrangements between players situated at different, but interdependent, levels in the production, whether upwards (supplier) or downwards (distributor or client). Within the universe of vertical agreements, the principal ones, from a competitive perspective, are the distribution agreements and the exclusivity arrangements that may raise market foreclosure concerns.

423. The scrutiny of a vertical agreement starts on whether the parties to the agreement hold dominant position, and whether, through the agreement, they are likely to behave in an anticompetitive fashion. The absence of market power within the vertical relation turns it to a likely acceptable case under CADE case law perspective.

424. Conversely, restrictive vertical agreements are to be held illegal if resulting or potentially resulting in a market foreclosure either in the downstream or in the upstream market, or in the creation of a double monopoly, whereby a dominant, monopolist or monopsonist undertaking achieves dominance, monopoly or monopsony in a downstream or an upstream market.

425. As opposed to horizontal concentrations, for which the CADE has published Guidelines for the Review of Horizontal Acts of Concentration,[40] which sets the procedures and principles adopted by the CADE (and indicating the competitive concerns in connection with such concentrations), and for predatory pricing, for which the SEAE has published Guidelines for the Economic Analysis of the Practice of

40. *Guia Análise de Atos de Concentração Horizontal*, approved by CADE on 27 Jul. 2016,

Predatory Pricing,[41] that seek to set the principles for the systematization of the analysis of such practice – no similar guidelines have been published in connection with vertical integration and restrictive arrangements.

I. Distribution

426. Distribution may involve distributorship, resale and agency agreements, whereby products are ultimately made available to final consumers and end-users. Such agreements are evidenced through multiple forms and reveal multiple levels of integration between producers and distributors, resellers and agents.

427. Distribution arrangements seek to enhance efficiencies in the supply of goods and services to the consumer. Consequently, producers are free to select the most efficient way of meeting the needs of demand, by selling its products and services either directly to the consumer or through distribution, or through a combination of both.

428. Based on such rationale, producers are not required to enter into distributorship agreements with all distributors interested in such contractual relation, provided that the selection of its distributor network is to be made on a non-discriminatory fashion. By the same token, the reduction by a producer of its distribution chain is a matter of the exclusive interest of the commercial policy of the firm, insusceptible of any governmental control, in the absence of any circumstantial evidence of injury to competition.

429. Commercial issues, such as prices, volumes and matters relating to termination of a distribution agreement, are questions not deemed to be competitive issues. Disputes on such matters are to be settled by the regular courts and not by the CADE. The imposition of quotas in a distribution agreement is acceptable especially whenever such provision shall seek to make viable a minimum production scale at the plant, save if it shall yield an increase in barriers to entry or result in an obstacle to the performance of the agreement.

430. Producers and distributors are not competitors with one another, since distribution arrangements seek to improve efficiency in the supply, by producer, of goods and services to the consumer. There are no competitive relations but only a contractual relation between them. Thus, for example, there is no impediment to the direct sale, by the manufacture, to the final consumer on more favourable competitive conditions than those extended to its own distribution chain.

431. Distribution and co-marketing arrangements entered between competitors or firms of the same industry, regardless of their location, are acts of concentration subject to the CADE notification requirements, since such arrangements are similar to agreements of association (associative contracts). Thus, acts of concentration that

41. *Guia para Análsie Econômica da Prática de Preços Predatórios*, attached to Ordinance SEAE No. 70, of 12 Dec. 2002, as published in the Federal Official Gazette issue No. 241-E, of 13 Dec. 2002, s. I, pp 138 and 139. In practice, however, the CADE is not inclined to condemn predatory pricing practices and has declined to issue any adverse decision in this respect. The argument is that predatory pricing can hardly be an effective anticompetitive conduct.

relate to concerns that do business in Brazil solely through exports to independent distributors are subject to Brazilian jurisdiction.

432. However, a distribution agreement entered on a non-exclusive basis between two companies that are already vertically integrated does not raise antitrust concerns.

A. Exclusive Distributorship

433. Exclusive distributorship is a kind of vertical integration that ordinarily yields no anticompetitive concerns, save in those cases resulting in market foreclosure. The latter are subject to the CADE notification requirements.

434. Vertical restrictive practices are restrictions imposed by producers/suppliers of goods and services to a given market (of origin) on vertically related markets – 'upstream' or 'downstream' – along the production chain ('target' market). Such provisions are anticompetitive whenever they result in the creation of mechanisms for the exclusion of rivals, either by increasing the barriers to entry of newcomers, or by rising competitors costs, or by increasing the probability of coordinated exercise of market power by producers/suppliers or distributors, through the creation of mechanisms that enable the overcoming of obstacles to the coordination that would otherwise exist.

435. The potential anticompetitive impact of exclusivity clauses are associated: (i) with the implementation of collusive conduct in the market 'of origin', when they are used as means to divide markets among substitute products, (ii) with the unilateral increase of market power by the concern imposing the exclusivity, by means of market foreclosure and/or of an increase of barriers to entry in the distribution segment (or in the supply of raw materials), a result that may result directly from the contractual provisions or indirectly through the raising of rivals' costs, or result in: (i) facilitating the evasion from return profits in regulated markets or (ii) restricting consumers' freedom in selecting their supplier. The possible benefits from the clause are related to transaction cost savings, by seeking to restrict free riders in defending sunk costs, such as investments in brands or in technology, or in the protection of specific assets.

436. Exclusivity clauses are not, in principle, anticompetitive, unless they result in a significant market foreclosure. In order to determine the level of foreclosure, it is of the essence to measure: (a) the market power of the parties (whenever a party controls 20% or more of a relevant market), and (b) the volume of trade affected by the restraint *vis-à-vis* the total trade volume, provided that, for the practice to be repealed, the level of foreclosure needs not to be total, but actually may be negligible, even in homogeneous markets.

437. Exclusive distributorship arrangements are sought for a variety of economic reasons, such as efficiency reasons or reasons attached to the interest of producer in preserving or enhancing its image or its product image.

438. The legality or illegality of exclusivity in distributorship arrangements may change from time to time in a given geographic market. An agreement that is valid and legal today in a given area may subsequently become illegal, should market conditions change to cause the arrangement to become a market foreclosure instrument. No anticompetitive concerns arise, however, whenever multiple distributors are available or can be duplicated.

439. Exclusive distributorship arrangements are a matter of frequent review by the CADE. In the Act of Concentration No. 08012.005846/99-12 involving the merger of the two largest brewery companies in Brazil (*Companhia Cervejaria Brahma and Companhia Antarctica Paulista Indústria Brasileira de Bebidas e Conexos*), forming *Companhia de Bebidas das Américas – AmBev*, for example, the CADE concluded that, as a result of the merger of the two producers, their respective distribution network were considered immune to duplication and, as such, constituting a new barrier to entry in the beer market.

440. Should a producer acquire the stock control of its exclusive distributor, such transaction shall constitute an act of concentration subject to the CADE notification requirement.

B. Exclusive Dealing

441. Similar to exclusive distributorship agreements, exclusive dealings are vertical integration restraints, the anticompetitive impact of which is to be reviewed under the rule of reason.

442. Generally, exclusive dealings are exempt from anticompetitive concerns when based on efficiency rationales, seeking to obtain efficiency gains and cost reduction. Conversely, such arrangements are illegal whenever solely seeking maintenance or creation of control on the supply of goods and services, or market foreclosure.

443. The CADE, for example, in reviewing cases of exclusive dealing within the context of abuse of dominance, has in multiple occasions held illegal the conduct of physicians' cooperatives (cases primarily involving the cooperative *Unimed*) – the Charter of which forced its members to accept an exclusive relationship with it. Doctors were required to abide by an exclusive dealing provision of the cooperative Charter and work solely within the *Unimed* network, provided that the cooperative enjoyed a dominant position in the relevant market, and its conduct was considered to negatively affect the social welfare in the respective geographic areas of operations. An essential element of the CADE Resolution was the fact that *Unimed* enjoyed a dominant position in the relevant market.

444. On its turn, the CADE reviewed the case of a central cooperative (*Cooperativa Central dos Produtores Rurais de MG – CCPR*), the Charter of which required all cooperative members to deliver to the central cooperative all of the milk produced by members of the former, and prohibiting such member cooperatives from any kind of industrialization of milk or cream products, and from distributing or selling milk and milk products to consumers residing in cities or towns located outside the area of activities of each such member cooperatives.[42] In such cases, the CADE ruled that such exclusive dealing requirement was legal, provided, however, the cooperative had no market dominance.

445. There is also no anticompetitive concern in the granting, by a manufacturer, of exclusivity rights to a third party for the marketing and after-sale technical assistance to its products, whenever the market is characterized by rivalry among multiple producers and products, and specially whenever such exclusivity clause shall facilitate

42. Preliminary Investigation No. 08012.101986/2006-01 (resolved on 1 Mar. 2011), in re. *SDE, ex-officio v. Cooperativa Central dos Produtores Rurais de MG - CCPR.*

to the manufacturer its control of compliance with regulatory obligations or ensure its higher levels of legal and economic assurances, enabling it to better control liability risks resulting from product malfunctions.[43]

446. Conversely, the option of a consumer (or customer) in selecting a supplier to have an exclusive relationship, as long as it is adopted independently and freely, is a legitimate option seeking to obtain cost, quality and innovation benefits. The competitors are due to offer similar advantages.

447. Special interest to the competition authorities embraces essential facilities, when duplication of a given infrastructure is impossible (such as in the case of natural monopolies). In most of such cases, the behavioural remedies found to the concern are based on the non-discriminatory sharing of the infrastructure with the market.

448. An interesting case of infrastructure sharing (also involving an issue of abuse of dominance) was discussed in Administrative Process No. 08012.003048/2001-31 (involving *Associação NeoTV v. Globosat et alii*), where exclusive dealings were entered in connection with the broadcasting (on pay TV) of national and State soccer championships. In such cases, the CADE resolved that the relevant broadcasting rights constituted an essential facility in the TV pay-per-view industry and held anticompetitive the underlying exclusivity dealing arrangement entered between *Globosat* and Net TV for the signal of SporTV channel (owned by *Globosat*). As a result, it ordered the relevant television broadcasting contents, technical information, maintenance and other after-sale services to be sublicensed or subject to compulsory sales to third pay-per-view players on a non-discriminatory basis. Again, an essential element of the CADE Resolution was the fact that *Unimed* enjoyed a dominant position in the relevant market.

449. On its turn, and in connection with JVs, exclusivity dealings shall yield no competitive concerns whenever resulting from a JV that discloses an organic growth, and the relevant production is essentially captive, especially whenever excess production is destined exclusively to exports.

450. Further, termination of a cross-corporate shareholding in essential facilities also does not cause antitrust concerns whenever: (a) it shall reduce the motivation for coordinated action between the relevant parties, and (b) there is no competition in the flow of products through the relevant facility, or (c) in the case of a natural monopoly, the activity is subject to regulation and to adequate control by the relevant regulatory agency.

C. Selective Distribution

451. Distribution arrangements seek to enhance efficiency in the supply of goods and services to consumer or end-user, reason why there is no competitive relations (but only contractual relations) between a producer and its distributor.

452. In entering into distributorship agreements, both parties (producers and distributors) enjoy full party autonomy in negotiating their commercial terms and conditions.

---

43. Preliminary Investigation No. 08700.000558/2008-75 (resolved on 13 Jul. 2011) in re. *RIOURBE — Empresa Municipal de Urbanização v. Ortosíntese Indústria e Comércio Ltda.*

453. Principal, therefore, is permitted to act selectively by appointing territorial restrictions on the business activities of distributor (as long as such restrictions do not result in market foreclosure, through exclusivity arrangements), or selective distribution targets (e.g., reserving the right to sell directly to certain customers or under certain circumstances). Territorial exclusivity clauses are generally legal, especially in reasonably preventing free riding conducts and ensuring the return of the investment without imposing unreasonable limits to competition in the relevant market.

454. However, generally, principals are not permitted to prohibit authorized retailers to supply the contractual goods to unauthorized retailers (save under certain circumstances leading to the discredit of principals' image or product). Actually, principal itself is not permitted to refuse to sell to unauthorized retailers, should the latter be willing to pay FOB at no discount and in cash.

455. Imposing a retail price to the retailer is also void, although suggested prices may be permitted under the following circumstances: (a) principal has no market power (market share in excess of 20%) or, if it enjoys market power, the price suggestion is supported by a legal economic rationale, (b) there is no direct or indirect imposition of the suggested price and no penalties are attached to an eventual non-compliance, and (c) the market conditions do not favour collusion.

456. Consequently, the analysis of the illegality of price suggestions greatly rely on the impact of the conduct in the market *vis-à-vis* the potential benefits yielding to the final consumer and the resulting economic efficiencies. The CADE's position on this matter is unstable.

457. Indeed, old decisions[44] have highlighted the potential harm of suggested prices to competition and prohibited the practice save: (i) if the relevant firm suggesting prices did not have a dominant position, and (ii) the suggestion would only be a mere reference and not an imposition, the other party being free to follow it or not.

458. Later, however, the CADE adopted a more flexible standard. In the Administrative Process No. 08012.0004363/2000 (resolved on 28 October 2009, in which *Companhia de Bebidas das Américas – AmBev* was investigated for, *inter alia*, allegedly fixing resale prices and discriminating distributors, the CADE concluded that the practice by *AmBev* of suggesting resale prices was legal because: (a) the practice was supported by an economic rationale (the resale price was taken as a basis for sales taxes, the calculation of which was based on the retail sales prices, but the payment of which, was incumbent on the manufacturer), and (b) the relevant market was not characterized as collusive in nature and remained competitive.

459. In November 2009, in Preliminary Investigations No. 08012.005994/2004-65, the CADE relieved the *Sindicato das Empresas de Artes Fotográficas/SP – SEAFESP*, a trade union, of the charges of anticompetitive conduct for referring to its members'

---

44. *See* : (i) Administrative Process No. 148/92 (resolved on 22 Oct. 1997), in re. *Sindicato das indústrias de Panificação e Confeitaria de São Paulo and Associação das Indústrias de Panificação e Confeitaria de São Paulo v. Indústrias Alimentícias Gerais* (AIG), (ii) Motion for Clarification No. 20/97 (resolved on 22 Oct. 1997), applicants Ferrero do Brasil Ind. Doceria and Alimentar Ltda. and (iii) Preliminary Investigation No. 08012.006744/97-16 (resolved on 10 Nov. 1999) in re. *ABRADES – Associação Brasileira de Distribuidores Exclusivos de Sorvetes v. Kibon S/A – Indústrias Alimentícias and Kraft Suchard Brasil S/A* (by majority vote, dissenting Councilors Marcelo Calliari and Ruy Santacruz).

average prices for the rendering of photographic services in the State of São Paulo. In this case, a distinction was drawn by the CADE between a 'price suggestion' and a 'reference to average prices' made by the union to its members. In any event, the CADE resolved that the conduct had no anticompetitive impact given that: (a) the relevant market was not characterized by structural conditions favouring the practice, given the lack of market power by *SEAFESP*, and (b) there was no effective mechanism available to the union to force its members to follow the reference prices.

460. Further, on 16 December 2009, the CADE, in reviewing Preliminary Investigation No. 08012.008443/2007-04 in connection with price suggestions made by sports tennis shoe manufacturers to retailers, resolved by the leading opinion of Councillor Fernando de Magalhães Furlan, that such practice was not illegal. In so doing, the Examiner, adopting the opinion of the SDE on the matter, expressed that no price suggestion would be illegal if the relevant party enjoyed no market power or, should it be a dominant firm, if the adverse impact of the practice shall be countervailed by efficiencies associated with the suggested resale pricing.

461. Based on such decisions, the legality or not of the price suggestion practices should on a case-by-case basis take into consideration:

(1) the presence of market conditions capable of inhibiting a possible harm to competition as a result thereof;
(2) determination of market dominance;
(3) determination of the economic rationale;
(4) determination of efficiencies; and
(5) lack of elements of coercion.

462. Such liberal presumption of legality of price suggestions, however, has drastically changed with the CADE ruling on the Administrative Process No. 080012.001271-44 (resolved on 30 January 2013) in re. *Procon/SP* v. *SKF do Brasil Ltda.*, a Brazilian auto-part manufacturer that, at the request of its dealers, suggested minimum resale prices to its network. In resolving the case, Councillor Marcos Paulo Veríssimo argued that such practice was presumptively (*iuris tantum*) illegal and that such a presumption was to be overruled with a reversed burden of proof vested unto the defendant. In adhering to such understanding, CADE's President stated that the resolution created an important new standard to the market and declared: '*Any behavior resulting in a direct restraint related to prices is the target of a CADE concern given that there is a skepticism with respect to the existence of efficiencies that may compensate the resulting anticompetitive risks, such as, of a stimulus to parallel conduct among firms*' (free translation).

463. Such understanding was subsequently reaffirmed in the decision made in Administrative Process No. 08012.004736/2005-42 (resolved on 29 January 2015) in re. *SEAE v. Shell Brasil Ltda.et al*, in which the CADE concluded that the practice of the fuel distributor company suggesting resale prices to its franchisee gas stations was illegal. The defendant claimed that prices were only a suggestion, but Councillor Alessandro Octaviani Luis argued that: '*It may be, then that the firm shall declare that it is making a "mere price suggestion", but its attitudes may reveal a sense of obligation attached to such recommendation. This is strongly perceivable when the firm shall enjoy a significant market power, and the downstream market player is dependent on such firm, thus consequently becoming vulnerable to its determinations. Such understanding is reinforced by the opinion of the SDE when it says that "even in case of a resale price suggestion, if there is a credible coercion system, the effect is the same of a formal imposition*"' (free translation). Such conduct, pursuant to the decision, would only be considered legal if the defendant could prove to the satisfaction of the CADE that it is accessory, necessary, proportional and essential to meeting a licit object.

464. Thus the current state-of-art is that the CADE treats resale price suggestions severely, similar to an actual price-fixing.

D. *Franchising*

465. Franchising, under Brazilian law, is a contractual relationship, whereby a merchant (franchisor) shall license the use of its trademarks or brands to another (franchisee) and shall include entrepreneurial organization services and the sale of franchisor's products or services for the purpose of exploitation of the royalties.

466. Franchise agreements and dealership agreements are similar, given that both establish the *modus operandi* of the business, standardizing the procedures and premises, including the use of uniforms, and providing for product or service exclusivity, they differ as to their respective competitive concerns. For example, while franchise agreements permit price-fixing clauses, dealership agreements generally do not (save for car dealership arrangements, which are governed by special legislation, e.g., 'Lei Ferrari') and are governed by general civil law.

467. Franchise agreements are somewhat located in-between a spot market and a full vertical integration.

468. The two basic elements of a franchise agreement are, therefore: (a) the trademark use licensing, and (b) the entrepreneurial organization assistance. In such transaction, the franchisor shall increase its capacity in meeting the needs of demand, without resorting to its own capital funds or to its own managerial activities. On its turn, the franchisee may use its capital and management capacity to perform an economic activity with a consolidated image or brand, organizational techniques and marketing strategies that have already been tested in the market.

469. Although initial CADE precedents required all franchise agreements to be subject to the CADE notification requirements, based on concerns yielding from abuse of dominant position and related vertical integration restriction issues (e.g., price-fixing and exclusivity clauses), it is currently a settled matter that such arrangements are generally to be presumed legal and exempt from anticompetitive concerns and, thus, free from notification requirements.

470. For no other reason, a mere change in the governance structure of a franchise network, with no change in the control of the rights that are relevant to competition, is not subject to notification requirements, since such transaction shall not yield any market concentration nor any change in the competitive conditions, even potentially.

471. A franchise network is to be viewed, from a competitive point of view, in its totality, given the full coordination on product strategy, location, innovation and pricing. Therefore, changes internal to the network, such as changes in rights of ownership on the exclusive distribution of a brand, generally have no competitive impact. Consequently, the eventual integration between a franchisor and its franchisee, although falling within the notion of concentration, yields no competitive concerns.[45]

472. Indeed, the purchase of a franchise by the franchisor, without change in the control of the relevant market decisions was considered by former Joint SDE/SEAE Ordinance No. 1, of 18 February 2003 (Article 6, item I) as a case eligible to be reviewed under fast-track procedures. The CADE's Resolution No. 2/12, governing fast-track review procedures, failed to include a similar enabling provision.

473. But in confirmation of CADE's positive view on acts of concentration involving franchises, in Act of Concentration No. 08011.000416/2011-61 (resolved on 23 March 2011), in re. *Totvs S/A* and *Gens Tecnologia e Informática Ltda.*, it was reaffirmed that, should there be no indication that the transaction shall change the market conditions, the purchase of a franchisee by the franchisor does not yield competitive concerns.

II. Technology Licensing, Know-How and Trade Secret Licensing

474. Technological cooperation agreements are generally deemed to be pro-competitive, as they permit securing technological spillovers internalization gains and, consequently, enhance investments in research and development. There shall be anticompetitive concerns, however, when such agreements shall result in market foreclosure or require restrictions to other developments or additional barriers to the dissemination of the innovation.

475. There is still some confusion in determining the relevant market as to what affects technology licensing, meaning that the licensing market is frequently confused with the relevant market of the product resulting from the use of the underlying technology. The CADE, however, has already made an important distinction between the research and development market and that of the final product resulting therefrom.

476. In Act of Concentration No. 08012.006556/08-48 (resolved on 27 August 2008), involving *Monsanto do Brasil Ltda. and Syngenta Seeds Ltda.* relating to the licensing of the *Monsanto* RoundUp Ready 1 (RR-2), RoundUp Ready 1 Yield (RR-2 Y), Bt11, G121, VipCot and Dicamba technologies applied to corn, soya and cotton seeds, for example, the CADE has ruled that biotechnology research and innovation constitutes a relevant product market in itself.

477. Further, in Act of Concentration No. 08012.001560/2009-09 (resolved on 29 April 2009), involving *Monsanto do Brasil Ltda. and Wehrtec-Tecnologia Agrícola Ltda.*, concerning the exploitation of *Monsanto*'s RoundUp Ready (RR) technology[46] by Wehrtec in the production and marketing of soybean seeds, the CADE ruled that

45. *See* Acts of Concentration Nos 08012.001031/2000-69 relating to the integration between the Coca-Cola group and a franchisee and 08012.000238/2009-54 (resolved in 17 Jun. 2009), in re. *Recofarma Indústria do Amazonas Ltda., Coca-Cola Indústrias Ltda. and Spaipa S.A.* – Indústria Brasileira de Bebidas, both concerning a transaction, in which the Coca-Cola group started operating directly in distribution along with Spaipa, a franchisee bottler.

46. The soyas that use the RR technology become tolerant to the herbicide glyphosate used on the beans.

there is no interchangeability between the market of exploitation of technology in the production and marketing of seeds and that of seeds, meaning that each segment constitutes a separate relevant market.

478. In addition, in Act of Concentration No. 08012.000797/2010-06 (resolved on 7 July 2010), involving *Bayer S.A. and CVR Plant Breeding Ltda.*, concerning the purchase by *BCS*, a company of the *Bayer* economic group, of certain genetic material – sector of traits and soybean crops – owned by *CVR* resolved that the geographic market of biotechnology research and innovation (sector of traits and soybean crops) is a Brazilian domestic market.

479. The courts have already been adopted in the separation between the technology market and the product resulting therefrom. In Ordinary Annulment Action No. 2008.34.00.011433-3 resolved at the trial court level – fifth Federal Court in Brasília – on 26 April 2010, in which *Dow AgroSciences Industrial Ltda. and Monsanto Company* sought to annul a CADE decision that imposed on such firms a fine for the late notification of a cross-licensing agreement entered in the US between *Monsanto Company and The Dow Chemical Company* concerning the development and obtaining of a genetic material sequence to be incorporated in new corn seed varieties (Act of Concentration No. 08012.01.2392/2007-15). The parties argued before the court that they believed that a technology licence agreement entered into outside of Brazil, between non-Brazilian subjects, and using no Brazilian assets, for the research and development of a new product was subject to the CADE notification requirement and that, thus, they could not be fined for the late submission failing to know CADE's unprecedented understanding on the issue. The court, in an introductory reasoning adopted the CADE understanding that: *'the transaction did not impact the corn seed market, but rather the market of development of new genetically modified corn varieties'* (free translation) and then resolved that:

> as CADE well pointed out, the (notification requirement) should not be a surprise to the plaintiffs, given that, pursuant to a large number of CADE precedents, the market of genetically modified seeds is a global market and, therefore, it includes Brazil, so that any change in the competitive relations shall also yield impacts in Brazil (free translation).

480. Nevertheless, although lenient and generally favourable to technology licensing on its merits, the CADE has taken the more costly and not necessarily efficient position that even if a transaction shall result in a market de-concentration, a technology licensing arrangement is to be considered as an act of concentration, and thus, is subject to the CADE notification requirements, whenever entered between competitors[47].

A. Patent Licensing, Trademark Licensing and Intellectual Property Licensing

481. Intellectual property rights relate to the rules that govern intangible assets, such as artistic and scientific inventions, discoveries and others. Industrial property is a segment of intellectual property, specially dedicated to industry applications.

482. Competition laws admit the role of intellectual property as a vehicle to differentiation and innovation, and as a significant competitive component, to the benefit of consumers. Preserving motivation to research and development is a fundamental element of competition policies.

483. Occasionally, however, intellectual property rights and competition policies collide. Under competition laws, intellectual property rights are not absolute, nor immune to the former.

484. Indeed, certain anticompetitive conducts yield from the exercise of intellectual property rights, such as those: (a) resulting from fraud or abuse in the intellectual property registration procedures, such as patent ambush, patent flooding and change of pending patents, and (b) resulting from the abusive exercise of intellectual property rights.

485. For no other reason, the current Brazilian Competition Law expressly introduced in the list of potentially anticompetitive conduct, the abusive exercise or exploitation of industrial property, intellectual, technology and trademark rights (Article 36, §3, item XIX). As a corollary, Article 38, item IV(a) contemplates compulsory licensing, as the applicable penalty in case such offence occurs, although the CADE, to date, has never considered such alternatives.

486. Transactions entered between competing concerns involving the purchase of patents, trademarks and intellectual property, including product formulations and registration, as well as of rights related to industrial property constitute acts of concentration subject to the CADE notification requirements, as such transactions may yield competitive concerns. The same applies to plant leases with associated trademark licensing.

47. Technology licence agreements are considered by CADE to be an associative contract, which must be notified once the thresholds set forth in CADE Resolution No. 10/2014 are met. Whenever constituting a vertical relationship between licensor and licensee, technology licence agreements are only reportable if: (a) at least one of the economic groups party to the agreement shall have a market-share equal to or higher than 30% (thirty per cent) and (b) if the contract shall provide for either (i) an exclusivity arrangement or (ii) a turnover or loss sharing arrangement between the parties. The mere collection of royalties, however, albeit calculated based on sales volumes has not been considered a turnover sharing arrangement in Act of Concentration No. 08700.004963/2016-72 (resolved on 15 Jul. 2016), by Dispatch No. 847 of the Superintendent-General of the CADE, Eduardo Frade Rodrigues, that approved Opinion No. 173/2016/CGAA5/SGA1/SG, in re. *Monsanto do Brasil Ltda. and DuPont do Brasil S.A.* Although, the parties have met the market-share threshold, lacking an exclusivity clause and a turnover/loss arrangement, the case was not cognized.

487. For example, a concerned analysis has been made in Act of Concentration No. 08012.009361/2011-55 (resolved on 14 March 2012), in re. *Bayer S.A. and Metropolitana Incorporações e Locação de Bens Ltda.* In such case, the CADE identified that transactions related to the purchase of genetic material and of the related intellectual property may result in a dominant position whenever the parties, thereto, are the owners of a germplasm portfolio that is made of matrixes that are the most promising ones in the principal research lines in a given culture. In such case, the transaction may foreclose the access of multiple competitors to such a kind of fundamental input for the R&D activities in the field.

488. Patent and trademark licence arrangements, especially if non-exclusive, are, in principle, pro-competitive, since they enable the sharing of know-how protected by a statutory monopoly with another company, provided that there is always caution whenever such arrangements shall yield a portfolio effect.

489. In principle, CADE has admitted that patent pooling arrangements may be precompetitive.[48] A patent pool may be beneficial, harmful or irrelevant to the competitive logic, depending on the impact that it yields. It may result in benefits favouring competition whenever it integrates complementary technologies, thus reducing transaction costs and promoting the dissemination of technology.

490. An incipient issue to CADE concerns the ability of proprietors of standard essential patents (SEP), especially in high technology markets, such as smartphones, tablets and computers, that have adhered to standards organizations (SSOs) and are bound to grant unlimited licences in FRAND fair, reasonable and non-discriminatory terms, to resort to the courts pleading for prohibitory injunctions against alleged infringers of their patent rights. Such disputes may involve two conflicting aspects, i.e., on the one hand the possibility of trolls abusing of their monopoly rights to demand abusive royalties or contractual terms, and, on the other hand, the desire of free riders seeking royalty free licences.

491. CADE has a limited experience in this field. In handling Administrative Process No. 08700.008409/2014-00 (resolved on July 2015), in re. *TCT Mobile Telefones Ltda. v. Telefonaktiebolaget L. M. Ericsson*, concerning alleged coercive negotiation of royalties for the use of a SEP for the implementation of a 3GPP standard and sham litigation by *Ericsson* in obtaining prohibitory injunctions in the courts against TCT, in contradiction with international trends eager to discuss the issue, sidestepped from the main debate by claiming that the case involved private litigation, alien to the jurisdiction of the competition authorities.

492. As to the concept of a portfolio effect, such is based on the theory that the creation of a vast brand portfolio through a merger is capable of indirectly creating or strengthening a dominant position in a given relevant market, despite the lack of an increase in market share. Furthermore, competitors who do not possess a complete product line are subject, under circumstances, to be excluded from the market in the long run, thus enabling the firm controlliing the portfolio to increase prices or to invest less in research and development.

48. Act of Concentration No. 08012.008810/2009-23 (resolved on 29 Jun. 2011), in re. *Sony Corporation, Koninklijke Philips Electronics N.V., Panasonic Corporation, Hitachi Consumer Electronics Co. Ltd., Samsung Electronics Co. Ltd. and Cyberlink Corp.*

493. The portfolio effect is evidenced, *inter alia*, by a better use of the distribution network, the leverage of advantages *vis-à-vis* the retail dealers and the sales channels, the management of more elaborated and aggressive pricing strategies, and the greater brand exposure. The impact of such effect may be either anticompetitive, as well as a source of efficiencies, meaning that, at the same time it may result in the reduction of transaction costs to the firms acquiring products, it may result in an important barrier to entry and affect rivalry by the other competitors, given that the latter may have their sales points either injured or blocked.

494. The CADE does recognize the pro-competitive nature of certain licensing, such as licensing for the development of new products. A general understanding is that such arrangements only raise competitive concerns whenever contemplating non-compete or exclusivity clauses.[49]

495. There are curious cases that CADE has been hearing in connection with industrial property rights.

496. In a first case (Act of Concentration No. 08012.002620/08-11, involving *TF Indústria e Comércio de Modas Ltda., Triton e Fórum Publicidade Ltda., TF Licenciamento de Marcas Ltda. and A.M.C. Têxtil Ltda.*), the CADE reviewed the peculiarities of the fashion world. Although non-competition clauses are generally permitted by the CADE, as long as restricted to a term of five years and to the relevant product and geographic markets, it has cleared an extravagant term for the life of the restrictive clause by recognizing that the brand name in such market is a particularly special asset, and much more so when related to the name of the creator.

497. In a second interesting case (Preliminary Investigation No. 08012.005181/2006-37, resolved on 29 April 2009, involving *Videolar S.A. v. Koninklijke Philips Electronics N.V*), also involving the issue of abuse of dominance, there was a complaint made against *Philips Electronics*, claiming that failure by the latter in enforcing its patent rights against the importation of non-licenced products constituted an abuse of a dominant position. The CADE dismissed the case.

498. In a third case (Preliminary Investigation No. 08012.002673/2007-51, resolved on 15 December 2010, involving *Associação Nacional dos Fabricantes de Autopeças – ANFAPE v. Volkswagen do Brasil Indústria de Veículos Automotivos Ltda., Fiat Automóveis S.A. and Ford Motor Company Brasil Ltda.*), there was a complaint by aftermarket auto-part manufacturers arguing that car manufacturers were abusing their industrial design registrations by preventing independent auto-part manufacturers from producing and marketing competing products. In such case, the CADE had resolved that the underlying industrial property rights resulted in a lock-in effect to the detriment of consumers that were unable to circumvent the legal monopoly in the aftermarket. Although recognizing and affirming the OEM manufacturers' intellectual property rights against other OEM manufacturers, the CADE concluded that such rights could not, prima facie, be opposed to aftermarket manufacturers since the legal monopoly was not justified by the need of: (a) recovering R&D investments, (b) preserving motivation to innovation, (c) ensuring quality and safety of the auto parts, (c) preventing independent manufacturers from falsely marketing non-OEM

---

49. *See* Act of Concentration No. 08012.006343/2010-31, resolved on 22 Sep. 2010, involving S.A. Basf & Meiji Seika Kaisha.

products as OEM and (d) preventing cream skimming practices by such independent manufacturers.

499. Not many cases were reviewed by the CADE in connection with copyrights. Pursuant to Article 5, item XXVIII, of the Brazilian Federal Constitution, as regulated by Article 7 of Law No. 9610/98, protection is extended to intellectual property representing 'creations of the spirit, expressed by any means or fixed in any support, tangible or intangible, either known or to be invented in the future' (free translation). A copyright is a group of prerogatives granted by law in favour of any intellectual creator on having his literary, artistic and scientific originality.

500. In Administrative Process No. 08012.004283/2000-40, involving *Comissão de Defesa do Consumidor, Meio Ambiente e Minorias da Câmara de Deputados v. Box 3 Vídeo e Publicidade Ltda. and Léo Produções Publicidade*, resolved in 15 December 2010, the CADE has reviewed the conduct of defendants that, claiming rights of ownership of copyrights registered with the Brazilian National Library in connection with a television programme gender, brought a large number of court actions (a few of which were successful) against alleged counterfeiters. The CADE has ruled that such was a typical case of objective claimless claim since the law (Article 8 of said Law No. 9610/98) expressly states that 'I – ideas, normative procedures, systems, methods, projects or mathematic concepts as such; and II – schemes, plans or rules to enable mental acts, games or business' shall, *inter alia*, not enjoy copyrights, and (although not being a copyright authority or office) that television programme genders were not a copyrightable creation, since it would, in the Panel's opinion, constitute a mere idea or a mental scheme, and its registration with the Brazilian National Library has no effect of granting rights, but only of affirming anteriority. Thus, the CADE further resolved that the multiple court actions brought by defendants were typical cases of sham litigation, illegally attempting to create an unlawful monopoly.

501. An important benchmark case on the subject was established in Administrative Process No. 08012.003745/2010-83 (resolved on 6 March 2013), in re. *Associação Brasileira de Televisão por Assinatura – ABTA v. Escritório Central de Arrecadação e Distribuição – ECAD et alii*. ECAD is a collective copyright management entity that was created by Law No. 5988/73 and operates under the aegis of the Brazilian Copyright Law (Law No. 9610/98), which authorized the creation of a system under legal monopoly for the collection and distribution of copyright amounts relating to musical and literary-musical works and phonograms. ECAD is formed by artists' associations and established a blanket licence mechanism for the collection of copyrights based on a shared repertoire platform, and the amounts to be paid were established by ECAD itself as opposed to by each of the artists' association. The CADE ruled that ECAD had the legal monopoly to collect and distribute copyright amounts, but not to fix prices, and considered the existing system a cartel arrangement.

502. Finally, although no actual case may be quoted in this respect, patent licensing, trademark licensing and intellectual property licensing are further subject to similar competitive concerns as in distributorship agreements. Thus, resale price maintenance is not permitted, while absolute territorial or client restrictions may be admissible if based on a rule of reason and economic rationale, where net consumer welfare and efficiencies can be demonstrated.

Chapter 2. Dominant Undertakings' Prohibited Practices

503. Pursuant to Article 36, §2, of the Brazilian Competition Law, dominance shall occur whenever an undertaking or group of companies shall control a significant share of the relevant market, as supplier, broker, purchaser or financial agent of a product, service or related technology. Such dominance is presumed whenever the undertaking or group of companies shall control 20% or more of the relevant market, provided that such percentage may be altered by the CADE in connection with specific fields of activity.

504. Abuse of dominance refers to those actions that, subject to the rule of reason, yield or may yield (potential effect) negative impacts on the social welfare. It is worth recalling that the Brazilian legal framework does not entertain per se offences.

505. A curious case on the possibility of abuse of dominance by omission is found in Preliminary Investigation No. 08012.005181/2006-37 (resolved on 29 April 2009) (in re. *Videolar S.A. v. Koninklijke Philips Electronics N.V.*), whereby Videolar claimed that Philips, the owner of patent rights in connection with recordable optical media storage products, abused its dominant position by failing to react against the importation into Brazil of unlicensed products, thus injuring competition of licensed products. In its final resolution, the CADE decided that a patent owner has the faculty, but not the obligation, to enforce its industrial property rights.

§1. Exploitative Practices

I. Excessive/Unfair Pricing

506. The Brazilian Competition Law in repealing former Law No. 8884/94 excluded excessive/unfair pricing as a potentially anticompetitive practice. The rationale behind such revocation is threefold: (a) price increases are a natural phenomenon of the full exercise of the constitutional principle of market freedom,[50] (b) the CADE is

50. In Preliminary Investigation No. 08012.008845/2006-10, resolved on 3 Mar. 2009, involving *SDE v. Copagaz Distribuidora de Gás Ltda. et alii*, in which certain home gas distributors were charged of not passing over to consumer certain tax reduction secured by the industry. The CADE then ruled that it is incumbent with ensuring competition in the market and not with restricting or controlling prices. Thus, lacking any evidence of an anticompetitive conduct destined to influence the pricing of the product subsequent to a tax reduction, the decision-making process of the relevant undertaking in connection with pricing is a matter not subject to the review of, or punishment by, the CADE.

not a price-control agency,[51] and (c) abusive pricing is not an autonomous illegal conduct, but only a circumstantial evidence of other eventual anticompetitive conducts.[52]

507. Notwithstanding, arbitrary profit increase (Article 36, item III, of the competition law) remains a punishable anticompetitive offence. Such standard is indeed close to that of an abuse of dominant position, save for being specific to monopoly or oligopoly power situations, as explained below.

508. The key word in the concept of 'arbitrary profit increase' is the adjective 'arbitrary', meaning the undertaking that is capable of acting solely pursuant to its own will, with no care for the reaction of the market or competition. An arbitrary profit increase shall only be characterized in the presence of market power, given that an 'arbitrary' action can only take place when the profit increase shall result from the exercise of market dominance (monopoly or oligopoly power).

II. Discrimination

509. A price discrimination is characterized by the sale of a given product to different clients under unjustified different conditions, representing the capacity of a market player of extracting the maximum of the willingness to pay by its different consumers in connection with a given product.

510. Discrimination is the breach of the constitutional command that all should be treated equally (principle of isonomy), provided that no such breach exists when different treatment is given to different circumstances. For example, different treatment of customers yielding different profit margins in connection with sales made to wholesalers and retailers is not discriminatory and licit, since such conduct is economically rational given that transaction costs tend to be reduced proportionately to negotiated volumes.

511. Discrimination may relate to multiple economic variables, such as price, discounts, payment terms, acceptance of return of inventory, technical requirements and other transactional issues relating to client idiosyncrasies, as well as legal or statutory issues. Price discrimination is the issue that raises the largest anticompetitive concerns.

512. Characterization of an illegal price discrimination requires: (a) dominant position, (b) anticompetitive effect or potential anticompetitive impact, such as the exclusion of rivals, profit squeeze, market foreclosure and (c) lack of a reasonable

51. For example, in Preliminary Investigation No. 08012.0013661/2009-15 (resolved on 19 May 2010), involving *Ministério Público Federal – Procuradoria da República de Minas Gerais v. TAM Linhas Aéreas S.A.* and *Gol Linhas Aéreas S. A.*, in which the Office of the Federal Attorney General in the State of Minas Gerais complained of abusive pricing by the defendant airline carriers, the CADE firmly confirmed not being a price regulator and that the Council should only dedicate its efforts to act on the competitive process, of which prices would only be the result, not the cause.

52. The discredit of abusive price increase as an autonomous illegal conduct was basically concluded, e.g., in Preliminary Investigation No. 08012.003648/1998-05, involving *Figueroa Campos Indústria e Comércio Ltda. v. White Martins S/A*, concerning the allegation of abusive price increase in the liquid oxygen market – resolved on 18 Aug. 2010).

economic justification neutral to competition, such as cost reduction, distinct negotiation costs among differentiated clients and competitive strategies to dispute different consumer niches. Price discrimination is at all times to be reviewed under the rule of reason.[53]

513. Furthermore, the CADE decided that the investigation of a discriminatory practice requires the assessment of, *inter alia*: (i) the history of the conduct of the accused undertaking, (ii) the history of the cases in the sector and (iii) the characteristics of the relevant industry.[54]

514. Price discrimination is threefold: (a) first level discrimination or perfect discrimination, whereby a different price is charged to each client, so that each shall pay the maximum price it is willing to pay per unit (such conduct results in a socially undesirable transfer of income, since the manufacturer shall operate less efficiently); (b) second level discrimination, whenever economies of scale enable cost and price (discounts) reductions to consumers willing to purchase larger volumes, thus expanding production and increasing consumers' welfare; and (c) third level discrimination, when supplier, using a competitive strategy, seeks to classify consumers into two or more categories pursuant to their distinct elasticity (demand prices) and establish a lower price to more sensible clients or to weaker demands (e.g., discounts to students or to senior citizens, differentiated air fares for the coach and the executive class, higher prices for premium beverages, promotional coupons or differentiated prices between industrial consumers and final consumers).

515. Examples of non-discriminatory technical requirements may be found in public tender bids, when, for instance, the bidding authority: (a) requires prospective large volume supply bidders to prove market experience and capacity through the demonstration of prior supplies, or (b) waives testing requirements in relation to certain products enjoying notorious technical characteristics and requiring tests to others. Granting of bonus in connection with scale, quality and production is another example of a licit strategy.

516. Case law on such discrimination matters is numerous.

517. In Administrative Process No. 08000.022487/97-81, resolved on 14 July 2004, in re. *Messer Griesheim do Brasil Ltda.* and *Oxitec Indústria e Comércio Ltda.*, for example, the CADE ruled that the inclusion, in a public tender bid, of a clause requiring bidders to demonstrate prior supplies of the relevant product, shall not constitute discrimination that seeks to injure potential bidders, but only a requirement of technical capacity and of demonstration of ability to fulfil the undertaking, thus representing a normal and licit requirement in bidding procedures involving large volumes.

518. In Preliminary Investigation No. 08012.006717/2000-46, resolved on 26 July 2006, involving *Labo Cine do Brasil Ltda. v. Eastman Kodak Company – Latin American Region,* it was decided that price differentiation based on objective criteria,

53. Administrative Process No. 08012.001099/1999-71 (resolved on 23 May 2012), in re, *Steel Placas Indústria e Comércio Ltda. v. Comepla Indústria e Comércio, Reprinco Indústria e Comércio Ltda, and Queiroz & Souza Comércio de Placas Automotivas Ltda.*

54. *See* Preliminary Investigation No. 08012.006274/2009-21, resolved on 7 Apr. 2010 in re. *Roberto Marinho Paredes v. Ambev Brasil Bebidas Ltda.*

such as: (i) volume discounts, (ii) minimum volume requirements and (iii) determination of incentives for the creation of a long-term relationship, is legitimate.

519. In Preliminary Investigation No. 53500.005669/02, resolved on 11 July 2007, involving *Empresa Brasileira de Telecomunicações S.A. v. Brasil Telecom S.A.*, there was a discussion on whether there would be discrimination in the charging of a lower price in fixed-term supply agreements as opposed to open-end agreements. The CADE concluded that no such discrimination existed, since the degree of uncertainty of an open-end term agreement permits the adjustment, thereof, to the price, thus resulting in a higher price.

520. The commercial policy of granting bonus for scale and quality in production was also found to be non-discriminatory, given that it is a mechanism that yields efficiencies, as ruled in Administrative Process No. 08012.009312/98-39, resolved on 11 April 2007, involving *Coopará – Cooperativa Regional dos Produtores Rurais de Pará de Minas Ltda. v. CCPR – Cooperativa Central dos Produtores Rurais de Minas Gerais Ltda. ('Itambé').*

521. Limited-term promotional campaigns adopted as a market entry strategy was also held a valid non-discriminatory initiative in Preliminary Investigation No. 53500.004242/04, resolved on 9 January 2007, in re. *Telemar Norte Leste S.A v. Telesp Celular S.A et alii.*

522. Preliminary Investigation No. 08012.0000387/2000-03, resolved on 12 December 2007, involving Brazilian Internet Association (ABRANET) – *Associação Brasileira de Acesso, Serviços e Informação de Provedores de Internet v. Telecomunicações de São Paulo – Telefônica et alii*, investigated whether the hiring by a financial institution of free of charge Internet access to its clients would constitute a discriminatory offer of services by the server and concluded for the negative since the action did not sought to conquer a specific market, and the server continued to be regularly paid for the rendering of the service to the banks.

523. In Motion for Settlement (*Requerimento*) No. 08700.001151/2012-41 (resolved on 25 April 2012), in re. *Telemar Norte Leste S/A, Telemar Internet Ltda., Brasil Telecom S/A* and *BRT Serviços de Internet S/A.*, in principle, the telephone carrier that directs its clients of Internet broadband connection services to its own providers, by unequally displaying competing providers' offers and discriminatory treatment via call centre.

524. An interesting case discussed whether the imposition by the CADE of remedies as a condition for the clearance of an act of concentration would create a discriminatory market condition to the affected party *vis-à-vis* its competitors. In Preliminary Investigation No. 08012.005307/2002-40, resolved on 26 November 2008, involving *Amadeus Global Travel Distribution S.A and Amadeus Brasil Ltda. v. Sabre International Inc.*, the CADE ruled that remedies imposed in merger review procedures shall only bind the party thereto and not its competitors, since such obligations result from the peculiarities and circumstances that are specific to the underlying transaction.

525. The classical issue whether a price differentiation would constitute discrimination was again debated in Preliminary Investigation No. 08012.007692/1999-11, of 17 December 2008, involving *Auto Posto Esmeraldas Ltda. v. Esso Brasileira de Petróleo Ltda.* In such case, the CADE updated its standards on the matter by ruling that price differentiation does not per se constitute an anticompetitive conduct and that to be held illegal, it is necessary that: (i) the defendant shall enjoy a dominant position, (ii) the conduct shall tend to yield an anticompetitive impact, such as the exclusion of rivals, profit squeeze, market raise or foreclosure and (iii) the price differentiation shall not be justified by legitimate commercial practices that are proven neutral from a competitive point of view.

526. In connection with supply arrangements, the adoption of a preference for a given material to the detriment of another does not represent an anticompetitive intent, nor the waiver of testing requirements in relation to one of the products, once based on technical differences between the two, does not characterize any discrimination, as decided in Preliminary Investigation No. 08012.006111/2003-53, resolved on 4 February 2009, involving *Agência Reguladora de Serviços Públicos do Rio Grande do Norte – ASERP* and *Companhia Energética do Rio Grande do Norte – COSERN* and *Neoenergia S.A.*

527. Distribution agreements from the perspective of discrimination were also the subject matter of Administrative Process No. 08012.0004363/2000-89, resolved on 28 October 2009, involving *Conselho Administrativo de Defesa Econômica; – CADE v. Companhia de Bebidas da América – AmBev.* In this case, the CADE resolved that there is no impediment to the direct sale, by a manufacturer, to large dealers, on more favourable competitive conditions than those extended to its own distribution chain.

528. In Preliminary Investigation No. 08012.001952/2008-89, of 20 January 2010, involving *Dry Color Especialidades Químicas Ltda. v. Colormatrix América do Sul Ltda.,* the constitutional principle of isonomy was clearly ratified. The resolution states that discrimination assumes the charging of different prices to clients under the same conditions, or of the same prices to clients in different conditions. Should prices be different because the clients are in different conditions, there is no discrimination.

§2. Exclusionary Practices

I. Predation

529. Predatory pricing and abnormally low pricing are the same concept under Brazilian Competition Laws, and there is no theoretical or practical difference between the two. Predation (or underselling) is defined by former CADE Resolution No. 20/99 as the initial pricing below the average variable cost with the purpose of eliminating competitors and subsequently exploiting dominance through supracompetitive pricing, closest to monopoly prices.

530. The CADE has traditionally despised predation as an effective anticompetitive conduct and has routinely dismissed such charges, alleging that predation most unlikely is a successful mechanism for driving competitors out of the market without attracting newcomers, at great loss.

531. In any event, it should be noted, however, that the sale at prices below cost is a legal practice, as long as justified and failing to reach the effects set forth in items I through IV of Article 36 of the Brazilian Competition Law. Indeed low pricing by more efficient players, even if resulting in higher market concentration levels or in the exclusion of competitors, is licit behaviour, subject to inhibiting a greater efficiency by the market players. Further, the mere verification that a given player practices prices below its rivals' costs does not necessarily mean that the latter's is lower than such player's own costs.

532. The comparative analysis of costs and prices is insufficient to the characterization of predatory pricing, since such method is only plausible in those markets the characteristics of which enable the recovery of the loss incurred during the phase of predation. The analysis of the market structural conditions is the most adequate path to achieve such purpose, even if it is determined that prices are lower than the average variable cost, and that the intention of the market player is clear, given that such route shall permit the assessment if the strategy of predation is economically rational or not.

533. Although predation could be determined based on total average costs, the CADE has, so far, generally given preference to average variable costs. Variable costs are the costs of labour, materials, power, promotional costs, plant depreciation and other costs that vary with production. However, in Preliminary Investigation No. 08012.001022/2008-25 (resolved on 25 January 2012), in re. S*indicato da Indústria da Extração do Sal no Estado do Rio Grande do Norte – SIESAL* and *Federação das Indústrias do Estado do Rio Grande do Norte – FIERN v. Sociedad Anónima Empresa Marítima – Empremar S/A,* the CADE ruled that avoidable average costs are to be preferred over average variable cost in determining predatory pricing.

534. In order to permit the end-result, predator must act in a market characterized by high barriers to entry, subject to acting irrationally and faded to failure, given the possible price war launched by newcomers taking advantage of excessive pricing by the former attempting to recover losses yielding from the predation. The assessment of the possibility of recovery seeks to evaluate the presence of economic rationality behind the alleged predatory pricing strategy, by determining if the structural conditions of the relevant market are capable of supporting such strategy.

535. Predation may initially benefit the consumer and temporarily enhance social welfare, but in the long run would reduce the number of incumbent players in the market and thus restrain trade and cause a loss of consumers' welfare. It should be noted, however, that selling at prices below cost is a legal practice, except only in the event the predation shall be carried out in restraint of trade.

536. The objective standards for the characterization of predation are notions related to dominant position, such as: (a) market dominance and (b) high barriers to entry in the relevant market, and, additionally, (c) availability of production capacity sufficient to meet the increase in demand in the short term and (d) financial capacity to stand the losses yielding from the predatory strategy.

537. The SEAE Ordinance No. 70/2002 provides guidelines for the analysis of predatory pricing and is to be interpreted in conjunction with SEAE/SDE Joint Ordinance No. 50/2001, governing the review of horizontal concentrations.

538. Pursuant to SEAE Ordinance No. 70/2002, the first step in determining predation is to define the affected relevant market and to determine its structure. For such purposes, the same methodology used for the determination of the relevant market for concentrations (hypothetical monopolist test) is to be applied. The test is defined as the smallest group of products and the smallest geographic area necessary for a monopolist to be capable of imposing a small but significant and non-transitory price increase (of 5%, 10% or 15% in a period not lower than one year, at the analyst's discretion). However, while in merger-control reviews the determination of the relevant market takes into account the parties overlapping products, in investigating predatory pricing the relevant market is identified solely by the product that is being undersold.

539. Once the relevant market is determined, the second step of the analysis is the determination of barriers to entry.[55] An entry shall be easy whenever timely (if capable of occurring within approximately two years) and probable (the entry must be profitable and viable). In such analysis, it may be considered the market share of the predator[56] (on a yearly basis, in the past five years) in terms of production, productive capacity, volume of sales and turnover.

540. Supply conditions are to be subsequently reviewed, since predation shall yield an increase in demand in the short run, and predator must be capable of meeting such additional demand. For such purposes, the authorities shall review predator's idle capacity and its capability of swiftly and economically expanding productive capacity.

541. Further, in order to be successful, predator must recognize that its initiative shall necessarily result in a short-term loss resulting from sales below cost, and further that it shall need financial support should it need to make investments in capacity expansion. The authorities, in such task, will consider the capacity of predator in securing financing through third parties, including through new investors.

542. The authorities will consider that predation is a viable strategy whenever at least one of the following pre-conditions is present: (a) competitors are dependent on third-party financing, (b) third-party financing to competitors is strongly conditioned to their initial performance (especially in the case of newcomers), (c) competitors are in a position to demonstrate that predation will make their third-party financial flow unfeasible, (d) competitors can show that predator is aware (or is capable of acknowledging it) that third-party financing is necessary to the former and (e) predator has safer and more stable sources of financing than its competitors.

543. Finally, whenever predation is considered a viable strategy, the final phase of the analysis shall be a cost/price analysis in order to determine if sales at a price below cost are 'unjustified', as required by Article 36, paragraph 3, XV, of the Brazilian Competition Law. In such analysis, due care is taken in differentiating 'underselling'

55. In Preliminary Investigation No. 08012.000204/2001-11 (resolved on 4 May 2011) in re. *Labnew Indústria e Comércio Ltda.v. Becton, Dickinson Indústrias Cirúrgicas Ltda.*, the CADE ruled that in the characterization of predatory pricing, it is not sufficient to determine the practice of below cost pricing, but also if the market offers conditions for the recovery of the losses incurred by the offender, as a result of the exit of competitors or the significant increase of barriers to entry, thus permitting the recovery of profits. Thus, there is no offence whenever the market offers favourable conditions to the entry of newcomers.

56. In Preliminary Investigation No. 08012.002084/2005-10 (resolved on 19 Jan. 2011), in re. *Centro de Educação Projeção Ltda. v. SESC - Serviço Social do Comércio*. The CADE decided that the characterization of an anticompetitive conduct, resulting from the fact that a player enjoys the benefit of a tax incentive, requires the demonstration that the defendant, by enjoying market power, is actually taking advantage of the incentive to practice prices below cost with the intent of eliminating competition.

or prices below cost and 'prices below market prices', such being a legitimate strategy, specially to meet the competition of new entrants. The charging of prices significantly lower than those practised by competitors and temporary promotional prices (even if at prices below cost) are valid commercial strategies.

544. Justification for underselling must be made from both the demand-side and the supply-side. For example, a sudden contraction of demand may justify a price war, since under such conditions, it may be preferable to realize at least some return on investments made in production. On the supply-side, an eventual excess capacity may justify underselling (e.g., in case of sudden demand retraction, for example, in seasonal industries). However, underselling may be held 'unjustified' if the firm is wilfully neglecting opportunities to increase prices in response to an increasing demand.

545. The line dividing predation and competitive pricing is rather grey, especially in markets characterized by strong rivalry among incumbent players and contestability, or whenever price reductions are the result of increased competitiveness.

546. Although predatory pricing charges are not uncommon, the CADE has demonstrated to have little concern with the practice, the anticompetitive nature of which is seldom affirmed.

II. Tying

547. Tying arrangements are void in Brazilian competition (Article 36, §3, item XVIII, of Law No. 12529/11) and consumer laws (Law No. 8078/90).

548. Tying is characterized by the imposition by supplier of the sale of a product or service (tying product) to the purchase of another product or service (tied or secondary product). The offensive conduct may also be affirmed in case of imposition on consumer of the obligation to purchase a volume in excess of that sought by the latter.

549. Illegal tying arrangements require the meeting of the following basic standards: (a) market dominance in the tying product market, (b) the presence of at least two products, the tying and the tied product and (c) coercion (there is no illegal tying in merely de-motivating the acquisition of a competing product or service, lacking any coercion).

550. The characterization of a tying arrangement requires that the tying product and the tied product be in the market separately. In such case, supplier cannot impose the sale of a kit, even if the total price is lower than the prices charged for each product separately. Conversely, in principle, there is no illegality in bundling or in the sale of kits at total lower prices, as long as the products remain available to consumer separately. Nevertheless, if prices for the separate purchase of each product are exorbitantly high in comparison with the joint sale of such products, illegality may be envisioned. In short, consumer choices must be at all times preserved.

551. Tying is not void if required by domestic or applicable foreign laws. An example of the latter was discussed by the CADE in Administrative Process No. 08000.016489/97-21 (resolved on 11 May 2005) involving *Antônio Carlos de Moura Campos v. Ficsatur Agência de Turismo Ltda., Kamel Turismo* and *Chamonix Operadora de Turismo Ltda.* In this case, a group of travel agencies required tourists interested in participating in the New York Marathon to purchase the airline tickets from them in order to participate in the event. This requirement was based on the fact that such requirement was imposed by the US immigration authorities.

552. Similarly, there is no illegal tying arrangement if, in public tender bids, the Public Administration, using its discretionary powers, chooses to select the services that best meet the needs of the relevant public body or entity and requires bidders to supply not only a certain product or service but also of the related supplies and technical assistance. Consequently, there is no illegal tying if a potential bidder imposes on its supplier the joint supply of all required products or services in order to meet the requirements of the tender summons (in Administrative Process No. 08000.024919/95-62, resolved on 30 August 2006, involving *Associação de Produtores e Distribuidores de Insumos Reprográficos – APRODIR v. Xerox do Brasil S/A.*).

553. The CADE has also ruled that there is, in principle, no illegal tying arrangement in the sale of products that are part of a same relevant market. A curious example is found in Administrative Process No. 08012.008064/97-82 (resolved on 19 January 2005), in re. *Associação dos Concessionários-Consumidores de Jazigos do Cemitério Morumbi v. Comunidade Religiosa João XXIII*, in which the latter imposed the joint sale of graves, tombstones and shelves for burial purposes. The CADE dismissed the charge based on the argument that there was no separate market for each of those products, given the final purpose thereof (burial) was the principal product.

554. In Preliminary Investigation No. 08012.004308/2005-10 (resolved on 13 July 2011), in re. *Ministério Público do Estado do Rio de Janeiro v. Informix do Brasil Comércio e Serviços Ltda.*, the CADE has also ruled that tying maintenance services by the same supplier of the purchased product is a customary practice in the software market.

III. Rebates

555. The granting of rebates is a licit strategy, provided that the criterion used to establish price discount policies is: (a) objective (e.g., volume or minimum volume, discounts based on credit or inductive discounts seeking the establishment of long-term relationships), (b) reasonable (economic rationale) and (c) proportional (e.g., highest discounts should not be excessively larger than lowest discounts).

556. There is no discrimination if non-authorized distributors shall enjoy no discounts *vis-à-vis* accredited distributors or, conversely, if greater discounts are granted on direct sales by manufacturer to large dealers acting in more favourable competitive conditions than those extended to producer's own distribution network.

557. By the same token, open-end contracts may entail higher prices in comparison with fixed-term agreements and provide for no or lower rebates, since the latter creates less commercial uncertainties.

558. Promotional prices or commercial terms for the launching of new products or used to facilitate entry in a market are legitimate non-discriminatory actions, as long such initiatives are limited in time and scope.

559. Rebates, leading to exclusivity arrangements, however, may be a mechanism of illegal market foreclosure. Such an anticompetitive conduct was extensively reviewed in Administrative Process No. 08012.003805/2004-10 (resolved on 22 July 2009), involving *Primo Schincariol Indústria de Cervejas e Refrigerantes v. Companhia de Bebidas das Américas – AmBev*, a dominant undertaking in the Brazilian beer market. AmBev created a loyalty-inducing programme (*Programa Tô Contigo*) for retailers by granting bundle-above cost rebates, but conditioning rebates on retail customers meeting multiple target-growth rates for their purchases of AmBev products.

560. AmBev's discount system, retail customers (usually bars and restaurants), consisted of system of prizes equivalent to a discount on the price of the beer boxes. The customers would accumulate points based on the volume of purchased boxes (a box of 600 ml bottles would be equal to one point). Points were ultimately exchanged for prizes at any time within one year, such prizes being a bonus of up to 3% of the average purchases by the customer. The maximum number of points would be 600 per month, provided that no customer would be eligible to participate unless it would accumulate a minimum of five points per month. There was no formal exclusivity requirement, but there was a clear perception by the customers that non-exclusive customers were not eligible, and compliance with such requirement was closely monitored.

561. The CADE has ruled that the obligations undertaken by interested retailers and the inducing endogenous economic mechanisms of the programme promoted exclusivity (thus preserving or increasing AmBev market share and raising rivals' costs) and prevented customers from turning to competing products of producers that could be just as efficient as or more efficient than AmBev. Affirming the illegal nature of the programme, the CADE imposed a fine on AmBev of BRL 352,693,696.58, representing 2% of the company's gross turnover.

IV. Refusal to Deal

562. Pursuant to Article 36, §3, item XI, of the Brazilian Competition Law, refusal to sell under normal payment conditions and pursuant to regular commercial usages and customs is a possible anticompetitive conduct, but always subject to the rule of reason,[57] especially because a market player, even if enjoying market power, cannot be forced to contract with another undertaking in any and all circumstances. It should be noted, however, that the refusal by an upstream dominant undertaking to supply inputs to a downstream competitor, so as to eliminate competition in the downstream market, is a potentially anticompetitive conduct.

563. Refusal to deal cases are not uncommon before the CADE, but in many instances associated with matters related to the enforcement of exclusivity or non-compete clauses.

564. In general, and inspired by consumer law principles, producer is not permitted to refuse the sale if the purchaser (even if such purchaser is a competitor or a non-authorized distributor) is willing to pay on sight, in cash, FOB, at list prices. However, the CADE, in reviewing the anticompetitive nature of a refusal to supply a certain input to a downstream competitor (Preliminary Investigation No. 08012.006899/2003-

57. *See* Administrative Process No. 08001.006274/00-93, resolved on 6 Dec. 2006, in re. *Vidraçaria Estrela – Klaier indústria e Comércio Ltda. v. Companhia Vidraçaria Santa Marina and Blindex Vidro de Segurança Ltda.*

06, resolved on 22 July 2009, in re. *Instituto Radiológico Bento Gonçalves (IRBG) v. Sociedade Dr Bartholomeu Tacchini*) (*SDBT*)) ruled that, in matters of refusals to sell, the following circumstances are to be taken into account: (1) if the supplier enjoys dominance in the upstream market, (2) if there are no objective justifications for the refusal by the supplier and (3) if the refusal to supply is actually capable of eliminating or significantly injuring competition in the market.

565. In this case, *SDBT* was the controlling entity of the Tacchini Hospital and of the Tacchimed Health Plan. This was the only hospital in the city of Bento Gonçalves, in the State of Rio Grande do Sul, and the Tacchimed Health Plan was the only health plan to which the hospital was accredited. Further, the hospital was the only accredited agent before the Health Plan to make radiographic and echographic exams and the Health Plan, in 2005, controlled approximately 90% of the health-plan market in the city. On its turn, *IRBG*, a radiology and echography service company, was located in the city of Bento Gonçalves and faced the refusal of the Health Plan to contract.

566. The CADE initially recognized that the verticalization of the hospital and the Health Plan could, in principle, yield efficiencies (transaction cost reduction) that could be passed on to the consumers. Further, the CADE concluded that the Health Plan, although originally enjoying an almost monopolistic condition (90.64% of the market) lost share, declining to 71% in five years, and *IRBG* was not excluded from the market as a result of the Plan's refusal to deal and continued to render services to important competitors of the latter (Bradesco, Ipê, Banco do Brasil, CEP, Banrisul, Sener Saúde, Amil, Ulbra Saúde and Unimed, most of which are leading banking institutions and health plans in Brazil) for more than twenty-five years. Then the CADE concluded that it had no effective means to monitor prices in the market, and that any intervention could eventually eliminate the efficiencies claimed by the defendants. Finally, it came to the conclusion that there was no sufficient evidence of an anticompetitive conduct.

567. Still in the health-industry area, in Preliminary Investigation No. 08012.011463/2007-54 (resolved on 19 January 2011), in re. *Prontomed Sociedade Simples v. Santa Casa de Arcos*, in principle, a refusal to deal or to contract is legitimate: (a) whenever a supplier of a medical service does not accredit a health plan that lacks the basic quality requirements, (b) whenever exclusively resulting from a price disagreement, (c) whenever the purchaser is a defaulting party, (d) whenever there is a justified stopping in production or deficiencies in the productive capacity and (e) whenever the contracting shall result in injury to the party's financial reliability, investment continuity or injury to the quality of the relevant product or service.

568. In a more direct resolution, in Preliminary Investigation No. 08012.003762/2005-53, resolved on 9 June 2010, involving *Mérito Assessoria & Consultoria Empresarial Ltda. (Med Life Saúde) v. Sociedade Matonense de Benemerência* (Hospital Carlos Fernando Malzoni), the CADE decided that there is no anticompetitive conduct in the refusal by a hospital to contract with a health-plan carrier, in its legitimate exercise of party autonomy.

569. Conversely and on the basis of the criteria indicated above, there is no illegal refusal, if producer does not have the product available, its production is committed with other clients and the product is available at alternative sources of supply, as ruled in Preliminary Investigation No. 08012.009264/03-5, resolved on 6

April 2005, in re. *Siderúrgica Oriente Ltda.* and *Massa Falida da Companhia Metalúrgica do Espírito Santo v. Companhia Vale do Rio Doce.*

570. Also there is no illegal refusal to deal if purchaser is insolvent and is unwilling to make payment in cash, as decided in Administrative Processes Nos 08000.022826/95-11 and 08000.001430/97-75, both resolved on 30 August 2006, involving *Fortrade Fibras Sintéticas Ltda. v. Nitrocarbono S.A.* Indeed, in this resolution the CADE affirmed that no authority to force enterprises to accept third-party losses in their private commercial transactions and, thus, subverting the trade logics with the purpose of keeping in the market companies characterized by a poor financial condition.

571. In a controversial case (Preliminary Investigation No. 08000.019594/97-12, resolved on 30 August 2006, in re. *Interlar – Hidráulica e Materiais para Construção Ltda. v. Indústria de Fundição Tupy Ltda.*), the CADE again strongly affirmed party autonomy, ruling that no non-exclusive manufacturer is required to deal with a middle businessman, to the extent that there are other suppliers available in the market. Indeed controversial, given that, under consumer law principles, no refusal to deal is permitted if the supplier has available goods in inventory and buyer is willing to pay in cash, FOB, at no discount list prices.

572. By the same token, refusal is permitted if purchaser does not possess required licences or technical qualifications to buy the product, as decided in Preliminary Investigation No. 08012.003882/1999-13, resolved on 10 October 2007 involving *SWC – Prestadora de Serviços em Taxímetros v. Fumaça Instrumentos de Precisão Ltda. e Silmar Eletrônica e Mecânica de Precisão Ltda.*

V. Price Squeeze

573. The concept of price squeeze is closely related to price discrimination, cross-subsidies and raise of rivals' costs.

574. A price squeeze occurs when a dominant firm, vertically integrated or not, that controls an essential facility charges excessive prices downstream to a rival, while charging low output prices, below marginal costs, to common consumers.

575. Price squeeze requires that no substitute products are available, subject to motivating newcomers to enter the market through competing products.

576. The CADE has a limited experience in handling price-squeeze cases. Administrative Processes (all resolved on 14 September 2005) Nos 53500.001821/02 (involving *Empresa Brasileira de Telecomunicações S.A. – EMBRATEL S.A. and Intelig Telecomunicações Ltda. – INTELIG v. Telecomunicações de São Paulo S.A – TELESP*), 53500.001823/02 (involving *EMBRATEL and INTELIG v. Telemar Norte/ Leste S.A*) and 53500.001824/02 (involving *EMBRATEL and INTELIG v. Brasil Telecom Participações S.A.*) review the matter in connection with the charging of interconnection tariffs (TU-RL) in the telecommunication market. In such cases, the tariff resulted from the fact that EMBRATEL and INTELIG were long-distance carriers (STFC-LDN) requiring the use of the local concessionaires' network (controlled by TELESP, Telemar and Brasil Telecom, respectively) to complete long-distance calls.

577. In reviewing this case, the SEAE compared the TU-RL and the final price charged to the consumer by the STFC-LDN. In this analysis, the agency resorted to the teachings of Professors Stephen King and Rodney Maddock (*Imputation Rules and a Vertical Price Squeeze*), where these authors identified two principal forms of assessing price-squeeze conducts, taking into account the final price charged by the undertaking allegedly practising the anticompetitive conduct, such being the 'revenue imputation test' and the 'marginal imputation test'.

578. In the 'revenue imputation test', the firm's income is to be compared with total costs, while in the 'marginal imputation test', the analysis is to be made by comparing the price of the final product with the firm's marginal cost.

579. The CADE examined the argument that an anticompetitive conduct could be found if the value of the TU-RL: (i) would be significantly higher than costs in the rendering of the service, and (ii) would cause competitor's profitability to be negative.

580. In its review, the CADE adopted the 'marginal imputation test' and decided that resorting to the 'revenue imputation test' by reviewing income based on the final price charged to the consumers would require learning on the demand for long-distance calls by time of call and by geodesic degree, and that would be an excessively costly path.

581. The CADE's final determination was that there was no evidence that the local carriers artificially raised the costs of the rival STFC-LDN's, resorted to cross-subsidies or practiced price discrimination. The charges were all dismissed.

Chapter 3. Concentrations

582. The concept of 'concentration' under Brazilian law is broader than the concept of mergers and acquisitions. It also applies to the associative contracts, *consortia* and JV (Article 90, item IV of Law No. 12529/11). The law does not define the meaning of an 'associative contract', thus currently leading to a large controversy as to which kind of collaboration or cooperation agreement falls under such category. Generally speaking, an association, within the meaning of the law, refers to the association of two or more undertakings acting in the same field of activity that partner to achieve a common commercial purpose.

583. In that sense, not every market concentration is illegal or unacceptable. By the same token, not every collaboration among competitors or market players is a cartel. In Brazil, pursuant to applicable law, the authorities are required to assess each specific circumstance prior to determining whether a given action is an anticompetitive conduct or not. In other words, a case-by-case approach is of the essence to determine, inspired by the rule of reason, if a certain conduct is in actual or potential restraint of trade.

584. However, although Brazilian law does not admit per se offences, not even in cartel cases, in fact, the CADE has shown an inclination to consider arrangements among competitors almost a quasi-per se offence. Such fact must be taken into serious consideration in case of formation of *consortia* or collaboration arrangements among competitors in Brazil or that may yield any impact in Brazil.

585. In short, any form of coordinated action among concerns or groups of concerns having the purpose or effect of misleading competition is an anticompetitive conduct subject to CADE's enforcement actions.

586. Collaboration among competitors from a conduct control point of view was reviewed in Chapter 1 of Part II. Collaboration among competitors from a structural point of view, in its multiple forms of acts of concentrations and mergers, is henceforth the subject matter.

587. The most common arrangements of this kind are fusions, mergers, JVs, *consortia* formed for a specific purpose or not, industrial property licensing, long-term supply arrangements etc.

588. Predatory practices, raising barriers to entry to newcomers and the abusive exercise of pricing policies may also result from a market concentration. Whenever the arrangement shall cover more than one level of a same production chain, there shall be a joint participation between the relevant market players, such as in the case of agreements entered between raw material producers and/or upstream manufacturers and/or dealers. Collaboration may be horizontal or vertical and, in certain cases, may be in restraint of trade.

589. In Brazil, the standards for the review of transactions that yield a market concentration are governed by Law No. 12529/11. Pursuant to Article 88 of this law, all such actions are subject to the notification requirement to the CADE, and notification may be made prior to the consummation (or closing) of the transaction (suspensory regime). Pursuant to §3 of said Article, closing a transaction prior to the CADE's clearance may result in the nullity of the transaction and the assessment of a fine of no less than BRL 60,000.00 and not exceeding BRL 60,000,000, without prejudice to the commencement of an Administrative Process to investigate the facts.

§1. Horizontal Mergers

590. Horizontal concentrations occur whenever two or more players operating in the same business, that is, in the same relevant market, merge their interests, while previously competing with each other. The main acceptable purpose of such merger is to seek cost reduction and increase of operational efficiency through administrative and productive synergies, economies of scale and scope etc.

591. A horizontal concentration assumes the sum of market shares of the relevant players through a fusion, merger, JV, stock purchase or any other means of concentration.

592. Whenever a horizontal concentration affects a regulated market such as an infrastructure market (electric power generation and transmission, telecommunications, oil and gas, etc.), the principal concern of the CADE is with the level of awareness of the relevant regulatory authority and effectiveness of regulatory provisions concerning principles of competition. The exercise of competition advocacy by the CADE before such authorities is a major concern, given the fact that the CADE cannot interfere in regulatory policies or in the competence and jurisdiction of regulatory authorities.

593. Indeed, it is not uncommon that regulatory agencies have little or no *ex ante* concern for competition matters and their impact in the marketplace.

594. Until recently, in handling market concentration in regulated markets, the CADE applied a jurisdictional test similar, by analogy, to the *state action doctrine* and the *pervasive power doctrine.*

595. The so-called state action doctrine was originally developed in the US as a standard to settle conflicts between sector regulation and LDCs, so as to determine the cases of antitrust exemption. Two standards would basically rule antitrust exemption: exemption would be granted: (a) not because a certain statute would vest unto a certain regulatory authority with powers to determine the basic economic variables (such as prices and volumes), but because regulatory decisions and rules would be governed by norms that clearly express and define the substitution of competition laws by regulation, and (b) if such regulatory agencies would effectively and actively monitor and enforce compliance with all obligations set forth in the relevant regulation.

596. Recently, however, resorting to the state action doctrine is a rare phenomenon at the CADE. The interference of competition authorities in regulated markets is increasing, based on a dubious concept of 'complementary competence' (in certain case, in explicit conflict with applicable laws) where the competition authorities would enforce competition laws ancillary to the alleged lack of experience of regulatory authorities in enforcing competition principles.

597. For example, in Act of Concentration No. 08012.004238/2010-62 (resolved on 9 November 2011), in re. *São Cristóvão Administração e Participações Ltda. and Empresa Auto Ônibus Manoel Rodrigues S.A.*, the CADE ruled that, in case of regulated markets, there is no conflict of competence between the CADE and the regulator, nor in exemption of general regulation, or even in overlap of regulators, provided that the regulatory analysis does not exclude the competitive assessment. In the particular case, in reviewing the regular public road passenger and suburban transportation market, the CADE decided that competition in the market may occur not only in terms of quality of the service, but also in tariff, even if the latter shall be regulated.

598. The conflict of authority between competition authorities and regulatory authorities is a matter yet to be settled by the Judiciary and in its early stages.

599. Conflicting standards between such authorities are not uncommon. For example:

(a) in the Administrative Process No. 08012.007443/1999-17, in re. *SDE, ex officio, v. Terminal para Contêineres da Margem Direita S/A – TECONDI et alii* (resolved on 27 April 2005), the CADE ruled as anticompetitive the charge by port terminals of a *Containers' Release Charge* (TLC), commonly known as *Terminal Handling Charge 2* (THC2), for the handling and release of containers to competing dry customs terminals, in addition to the box rate charged to the ship owners. The defendants argued that such a charge was justified given that separating/segregating goods and containers to be delivered to other terminals was an onerous and separate service, requiring special equipment and manpower, while the CADE considered that such a charge only sought to raise rivals' costs and were to be included in the box rate charged to the ship owners. The port regulatory authorities (*Agência Nacional de Transportes Aquaviários – ANTAQ*) considered such charge legitimate and ultimately regulated its collection (ANTAQ Resolution No. 2389, of 13 February 2012). The courts affirmed ANTAQ's authority to govern such matter, but the CADE insisted in finding such charge anticompetitive, notwithstanding. The matter is currently under appeal by the CADE before the Judiciary;
(b) in Administrative Process No. 08000.009354/97-82 (resolved on 20 August 2014), in re. SDE, *ex* officio, *v. Agip Liquigás do Brasil S/A et alii*, the distributors of liquefied petroleum gas in the cities of Porto Alegre and Canoas, in the State of Rio Grande do Sul, have established a market-sharing system, whereby each distributor was allocated a certain day during the month to sell cylinders to the dealers on an exclusive basis. The GLP market was then free of price-control mechanisms, but the system adopted by the distributors was inspired by a prerviously existing distribution system established and regulated by the regulatory authority (*Agência Nacional do Petróleo, Gás Natural e Biocombustíveis – ANP).* ANP was fully aware of the practice and agreed with it, but the CADE ruled such system anticompetitive, notwithstanding, in conflict with ANP's view that such system would prevent piracy and freeriding.

600. Horizontal mergers are reviewed based on objective criteria as described by the Guidelines for the Review of Horizontal Acts of Concentration (2016), also known as H Guidelines.[58] The H Guidelines set forth common principles for the systematic and deep analysis of horizontal acts of concentration, seeking to permit a

58. The comments below and *passim* are only a summary of the main points of the H Guidelines, and not a comprehensive description of the contents of the document. For a complete reading of the H Guidelines, *see* http://www.cade.gov.br/acesso-a-informacao/publicacoes-institucionais/guias_do_Cade/guia-para-analise-de-atos-de-concentracao-horizontal.pdf. Accessed on 30 Jul. 2016.

greater assurance to the market players as to applicable rules, as well as transparency and prompt action in administrative proceedings.

601. The H Guidelines are similar to the US FTC Horizontal Mergers Guidelines (of 19 August 2010), the contents of which inspired the elaboration of the Brazilian document.

602. The H Guidelines also describe the main concepts, procedures and principles to be followed by the CADE to review the transaction.

603. Such procedures and principles articulate the main phases of the merger review and, in practice, seek to be an instrument of applicability of the rule of reason and of transparency of the Public Administration by describing the objective criteria and phases that are to be followed by the CADE in performing its duties under the LDC. Consequently, the H Guidelines limit the discretion of the CADE's acts.

604. As mentioned, such procedures are applicable to horizontal concentrations that are, to mergers and acquisitions involving competing producers of goods and services, or players that operate at the same business level, including JVs between potential competitors, incorporating a new firm under joint control.

605. The review procedures adopted by the CADE take into account five main phases and are based on a 'structure-conduct-performance' paradigm.

606. The first two are: (i) determination of the relevant market; and (ii) determination of share or market control. Such phases respond to the 'structure' portion of the paradigm.

607. In order to determine the relevant market, the authorities take review of the market characteristics from both the supply-side (production inputs: raw materials, technology, level of unionization, legal framework etc.) and the demand-side (structure preferences: demand elasticity, product interchangeability, growth level, season characteristics etc.). The H Guidelines also considers the time/seasonal aspect, relating to the period of time that the market operates, especially in connection with industries with service and production peaks versus natural idle periods (such as in the case of the transportation and electric power industries, or industries with seasonal variations (i.e., the food industry). The very same definition of relevant market is carried out both in the conduct control and in the merger review.

608. It should be noted that the guidelines below refer to the determination of the relevant market in concentration cases only. Although the determination of a relevant market in a merger case is not mandatory and in many cases has been simply disregarded or left open, such determination in conduct cases is even less important (there are arguments suggesting that the relevant market needs not to be determined in reviewing anticompetitive conducts), and, in such cases, the market is frequently restricted to the specific product under investigation, or the specific location or the specific parties.

609. In any event, in dealing with concentrations, once the market is determined, the analysis shall proceed to determining its structure: number of incumbent players, product differentiation, etc. Market share will be assessed primarily through the sales (volume and value) of the relevant parties *vis-à-vis* total market sales (demand-side).

610. In determining the relevant market (both in its product-product interchangeability from its supply-side and demand-side approaches and geographic – area where substitute products effectively compete – dimensions), the CADE will use the so-called hypothetical monopolist test, which consists of determining the market by the smallest group of interchangeable goods and services and the smallest geographic area that would enable a hypothetical monopolist to impose a small but significant and non-transitory price increase (SSNIP) on consumers.

611. One of the standards to be met in determining if a given transaction shall cause a negative impact on the consumer welfare and on competition is the fact that the company resulting from the merger shall control a significant share of the relevant market.

612. The Herfindahl-Hirschman (HHI) index may be used to calculate the level of market concentration and, consequently, of competitive concerns.

613. Based on the use of the HHI index, the markets are:

(d) not concentrated: with HHI lower than 1,500 points;
(e) moderately concentrated: with HHI between 1,500 and 2,500 points;
(f) highly concentrated: with HHI above 2,500 points.

614. Transactions that yield an HHI variation lower than 100 points and, in the case of a non- concentrated market (if the market, as a result of the transaction shall remain with an HHI lower than 1,500 points) generally do not result in negative competitive effects, and thus, require no further analysis.

615. Conversely, the following transactions yield competitive concerns:

(d) in the case of moderately concentrated markets, if the transaction shall result in a market with HHI between 1,500 and 2,500 points and involve an index variation exceeding 100 points ($\Delta HHI > 100$);
(e) in the case of highly concentrated markets, if the transaction shall result in a market with HHI exceeding 2,500 points and involve an index variation between 100 and 200 points ($100 \leq \Delta HHI \leq 200$); and
(f) transactions resulting in a market with HHI in excess of 2,500 points and involve an index variation exceeding 200 points ($\Delta HHI > 200$).

616. The use of the HHI index, however, is not decisive, but only indicative of a causal nexus and a starting point for the analysis of market power. As a matter of fact, the HHI index is to be used with caution in markets with a large fringe and a high market dispersion. It should also be flexibly used: (a) should there be indicia of coordination among market players, (b) should one of the parties be a maverick or practice a disruptive market strategy, (c) whenever the merger shall refer to a newcomer, (d) should there be a significant cross shareholding between the parties and its competitors, (e) should the degree of market concentration not reflect the actual competitive dynamics of the market and (f) should the merger increase a portfolio power.

617. Transactions that result in a high market concentration shall precede to the second phase of analysis of probability of exercise of market power, the 'conduct' portion of the paradigm. Such phase will primarily review the presence of barriers to entry, entry thresholds and of rivalry among the incumbent players.

618. The mere fact that a transaction shall result in a sufficiently high market concentration level does not necessarily imply that the resulting company shall actually and unilaterally exercise market power, or that the relevant companies shall act in coordination.

619. However, given that the actions of the competition authorities in merger review procedures are preventive by nature, the mere potential of an abusive exercise of market power, whether unilateral or in collusion, are sufficient to cause competitive concerns, and prompt the authorities to either order full or partial divestiture orders or behavioural remedies to curb the potential risk.

620. Market power means the control of a significant portion of a relevant market capable of causing a price variation for a reasonable period of time through a restriction in volume output. The exercise of market power resulting from an act of concentration requires that the demand be or become inelastic to prices as a result of the transaction.

621. Whenever the supply by an individual company or by a group of companies shall be sufficiently high *vis-à-vis* the total supply in a given relevant market, such company or companies, joint or separately, shall be capable of modifying the market conducts in comparison with those conducts that would otherwise be found in the case of a freely competitive environment, once the rivals would not be capable of meeting alone a significant portion of demand. In such cases, the relevant concern or group of companies would control a significantly high share of the relevant market and would, therefore, be capable of exercising market power.

622. This portion of the analysis shall consider all variables that may inhibit the exercise of market power either unilaterally by the relevant parties or in coordination with others. The most important variables are: availability of importation of competing products, possibility of entry of newcomers in the market, degree of rivalry, bargaining power of consumers, etc.

623. As mentioned earlier, in the review of the probability of exercise of market power, the authorities will take into account multiple aspects, such as those relating to the availability of imports, the possibility of entry of newcomers, barriers to entry, sunk costs, high minimum scales, etc.

624. In terms of market power contestability, actual importation or the possibility of importing is, for example, circumstances that may deter (or contest) the exercise of market power, since the greater the share of imported products in the marketplace the lesser shall be the probability of exercise of market power. However, a smaller volume of imported products is insufficient to consider probable the exercise of market power. Furthermore, one must consider that the mere possibility of importing at economic prices and conditions or of increasing the volume of actual imports, in response to a 'small but significant and non-transitory' price increase may reduce or eliminate competitive concerns.

625. In such line of thought, it is necessary to verify the elasticity of imports *vis-à*-vis the barriers to entry hindering such imports in the relevant market, such as: distribution costs, degree of dependency of the import in relation to local producers, the presence of exclusivity arrangements among local importers and foreign producers, and the capacity of importers to accommodate import increments without the need of resorting to investments in new tangible assets.

626. The possibility of entry of a newcomer is another relevant circumstance capable of deterring the exercise of market power. Such entry, for such purposes, must be 'probable', 'timely' and 'sufficient'. In the entry condition analysis, the CADE shall take into account the conduct that the hypothetical newcomer would have to adopt. Examples of companies entering the market in the past five years can be used as evidence of favourable entry conditions.

627. Other fundamental aspects denoting a probability of exercise of market power refer to the indexes obtained in the review of: (i) a probable entry, (ii) a timely entry, (iii) a sufficient entry, (iv) sales opportunities, (v) minimum viable scales (*EMV*), (vi) barriers to entry, (vii) *sunk costs* in capital requirements, (viii) legal and regulatory barriers, (ix) scale economies, (x) effectiveness of rivalry, (xi) economies of scope etc.

628. The principal barriers to entry (meaning natural or artificial limits to access) are: institutional barriers (governmental barriers, legal monopolies, industrial property, tariffs, etc.), economies of scale, idle capacity, sunk cost requirements, brand and advertising requirements, distribution requirements and difficulties of entry/exit from the relevant market, etc.).

629. Subsequent to the review of barriers to entry, the assessment of rivalry among incumbent players plays a significant role, and it has permitted clearance of transactions even in the presence of high barriers. The rivalry analysis seeks to determine if, should a firm resulting from the transaction shall unilaterally exercise its market power, the consumers shall have means to redirect their demand to other market competitors. Rivalry is the circumstance in which the firms are able to inhibit the exercise of market power, so that any attempt to alter the market structure is fought efficiently by the competing firms, thus causing that the competitive conditions shall not be changed significantly.

630. It is a necessary and sufficient condition to affirm rivalry in a given market that the competing concerns shall have the capacity of absorbing the eventual demand shift as a result of a price adjustment made by the parties to the act of concentration, aside from adopting an aggressive competitive behaviour among them. The elements in evidence of such circumstances are the distribution of the idle capacity and the market-share structure.

631. Idle capacity is a bi-directional standard in the assessment of rivalry. If, on the one hand, a high market idle capacity tends to reduce the possibility of entry by a newcomer, on the other, such is a rivalry factor, given that the market players that have idle capacity tend to minimize their losses (or maximize their profits) by optimizing the use of their respective installed capacities.

632. The best form to assess if there is an actual rivalry among players is by comparing the idle capacity of the incumbent concerns and size of the market. In addition, one should review the evolution of the market shares, given that the similarity of behaviour or the change of ranking among the players may indicate the presence of rivalry.

633. Conversely, a merger may reduce rivalry by increasing the probability of explicit or tacit collusion or by enhancing or expanding pre-existing strategies of coordination, and thus injuring consumers' welfare. Thus, the review process shall assess if the merger shall make coordination more probable to the detriment of rivalry and permitting a lucrative joint price increase and negate modification of other competitive variables, such as innovation and quality of products.

634. Should the review come to the conclusion that the exercise of market power is improbable to any of the parties involved (e.g., a market characterized by low barriers to entry or high rivalry) in the transaction, it shall enjoy a favourable recommendation by the authorities. Otherwise, the latter shall proceed to the next phases of analysis: the review of efficiencies yielding from the transaction; and the assessment of the resulting costs and benefits to the Society's welfare, whereupon a final technical opinion will be issued.

635. Efficiencies are threefold: innovation, production/productivity efficiencies and allocative efficiencies. In such a review, the authorities will consider the efficiencies that necessarily result from the transaction in light of economies of scale and scope, introduction of more productive technologies, appropriation of positive externalities and elimination of negative externalities, etc. Once the analysis reaches this level, the interested parties bear the burden of proof for the efficiencies.

636. Pursuant to Article 88, §5, of Law No. 12529/11, the acts of concentration that result in the elimination of competition or of a substantial part of the relevant market, or that may create or reinforce a dominant position, or that may result in the domination of a relevant market, are prohibited, unless efficiencies may be caused thereby, resulting in a positive net effect to the Society. However, whenever an act of concentration yields the control over a significant market share, the CADE is not authorized to clear the transaction simply in light of efficiencies, no matter how high, yielding therefrom.[59]

637. Economic efficiencies that enhance economic welfare must be necessarily resulting from the act of concentration, meaning that they cannot yield from any other manner (efficiencies specific to the concentration). Efficiencies specific to the concentration are those that cannot be achieved in less than two years through other alternative means or that involve greater risks to competition.

638. Efficiencies cannot be speculative or result in a mere pecuniary gain as a result of an increase of market share, or represent only a transfer of income between market players, provided that, as such standard is concerned, the efficiencies are accountable only when derived from variable costs (or predominantly of variable costs) and by disregarding reductions exclusive to fixed costs.

639. Furthermore, efficiencies must be quantifiable and capable of being proved and verifiable, and the alleged benefits must be equitably shared with consumers, and cannot be entertained, even in the national interest, if the transaction shall cause injury to consumers. As to the benefits to the consumer, efficiencies are accountable only when derived from variable costs (or predominantly of variable costs) and by disregarding reductions exclusive to fixed costs.[60]

640. The review of economic efficiencies shall depend on the analysis of certain concentration factors, such as, the index of economies of scale and of scope, fixed costs (costs that are not dependent from volume, such as start-up costs), average

59. Act of Concentration No. 08012.007776/2008-99 (resolved on 21 Jul. 2010), in re. *Cobb-Vantress, Inc.* and *Hendrix Genetics B.V.*

60. In connection with the standards of efficiencies, *see* Act of Concentration No. 08012.004423/2009-18 (resolved on 13 Jul. 2011), in re, *Perdigão S.A.* and *Sadia S.A.*

production levels and costs, work productivity (relation between the final volume and the volume of work required to produce it), introduction of new technology, generation of positive externalities, elimination of negative externalities, etc.

641. Should the net effect of the efficiencies be equal to or superior to the costs of competition, the authorities may recommend the clearance of the transaction. If the efficiencies are not greater than the anticompetitive effects, the authorities recommend total or partial divestitures (structural remedies) or behavioural remedies. It is a trade-off analysis of the transaction.

642. In practice, however, clearance of a transaction based on efficiencies only is a rare phenomenon. Despite being the only statutory requirement for the clearance of a merger, the CADE generally disregards efficiencies as a *leit motiv* for approval of a transaction. Efficiencies are hardly recognized by the CADE and, when doing so, efficiencies are only a *plus factor* for approval.

643. In Act of Concentration No. 08012.001697/02-89, resolved on 14 July 2004, involving *Nestlé Brasil Ltda.* and *Chocolates Garoto S/A.*, whereby the transactions was rejected by the CADE. Since then, the authorities have virtually restricted themselves to accepting a price standard, whereby efficiencies should be of such nature and impact that the necessary result thereof shall be a reduction in prices of the relevant products.

644. Firms that resort to judicial protection against insolvency (Judicial Recovery)[61] under Law No. 11,101/2005 may have their agreement with creditors subject to the CADE notification requirement if applicable notification thresholds are met. In such cases the failing firm defence (FFD) is reviewed under the chapter of efficiencies.

645. FDDs are seen with scepticism and caution by CADE and, pursuant to the H Guidelines, may eventually be entertained only if the following criteria are met on a cumulative basis:

(a) should approval to the transaction be negated, the firm would exit the market or be prevented from meeting its financial obligations as a result of its economic and financial difficulties;
(b) should approval to the transaction be negated, the assets of the firm would remain in the market, causing a reduction of supply, a greater level of concentration in the market and a reduction of economic welfare; and
(c) the firm shall have demonstrated efforts in searching alternatives that are less harmful to competition (i.e., by means of alternative purchasers or of engagement in a judicial recovery process) and that there remains no other solution for the maintenance of its economic activities other than the approval of the transaction.

646. The burden of proof of such requirements are vested unto the applicant firm.

647. In order to clear an act of concentration that results in a significant market share (phase II) in a market where conditions of exercise of market power exist (phase III), based on yielding efficiencies (phase IV), it is necessary to demonstrate that the impact of the transaction on the Society's welfare is not negative.

61. Law No. 11101, of 9 Feb. 2015, also known as the Judicial and Extrajudicial Recovery and Bankruptcy Law.

648. Aside from the classic methodology described above governing the CADE review process of horizontal mergers, the H Guidelines lists, on a non-exhausting basis, certain complementary or alternative methods for the antitrust analysis:

(a) counterfactual analysis, by comparing different scenarios in searching evidence that demonstrates the competitive impact of the merger, disregarding the definition of the relevant market and of the market share of the firms;
(b) use of simulations, whereby mathematical and econometric models simulate the impact of the transaction, again disregarding the determination of the relevant market and of its structure, by seeking to estimate some actual parameters of demand and supply targeting to assess what can happen in the future (after the merger) with respect to market prices and controlling eventual levels of efficiency gains yielding from the transaction; and
(c) consideration of other factors, such as:[62] (i) the possibility of elimination of mavericks and of potential competition,[63] (ii) the combination of a horizontal concentration and of a vertical integration, even if the parties shall not directly operate in each phase of the production chain, (iii) the impact of the merger on two-sided markets and (iv) the impact of acquisition of partial control, yielding active shareholding that may grant the purchaser a control power (jointly or severally) or the power to exercise a relevant influence on the commercial behaviour of the target company.

649. Once their review process is completed, the GS will clear the transaction, if no harmful effect is found to competition, or will issue a non-binding technical opinion challenging the transaction before CADE's administrative tribunal, by recommending a partial or total divestiture. Such opinion is certainly of importance in the CADE's final determination.

650. On a systemic perspective, the actual role of competition laws is not to control or to intervene at the discretion of the Public Authority in the existing market structures, but rather, given the fact that acts of concentration shall permanently modify the relevant market structure, to ensure the latter's free functioning and the free initiative

62. Such criteria was adopted, for example, in the opinion of Councillor Elvino de Carvalho Mendonça in Act of Concentration No. 08700.00398/2012-90 (resolved on 30 Jan. 2013) in re. *Unimed Franca - Sociedade Cooperativa de Serviços Médicos e Hospitalares S.A. and Hospital Regional de Franca.*

63. *Potential competition manifests itself in two ways: (i) Perceived Potential Competition, when the incumbent market players market fear that high profits will attract new competitors, a perception which induces reduction of costs and prices and, (ii) Effective Potential Competition, when the entry shall increase competition in a given market, disciplining the behaviour of prices, volumes and innovation. The analysis of Perceived Potential Competition requires proof of the effects of the imminent entry on the actual behaviour of the incumbent firms, while the Effective Potential Competition requires proof that the acquiring/acquired firm would be able to enter independently, resulting in future effects on competition. See* Dispatch No. 991 of the Superintendent-General of the CADE, Eduardo Frade Rodrigues, that approved the Opinion No. 262 of the Superintendency-General in the Act of Concentration No. 08700.003748/2014-92 (resolved on 20 Aug. 2014), in re. *Bionovis S.A. - Companhia Brasileira de Biotecnologia Farmacêutica, Ares Trading AS* and *Merck KGaA.*

of market players. In addition, the purpose of the merger review process is also of assessing the economic impact of the underlying transaction, impeding the consummation of actions that may yield restraints to the economic efficiency and/or to social welfare. In such context, the CADE may recommend: (a) the unconditional clearance of the transaction, whenever it shall be incapable of causing injuries to the competitive environment; (b) the conditional clearance thereof, avoiding that it may cause an adverse impact to consumer welfare or to economic efficiencies through a structural or behavioural remedy; and (c) full divestiture, whenever a conditional clearance would be insufficient to avoid the adverse impacts of the deal on the market.

651. In short, the following are the circumstances under which an act of concentration shall be approved:

(a) lack of control of a significant share of the market;
(b) despite the control of a significant share of the market, the exercise of market power subsequent to the merger is improbable; or
(c) although there is a probability of exercise of market share subsequent to the merger, the net effect of the transaction is positive to the market and consumer welfare.

§2. Vertical Mergers

652. Vertical integrations occur when companies operating at different levels, whether upstream or downstream, in the industrial chain unite their efforts on a common purpose. Such is the case, for example, of the merger of a car manufacturer with an auto-part supplier, or of the merger of a crushed-stone producer with a concrete-disposal company.

653. Generally, the underlying purpose of such deals is to mitigate transaction costs and eventual externalities resulting from the existence of imperfect market structures, or to achieve economies through integrated operations, such as stock and production planning, logistics, optimization of distribution channels.

654. Vertical integrations are primarily the concern of the CADE only in those cases where the underlying transaction shall result in the possibility of: (i) upstream market foreclosure, when the downstream undertaking enjoys market power and has incentives to purchase inputs only from the verticalized company, and (ii) downstream market foreclosure, when the upstream undertaking enjoys market power and has incentives to direct its production to the verticalized company or to practise conducts tending to market foreclosure, such as price discrimination. In the case of captive use production, there is no possibility of market foreclosure as a result of a vertical integration, given that, in such cases, there is no causal nexus between the transaction and the risk of foreclosure.

655. Generally, vertical restrictive practices are restrictions imposed by manufacturers and/or suppliers of goods and services in a relevant market on other markets vertically related to it in the productive chain. Vertical restrictions are anticompetitive whenever they create mechanisms of rival foreclosure, either because such actions raise barriers to entry to potential newcomers, or because they raise competitors' costs, or enhance the probability of coordinated market power by producers, suppliers or distributors through the creation of mechanisms that permit overcoming obstacles to coordination that would otherwise exist.

656. The analysis of the interaction between different relevant markets may also be made from contractual clauses, such as in the case of exclusivity arrangements between suppliers and distributors, should they result in market foreclosure. However, an interesting case is found in Act of Concentration No. 08012.001205/2010-65 (resolved in February 2011), in re. *Braskem S.A., Petróleo Brasileiro S.A., Petrobras Química and Quattor Participações S.A.*, in which the CADE decided that, although the eventual attempt of market foreclosure through the execution of an exclusivity arrangement between a domestic monopolist and a foreign maverick type competitor can be considered illegal, there is no reason, in itself, to prevent such contracting.

657. Similar to horizontal restrictions, vertical restrictions also assume the presence of market power in the relevant market 'of origin', as well as the impact, thereof, on a significant portion of the 'target' market, so as to characterize a risk of injury to competition. Although such restrictions may eventually constitute a restraint to free competition, they may conversely promote economic efficiencies permitting, in such instances, their adoption based on the principle of reasonability.

658. Thus, again similar to horizontal overlaps, once it is determined that the upstream market player enjoys market power, and that it is capable of using such power effectively by applying vertical restrictions affecting the downstream market, specially whenever such player shall enjoy proprietary rights over an element essential to such downstream market, the competition authorities are bound to act to deter the resulting dominance through the imposition of the penalties set forth in Law No. 12529/11.

659. The most common types of vertical restrictions are: resale price maintenance, territorial restrictions, client restrictions, exclusivity arrangements, refusals to deal, tie-in arrangements, price discrimination, etc.

660. In various occasions, the CADE has addressed the issue of vertical restrictions and vertical integrations. Generally, vertical restrictions are reviewed in investigating anticompetitive conducts, such as in the case of *Power-Tech v. Matel* (Administrative Process No. 08012000172/1998-42), concerning the refusal by *Matel* to supply spare parts for the maintenance of the MD 110 PBX model.

661. In ascertaining the anticompetitive conduct, the CADE affirmed that the refusal to sell yielded a harmful effect on the market to the extent it was the result of *Matel's* unjustified exercise of monopoly power. The Council then ruled that such conduct characterized a market foreclosure, as well as the creation of difficulties to the operations of a rival through obstacles to access to input sources.

662. *Matel* was held accountable for the offence to former Article 21, items IV, V and VI, combined with former Article 20, items I and IV, of Law No. 8884, and the CADE imposed a fine (minimum statutory fine) of 1% of the company's turnover in the year preceding the commencement of the Administrative Process, all in accordance with former Article 23 of Law No. 8884/94 and Article 11 of Law No. 9021.

663. An example of the CADE addressing vertical integrations in the control of market structures is the case *Cimpor – Embu* (Act of Concentration No. 08012.001230/2007-43), concerning the purchase by *Cimpor* (a cement company) of the stock control of a concrete- disposal company (*Embu*). This case became a benchmark in the review of vertical integration cases in the civil construction field (more precisely in the cement, sand and concrete-disposal markets).

664. The transaction involved the purchase by *Cimpor Cimentos do Brasil* of such assets as vehicles, machinery, equipment, furniture, utensils, tools, components, spare parts, office material and client lists, and the potentials of the business, all such assets being related to the production units of the concrete-disposal services owned by *Embu Engenharia Ltda.*

665. In reviewing the merits of the case, the CADE came to the conclusion that, although resulting in a vertical integration, it was not possible, nor probable, for the transaction to foreclose any downstream or upstream market.

666. Pursuant to the CADE opinion, the market shares of the applicant parties were not significantly high (lower than 20%) both in the upstream market (production and sale of cement) and in the downstream market (concrete-disposal market).

667. Furthermore, the Council considered the fact that the total concrete-disposal market represented only 15% of the total supply of cement at the time. Thus, the transaction was cleared, conditional only upon the restriction of the geographic scope of the non-competition clause agreed upon by the parties to the Metropolitan Area of São Paulo city – the area where *Embu Engenharia* operated.

668. The CADE has generally considered cases of vertical integration favourably, although limiting the scope of unjustified vertical restraints (e.g., restrictions on the use of essential facilities, or in the use of distribution network channels, or resulting in resale price maintenance). An example of such a trend may be found in Act of Concentration No. 08012.009537/2011-79 (resolved on 8 February 2012), in re. *Boston Medical Device, Inc.* and *ConvaTec Inc.* in which the CADE ruled that there are no competitive concerns in the acquisition of the stock control of a distributor, the relations with which pre-existed the transaction.

669. In a more significant precedent, in discussing whether the formation of a JV (*EMDAPI — Empresa de Destinação Adequada de Pneumáticos Inservíveis Ltda.*).by all domestic competing OEM tyre manufacturers for the management and marketing of services and products resulting from the collection and final destination of unusable tyres (Act of Concentration No. 08012.001818/2012-64 (resolved on 9 May 2012), in re. *EMDAPI – Empresa de Destinação Adequada de Pneumáticos Inservíveis Ltda., Goodyear do Brasil Produtos de Borracha Ltda., Pirelli Pneus Ltda., Bridgestone do Brasil Indústria e Comércio Ltda., Sociedade Michelin de Participações Industria e Comercio Ltda., and Continental do Brasil Produtos Automotivos Ltda.)* – the CADE gave heavy weight and consideration to applicable environmental laws and rules that such a JV did not represent a vertical integration and cleared the transaction.

§3. Market/Product Extension Mergers

670. The expressions 'fusion of market extension' and 'fusion of product extension' consist of the two basic kinds of fusions that have become most common in modern configuration of the financial market, since each time more of the companies are seeking to enlarge the base of their operations and their product portfolio offered to the consumers.

671. The fusion of market extension occurs between two players that manufacture the same product or render the same service, but operate at separate segments of the market. The principal scope of such kind of fusion is to ensure to the relevant players that the merging companies can have access to a broader market, thus expanding their respective base of operations and assuring the parties access to the pool of clients of that certain market.

672. A good example of a fusion of market extension case in Brazil was the merger between *Banco Santander and Banco ABN Amro Real* (Act of Concentration No. 08012.010081/2007-11. applicants: *The Royal Bank of Scotland Plc, Fortis N.V/ Fortis S.A/ N.V and Banco Santander Central Hispano S/A*), given that the former had as its target a low and average income clientele, while the latter was dedicated to specific segments, such as the package of services to university students and prime clients (through the prime segment called 'Van Gogh').

673. On its turn, a 'fusion of product extension' occurs whenever two corporate organizations operate in the same market, but with different products functionally related to each other. The product-extension concentration permits the merging relevant companies to integrate their respective product lines and thus have access to a larger group of consumers.

674. In Brazil, a good example of product-extension fusion was the merger of federal public banks with State public banks, such as the case of *Banco do Brasil* acquiring the control of *Banco Nossa Caixa, a State Bank of the State of São Paulo* (Act of Concentration No. 08012.011736/2008-41), *of Banco do Estado de Santa Catarina S.A.* (Act of Concentration No. 08012.009986/2008-11) *and of Banco do Estado do Piauí S.A.* (Act of Concentration No. 08012.011505/2008-38).

675. The CADE has already cleared the *Banco do Brasil – Banco do Estado do Piauí* transaction. Other cases on this topic will be subsequently addressed.

§4. Pure Conglomerate Mergers

676. The economic concept of a conglomerate relates to a kind of oligopoly where many companies acting in different fields unite their efforts in their attempt of dominating a certain supply of goods and/or services and are usually managed by a holding company, the purpose of which is to ensure managerial stability to the member companies. An example of a conglomerate is a group of large corporations that is engaged in business from the exploitation of a raw material to the transportation of the final industrialized product.

677. Example of global conglomerates are Mitsubishi that manufactures from cars to pens, and General Electric that produces a large variety of products, from light bulbs, to ovens, freezers, etc.

678. Many trusts formed at the end of the nineteenth century, and early twentieth century, changed themselves into conglomerates and is the result of a broad process of concentration and capital centralization that sought dominance of supply of certain products to the market.

679. The horizontal concentration, the vertical integration and the conglomerate mergers differ from one another by kind of economic activity performed by the merging companies, considering the type of business in which each such company is engaged or the part of the production process to which each is dedicated.

680. Differently from a horizontal merger and a vertical integration, conglomerate mergers occur whenever the relevant merging companies operate in different fields of activity, thus resulting in the expansion of their product lines.

681. Conglomerate mergers can be grouped into three characteristic kinds, pursuant to the extension that they entail: (i) product extension: it occurs whenever the product lines are expanded, and the fusion takes place between companies that are somewhat related to each other; (ii) geographic market extension: it involves the merger of companies the operations of which are conducted in different geographic areas, for example, a company acting in the domestic market and the other in the international market; and (iii) pure conglomerate: meaning a fusion that involves companies that operate at different, unrelated business fields.

682. The CADE's position has to date been generally favourable to market/product extension mergers and pure conglomerate mergers. Example of such favourable approach is the act of concentration involving *TPG Partners IV. L.P., T3 Partners II, L.P. and Isola AG*. In such cases, there was neither horizontal concentration nor any vertical integration, thus permitting its unconditional approval.

683. However, the CADE has expressed concerns whenever the transaction shall yield an increase of portfolio power, or in the creation of such power, indicating that such effects are to be carefully reviewed on a case-by-case basis.

684. In the *Braço S.A., Companhia de Bebida das Américas – AmBev, and Interbrew N.V.S.A.* case, the CADE ascertained the portfolio effect resulting from the fact that the applicant parties controlled most of the brands in the beer market.

685. In this case, the Council came to the conclusion that an eventual statement of objection or a motion for the imposition of remedies based on the risk of potential adoption of anticompetitive conduct by any of the parties to the transaction could be overruled if such risk would necessarily result from the deal. The CADE decided that, in such cases, the eventual and actual abusive exercise of market power would characterize an anticompetitive market conduct that could be reviewed a posteriori in an Administrative Process, and not in the course of review of the act of Concentration.

686. In connection with the portfolio power, the CADE stated that such power may, as a result of the acquisition of a significant number of brands through an act of concentration, directly or indirectly create or strengthen a dominant position, regardless of any increase in market share. Under such circumstances, competitors having no complete product lines risk being excluded from the market in the long run, thus permitting the dominant concern to increase prices or to make less investments in research and development.

687. Nevertheless, the eventual decision to order the divestiture of a transaction or the imposition of significant restrictions thereon, based on the risk of abusive exercise of power of portfolio requires ascertaining that, in the underlying case, the economies of scope are irrelevant, and that the market conditions are particularly favourable to the abuse of dominance.

688. In the *Braço S.A., Companhia de Bebida das Américas – Ambev and Interbrew N.V.S.A.* case, the CADE ruled that the transaction would yield a non-significant market concentration, of only 0.001%, and would actually result in the entry of a new player in such market. Consequently, the case was approved because it did not raise any antitrust concern.

689. A similar issue was reviewed in the case *Recofarma Indústria do Amazonas Ltda. (Coca-Cola) and Leão Junior S.A.* (a ready-to-drink tea company). In this case, the CADE analysed the effects of the power of portfolio and the risks associated with its potential abusive use to free competition, especially when one of the parties (Coca-Cola) is a conglomerate.

690. In handling such matters involving the power of portfolio and conglomerates, the CADE frequently resorts to the OECD guidelines on the subject and concludes that such transaction may yield anticompetitive, as well as pro-competitive, effects, since such transaction would permit aggregating complementary products. The complementary impact yielding from such acts of concentration differ from the complementary impact as viewed in classic economies. They cover both 'technical' complementary impacts (products that, for technical reasons, can be jointly consumed) and 'commercial' complementary impacts (products that are part of a group of products that distributors may supply, such as alcoholic beverages and soft drinks).

691. The CADE came to the conclusion that the *Braço S.A., Companhia de Bebida das Américas – Ambev and Interbrew N.V.S.A.* case yielded commercial complementary impacts, and that such effect was an efficiency, as claimed by the applicants.

692. Based on that conclusion, the CADE, although deciding that the exercise of portfolio market could eventually facilitate market foreclosure to competing brands (by making their operations more difficult or even impeding them, thus resulting in an eventual reduction in the total supply of products to the market and limiting the choice of consumers to the brands offered by the conglomerate), the transaction could conversely result in certain gains to welfare in the short term (as a result, for example, of the economies of scope and of scale), since Matte Leão would be thereby benefited by being able to use the more extensive and efficient Coca-Cola distribution network.

693. The foregoing, notwithstanding, the CADE signalled that the transaction was not free from competitive concerns, bearing in mind that such short-term efficiencies could be subsequently prejudiced in the long run, as a result of an eventual market foreclosure to rivals. Such foreclosure would probably have a much greater negative effect on the general welfare.

694. The greatest concern was related to the possibility of the parties engaging in illegal tie-arrangements supported by the greater attraction exercised by a product portfolio controlled by a dominant firm in comparison with the individual products offered by smaller firms. By being able to offer a portfolio of many products, the transaction would possibly enable the parties thereto to raise rival's costs, especially because, under such circumstances, purchasers would be motivated to acquire various products from a single supplier.

695. Such risks are even greater if the distribution network channels would also result in foreclosure and eventually dedicated to the marketing of only a few brands, the conglomerate brands. In such cases, prices charged by the conglomerate would tend to rise subsequent to the transaction, since competitors would probably be unable to enter or re-enter the market at ease. Indeed, in such a scenario, the distribution channels would be limited and occupied by the conglomerate brands. Another possible consequence would be that the number of options offered to the consumer would be reduced.

696. In consideration of such concerns, the CADE concluded that the transaction could excessively concentrate the market, bearing in mind that the relevant market was already highly concentrated, and presented high barriers to entry. Furthermore, the foreclosure of the main distribution channels would contribute to prevent other competing brands to reach the market and to contest the market power of the applicants.

697. The transaction was ultimately cleared, by conditional upon Coca-Cola not participating in the marketing of the brand Nestea, the principal ready-to-drink tea brand of Matte Leão.

698. An important conglomerate merger was analysed by the CADE in connection with the Act of Concentration No. 08012.004423/2009-18 (resolved in 13 July 2011), in re. *Perdigão S.A.* and *Sadia S.A*, which resulted in the merger of the competing national champion domestic players in the refrigerated food market. The transaction had two basis features: (a) although not using the failing firm defence, *Sadia* claimed to be facing a severe financial condition; and (b) the transaction would involve national interest, by creating a significantly strong player in the global market.

699. In connection with the national interest argument, the CADE expressly affirmed that, in cases, such as this one, resulting in a significant elimination of competition in the Brazilian domestic market, '*the Law expressly prohibits the approval of acts (of concentration) that yield injuries to the consumer or to the final user, even in cases involving alleged preponderant motives of the national economy, thus indicating that the consumer welfare is superior to any other interest*'. '*The strengthening of a firm, regardless whether a Brazilian firm, and the increase of exports eventually resulting therefrom, cannot supersede, in absolute, the welfare of the Brazilian consumers. An act of concentration that yields severe damages to the domestic consumer cannot be cleared under the argument that such would create a strong firm, capable of competing globally and of exporting its products*' (free translation).

700. A key argument placed by the applicants was based on efficiencies, but the CADE failed to recognize their existence or positive net effect on competition and on the domestic consumers; consequently, the transaction was ultimately approved but subject to severe structural remedies (partial divestiture). Indeed, the CADE concluded in reviewing the brand portfolio effect that, the merged firm, through its principal trademarks, would be capable of practising higher prices and still sell a volume of products much higher than its remaining rivals, thus indicating its capacity of increasing prices. Such firm would not be contestable by newcomers or by any other incumbent player.

701. In the opposite direction of national interest concerns, the CADE cleared Act of Concentration No. 08012.001205/2010-65, in re. *Braskem S.A., Petróleo Brasileiro S.A., Petrobras Química* and *Quattor Participações S.A.*, which resulted, based on clear national interest arguments, in the creation of a national champion in the petrochemical industry with global presence and a domestic monopolist condition in multiple petrochemical markets (the CADE concluded that the relevant geographic markets in connection with such products was, in each case, an international market).

702. The consolidation process had started in 2002, when Braskem was incorporated with the specific purpose of integrating the second generation petrochemical firms and such firms with their respective raw material suppliers (first generation firms), seeking to achieve scale and synergies, aside from significantly increasing its investment and R&D capabilities. In such a scenario, the Braskem/Quattor merger was the final phase of the restricting and consolidation of the Brazilian petrochemical industry, capable of permitting its insertion in the global market.

703. The transaction consolidated strategic areas of the Brazilian domestic economy and created favourable conditions for investments and expansion of the Brazilian domestic petrochemical industry and, therefore, enhanced its international competitiveness and created value, with positive impact on the domestic economic growth and generation of foreign currency to the country. Braskem argued, for example, that the transaction would result in important economies of scale, and that many countries had only one petrochemical company.

704. Although the transaction was ultimately approved, it raised competitive concerns to the Brazilian domestic consumer of resins. *ABIPLAST – Associação Brasileira da Indústria do Plástico*, a trade association, filed a statement of objections, given Braskem's recurrent practice of seeking the imposition of antidumping duties against foreign competitors to protect its domestic market, claiming that the CADE should order Braskem not to file new antidumping cases in the future in the field of thermoplastic resins. ABIPLAST claimed that the existence of: (i) antidumping duties imposed on US and Mexican exports, (ii) certain commercial agreements entered by and between Braskem and certain foreign companies; and the (iii) high import duties affecting the importation of thermoplastic resins could result in market foreclosure for Brazilian third generation companies, which would thus be prevented from importing such foreign competing products and contesting the monopoly power of Braskem.

705. The CADE, in hearing the case, ruled that it had no authority to require from a company not to plead for, or support the, assessment of antidumping duties, and in such area that it could only, in the exercise of the competition advocacy, recommend the Brazilian international trade authority (CAMEX) to more carefully review the impact of antidumping duties on prices in the relevant market.

§5. Joint Ventures

706. The CADE usually favours the creation of JVs to the extent such transactions seek to promote competition in the relevant market. JVs tend to promote efficiencies, economies of scale, mitigation of sunk costs, reduction of transaction costs, minimization of free riding problems and better logistics in the marketing of products and services.

707. For example, Councillor Lúcia Helena Salgado e Silva stated in Act of Concentration No. 08012.005243/98-76, involving *Remy Holdings do Brasil Ltda. and Irmãos Zen S.A.*:

> As to the merits, I consider that the underlying transaction submitted to the CADE review is incapable of yielding any anticompetitive impact. On the contrary, the reported Joint Venture tends to increase competition in the starters′ market, since it results in the creation of a new domestic competitor. The Joint Venture is mostly important in the original equipment market (vehicle manufacturers), where there is a large demand for the component as a whole, and not for specific starting auto parts, that are restrict to the aftermarket. Therefore, I conclude that the circumstances described in the caput of Article 54 (of Law No. 884/94) are not present, meaning that the transaction does not injure or restrain competition in any way, reason why I unconditionally approve it (free translation).

708. As noted, the decision concluded that there was no anticompetitive concern in the eventual coordination between two auto-part manufacturers that, although operating in different fields of activity, decided to form a JV at the request of a vehicle manufacturer that decided to acquire complete kits from a single supplier as opposed to purchasing kits of separate parts. Indeed, the market power enjoyed by the vehicle manufacturer was sufficient to prevent any anticompetitive coordination by the associated members to the joint venture.

709. In an additional demonstration of a more lenient approach in relation to joint ventures, Article 90, sole paragraph, of the Brazilian Competition Law expressly excluded JV companies formed for the specific purpose of participating in public tender bids promoted by the direct and indirect administration, and the respective administrative contracts, from the concept of 'act of concentration'. Thus, such ventures and contracts are exempted from the CADE notification requirements.

710. Also, the CADE Resolution in Act of Concentration No. 08012.001818/2012-64 (resolved in 9 May 2012), in re *EMDAPI – Empresa de Destinação Adequada de Pneumáticos Inservíveis Ltda., Goodyear do Brasil Produtos de Borracha Ltda., Pirelli Pneus Ltda., Bridgestone do Brasil Indústria e Comércio Ltda., Sociedade Michelin de Participações Industria e Comércio Ltda. and Continental do Brasil Produtos Automotivos Ltda.* that permitted the creation of a JV among all of the OEM tyre manufacturers for the management and marketing of services and products resulting from the collection and final destination of unusable tyres.

711. The JV resulted in the incorporation of *EMDAPI*, a company formed by the OEM tyre manufacturers seeking to jointly comply with environmental laws[64] that require such manufacturers to collect and dispose of unusable tyres originally manufactured by them. The JV, in which each manufacturer would have a participation of 20%, sought to reduce common costs and create efficiencies in the collection and disposal of used tyres. The CADE decided that there was no vertical integration between the JV company (*EMDAPI*) and its shareholders and, thus, found no competitive concerns.

712. By the same token but conversely, as previously said, the CADE is permanently suspicious of JVs as shown in Act of Concentration No. 08012.004907/2010-09, involving *CPLPAR Holding S.A., CPA Trading S.A* e *Cattalini Terminais Marítimos Ltda.*, when it stated that:

64. CONAMA Resolution No. 258, of 26 Aug. 1999.

> such (JV) structure may increase the risk of collusion, especially with respect to price fixing, to matters concerning commercial policies (sale terms and conditions, costs, client and/or supplier definition and on which market to do business – products and territories, among others) and to other competitive variables (free translation).

713. One of the main aspects of a JV is the strict compliance by the members thereto with their non-compete obligations, since the eventual competition between any of the participants and the JV would annihilate the common purpose of the association and of the venture itself, since it would not be possible that the participants would at the same time compete and cooperate with each other in the same market. For no other reason, the CADE fully accepts non-compete clauses effective for the life of the JV, as well as for a reasonable time thereafter (usually for an additional term of five years).

714. In Act of Concentration No. 08012.011642/2008-72, involving *American Safety Razor do Brasil Ltda., ASR Exportação, Importação, Comércio e Indústria de Produtos de Barbear Ltda. and Hypermarcas S.A., Councillor Vinícus Marques de Carvalho* stated:

> The Office of the CADE Attorney ('ProCADE') noted the need of assessing the three main points, as follows: (i) the actual need of the non-compete clause as a requirement for the viability of the transaction; (ii) the consistency of the material, geographic and time, aspects of the non-compete clause to the minimum parameters; and (iii) the analysis of the justifications made for the non-compete clause should it fail to comply thereto. In reviewing such issues, the ProCADE concluded that the proposed clause is admissible, since, aside from being adequate as to the material and time aspects, the clause is justified and supported by CADE precedents, and make special note that the clause is consistent with the very purpose of the contract and that the nature of the transaction permits such exception to the rule that restricts the validity of the non-compete clause to the term of 5 years subsequent to the transaction being perfected (free translation).

715. The Brazilian Civil Code of 2002 imposed on the seller of a commercial enterprise the obligation not to compete with the purchaser for a term of at least five years, as of the date the business is transferred, save if the parties expressly agree otherwise.

716. However, and based on such provision of the Civil Code, the CADE has affirmed the validity of non-compete clauses, but for a maximum term of five years, save for certain exceptional cases in which it has accepted longer terms. The CADE requires, furthermore, that the scope of its application be restricted to the geographic area of the relevant market.

717. Examples of decisions where the CADE has consented to a period longer than five years are the following. In Act of Concentration No. 08012.006897/2001-47, involving *Libra Terminal Rio S/A and Multi-Rio Operações Portuárias S/A*, Councillor Thompson Almeida Andrade stated (emphasis added):

> However, it is not possible to consider a time limit for a non-compete clause of this nature. Indeed, the Applicants have jointly supported with the expansion of the water access seeking the joint servicing of large size vessels, it would be totally absurd if one of the Applicants would be permitted to separately compete with the Joint Venture, formed solely and exclusively to service vessels of the same type.
>
> In such case there is no offence to precedents made by this Council. Such is a totally different case from those that are generally reviewed by the Brazilian Competition Defence System.
>
> Thus, it is my opinion that the non-compete clause inserted in the Operational Agreement is perfectly acceptable and that it does not injure the market (free translation).

718. In Act of Concentration No. 08012.004771/2001-39, involving *Vega Engenharia Ambiental S/A and Koleta Ambiental S/A*, Councillor Cleveland Prates Teixeira stated (emphasis added):

> It makes sense, therefore, that the non-compete clause be effective for the life of the agreement entered by the parties. As to the five years immediately subsequent to the end of the association between the companies in Koleta Ambiental, I consider that they are consistent with the CADE precedents, which admits as reasonable that such term ensures the continuity of the business without the competition of the former participant. Should such limitation fail to exist, at the end of the agreement, the former partner could take advantage of the knowledge and of the corporate relationships acquired **during the life of the joint venture to conquer the latter's clients.** For such reason I do believe that the clause, as worded in the contract, is reasonable (free translation; emphasis added).

719. Such understanding has become settled, and on 12 August 2008, the CADE has enacted Abstract No. 4, worded as follows (free translation):

> Agreement on a non-compete clause effective for the life of a Joint Venture is licit, as long as it shall have a direct relation with the object thereof and be restricted to the relevant markets where it shall do business.

720. An Abstract, under Brazilian law, means a summary containing the settled interpretation of a court in connection with a specific issue, with the twofold purpose of making such understanding a matter of public knowledge and of promoting uniformity among the decisions. The CADE Abstract No. 4 seeks to render crystal clear the settled understanding of the Council in connection with non-compete clauses relating to JVs.

721. On its turn, CADE Abstract No. 5 rules that non-compete clauses related to the sale of a commercial business is licit, provided that its term shall not exceed five years and that it is effectively related to the relevant trade, meaning to the protection of the trade secrets of the affected company, to its know-how, client portfolio and distribution and supply networks. Again, such five-year term was being considered by the CADE, for a long time, a sufficient term of validity for such.

722. Despite the fact that the CADE generally considers JV arrangements pro-competitive, it has not failed to raise competitive concerns under certain circumstances.

723. In the *consortium* created by and between *Votorantim Celulose e Papel (VCP) and Suzano* to acquire the stock control (on a 50%–50% basis) and plant of Ripasa (Acts of Concentration Nos 08012.010192/2004-77 and 08012.010195/2004-19), all being paper and pulp companies, the CADE expressed one of such concerns. As a result of the transaction, Ripasa would cease to be an independent producer and change into a joint captive producer to the purchasers.

724. In reviewing the transaction, the CADE came to the conclusion that the *consortium* could motivate a tacit collusion between the parties in an already highly concentrated segment of the market (the uncoated cut size paper market), given that the transaction would permit a permanent interaction between the parties, risking an undue exchange of competitively sensitive information. Thus, the deal would reduce the asymmetry of information between the parties and their independence in their respective decision-making processes. It concluded that the transaction could only be cleared by requiring the parties to enter into a Settlement Agreement (*Termo de Compromisso de Desempenho*), whereby certain remedies would be imposed to reduce the possibility of the *consortium* becoming a *forum* for collusion or enabling instruments of retaliation deterrent of aggressive competitive strategies of one another.

725. The second benchmark case was related to a cooperative JV, involving competitors *White Martins and Air Liquide* (Act of Concentration No. 08012.011196/2005-53), incorporated with the purpose of constructing a new productive capacity to supply gas to a single consumer, *Companhia Siderúrgica do Atlântico* (*CSA*), a steel company the plant of which is still under construction.

726. Again the CADE concluded that the JV could motivate a tacit collusion between the parties, since the arrangement could facilitate the exchange of sensible information between competitors (i.e., the transaction would reduce the costs of coordination between the parties). Furthermore, the CADE reached the conclusion that the deal did not disclose factors that could mitigate the full exercise of market power resulting from the coordinated action of the applicants. Ultimately, the case was cleared through a Settlement Agreement (*Termo de Compromisso de Desempenho*) whereby *White Martins* was prohibited from participating in the management of the venture. An independent manager approved by the CADE would represent the interests of the company.

Part III. Administrative Procedure

Chapter 1. Administrative Investigations Before the Antitrust Authority

§1. Initiative

I. General Sectors Enquiries and Ex Officio Investigations

727. The GS has the statutory authority of permanently monitoring market practices by individuals and legal entities enjoying a dominant position and of requesting information and documents from both public and private parties.

728. Paying close attention to the general media or to enforcement actions in other jurisdictions on matters possibly affecting the Brazilian markets, the competition authorities not infrequently engage into informal investigations called preparatory proceedings or internal studies to determine if a given market phenomenon may cause antitrust concerns. In such tasks, the GS often engage into enquiries before the relevant sectors, by requesting information to, or seeking comments from, legal entities, trade associations or other public authorities.

729. A large number of investigations are commenced by the GS ex officio, at the authority discretion. Presence of minimum evidence of anticompetitive conduct is not required for the GS to engage into a preparatory proceeding or industry study, but minimum circumstantial evidence of an offensive conduct is mandatory for the commencement of a formal administrative investigation, preceding an Administrative Process, when a formal charge is made.

730. Preparatory proceedings in virtually all cases, and many administrative investigations, are carried out *in camera*, in order to protect the investigation from undue interference or obstructive actions by the interested parties. Experience has shown, however, that the authorities have little care for parties' intimacy or privacy rights, or for the parties' constitutional rights to presumption of innocence.

731. The GS is a quite active competition authority, engaged in more than 100 investigations every year. In the course of the first anniversary of the current Brazilian Competition Law (effective as of 29 May 2011), the CADE heard twenty-three administrative proceedings related to anticompetitive conducts, out of which, eleven resulted in condemnation.[65]

732. The principal current cases (April 2013) under investigation at the GS are:

(1) Administrative Process No. 08012.005255/2010-11, involving *SDE ex officio and Elpida Memory, Inc. et alii* concerning the investigation of a possible international cartel, with impact in Brazil, in the dynamic random access memory (DRAM) market.
(2) Administrative Process No. 08012.009885/2009-21, involving *Companhia de Saneamento Básico do Estado de São Paulo – SABESP and Saenge* Engenharia *de Saneamento e Edificações Ltda. et alii* concerning the investigation of a possible cartel formed to defraud a public tender bid carried to perform services in connection with the works of certain water reservoirs in the metropolitan area of Santos, State of São Paulo.
(3) Administrative Process No. 08012.004365/2010-66, involving *Ministério Público do Estado de Santa Catarina v. Farmácia Frei Rogério et alii*, concerning the investigation of a ridding system created by nine pharmacies in the city of Curitibanos, State of Santa Catarina, whereby each week, a different pharmacy would grant higher discount than the other and established maximum discounts to be granted to consumer.
(4) Administrative Process No. 08012.011980/2008-12, involving *SDE ex officio v. Chunghwa Picture Tubes Ltd. et alii*, concerning the formation of a possible international cartel, with impact in Brazil, of TFT-LCD displays.
(5) Administrative Process No. 08012.002608/2007-26, *involving Cervejaria* Kaiser *Brasil S.A. v. Companhia de Bebidas das Américas – AmBev and Cervejarias Reunidas Skol Caracu S.A*, concerning exclusivity arrangements entered by AmBev with retailers preventing rival beer companies from entering certain sales outlets, including by the offer of exclusive freezers one for each AmBev brands.
(6) Administrative Process No. 08012.008554/2008-93, involving *Cervejaria Kaiser* Brasil *S.A. v. Companhia de Bebidas das Américas – AmBev and Cervejarias Reunidas Skol Caracu S.A.*, concerning the investigation of the launching by AmBev of certain beer brands ('Puerto Del Sol' and 'Puerto Del Mar') simultaneously with the launching of the beer 'Sol' in the Brazilian market, given that the two brands and the marketing plans of such competing brands were quite similar to those adopted by the 'Sol' producers in other countries, possibly seeking to mislead the consumers and create a barrier to entry to the competitor.
(7) Administrative Process No. 08012.001772/2009-88, involving *SDE ex officio v. Associação Brasileira da Indústria de Chocolates, Cacau,* Amendoim, *Balas e Derivados (Abicab) et alii*, concerning the investigation of the dissemination of commercially sensitive information that may eventually result in the adoption of a uniform conduct by that chocolate industry trade association.
(8) Administrative Process No. 08012.009264/2002-71, in re. *Secretaria de* Acompanhamento *Econômico – SEAE/MF v. GSL Carbon AG et alii*, concerning the possible formation of a global cartel in the graphite electrode market.

65. *See* http://www.cade.gov.br/Default.aspx?ca7e8c9d77ac43c055e275cd65ed.

(9) Preliminary Investigation No. 08012.009696/2008-78, involving *Associação Brasileira dos Provedores de Acesso, Serviços e Informações da Rede Internet – ABRANET v. Telecomunicações de São Paulo S.A.* – TELESP, concerning ABRANET's motion for precautionary measures against TELESP in the Internet broad band connection service in the State of São Paulo.

(10) Administrative Process No. 08012.000291/2004-41, involving *Agência Nacional de Energia Elétrica v. Conservo Brasília Empresa de Segurança Ltda. et alii*, concerning investigations on the formation of a possible cartel to defraud public tender bids made by public bodies in the Federal District (Brasília) in connection with the outsourcing of technical and operational support related to cleaning, security, transportation and computer services.

(11) Administrative Process No. 08012.012081/2007-48, involving *Conselho Administrativo de Defesa Econômica – CADE v. Multiplan* Empreendimentos *Imobiliários S.A. (Shopping Morumbi) et alii*, concerning the legality of non-compete clauses (radius clause) in connection with the rental of commercial space in shopping centres, whereby shops are prohibited from opening branches in certain streets, commercial centres or shopping centres.

(12) Administrative Process No. 08012.012740/2007-56, involving *Ministério Público Federal – Procuradoria da República no Rio Grande do Sul v.* Administradora *Gaúcha de Shopping Centres S/C Ltda. (Shopping Iguatemi) et alii*, also concerning an investigation on the legality of radius clauses adopted by shopping centres.

(13) Administrative Process No. 08012.002474/2008-24, involving Associação dos Fabricantes de Refrigerantes do Brasil (Afrebras), *Cervejaria Imperial, Associação Brasileira de Bebidas (Abrabe) and Cervejaria Kaiser Brasil S/A. v. Companhia de Bebidas das Américas – AmBev*, concerning investigations on the legality of the launching by AmBev of a returnable amber 630 ml glass beer bottle with the embossed engraved inscription 'AmBev' in the markets of the States of Rio Grande do Sul and Rio de Janeiro.

(14) Administrative Process No. 08012.003321/2004-71 involving *SDE ex officio v.* Baxter *AG et alii*, concerning investigations on the possible formation of a cartel in connection with tender bids for the acquisition of blood products – Factor VIII (used in the treatment of homophile) promoted by the Ministry of Health between 1998 and 2003.

(15) Administrative Process No. 08012.004674/2006-50, involving *Senator Eduardo* Matarazzo *Suplicy v. ABIEF – Associação Brasileira de Embalagens Flexíveis et alii*, concerning investigations on the possible formation of a cartel in the flexible, especially in the segment of retrogravures.

II. Complaints

733. Third-party complaints, along with ex officio actions, are virtually equal in volume of investigations.

734. Since Brazilian Competition Law rules that free competition is a constitutional right, and the legal interest, of all of the Brazilian Society, complaints may be made by any individual or legal entity, having legal standing or interest, or not, on the underlying subject matter or facts.

735. Complaints are subject to no formality. They may be made orally, by telephone, or in written or electronic form. No special form or document, and no minimum evidence, is required. Anonymous complaints are not uncommon, although legally controversial. In such cases, the GS qualifies the case as an ex officio investigation to circumvent the potential illegality of the private complaint. The GS website[66] displays an icon Click Complaint (*Clique Denúncia*) inviting the public to place electronic complaints.

736. Complaints are only outrightly rejected in case they are prima facie a private issue only, given that the CADE has no authority to settle private disputes, or when they are unintelligible.

§2. Powers

I. Requests for Information

737. All Brazilian competition authorities (CADE, through its bodies administrative tribunal and GS, SEAE, the ANATEL, in the telecommunication market, and the BACEN, in the financial institutions market) have statutory authority to request information and documents from any individual, legal entity (both private and public) and public authorities. No party is immune from such authorities' investigative actions.

738. Parties, however, are not required to produce incriminating evidence against themselves, and they have the right to remain silent. Only witnesses, third parties other than the undertaking subject to the investigation, make depositions under oath and may be liable for perjury.

739. The unjustified refusal or omission in the supply of information or documents to the CADE or the SEAE, or the supply of misleading information or document, is a punishable conduct, subject to a daily fine of BRL 5,000 that may be multiplied up to twenty times, to ensure effectiveness of the relevant order (Article 40 of Law No. 12529). Failure to comply with the authorities' enquiries may also eventually constitute a criminal offence, subject to jail sentence (detention) of two to five years, or a fine.

740. Such statutory provisions governing the unjustified refusal or omission in the supply of information or documents to the competition authorities, or the supply of misleading information or document not infrequently conflicts with the constitutional principles of ample defence.

741. Therefore, the mere use of misleading allegations by a defendant party in responding to an administrative charge of anticompetitive conduct is insufficient for the assessment of a fine based on the supply of 'misleading information'. The misled

66. http://www.cade.gov.br/Default.aspx?43e324ec33d152e87fc095.

information must be in response to a specific official request made by the competition authorities.[67]

742. By the same token, the mere fact that a party has made comments making its own interpretation of the facts is likewise insufficient,[68] provided, however, that the CADE has warned that should a party file a motion giving its interpretation on a certain contractual clause, its eventual and subsequent attempt, in or out of court, to secure a different interpretation shall constitute a misleading conduct and subject the offender to the fine set forth in Article 40 of Law No. 12529, without prejudice of the revision of the CADE Resolution handed based on said original motion, all pursuant to Article 91 of the same law.[69]

743. A fine may also be imposed on a defendant or a third party, in case of unjustified refusal to give oral explanations in the course of an administrative investigation or proceeding.

II. Investigating and Search Powers

744. Large investigating powers are vested unto the competition authorities in performing an investigation. The authorities routinely make written enquiries and requests take oral depositions and request perusals in the course of the proceedings.

745. The Administrative Court, the Councillor Examiner and the GS have, further, the statutory authority of performing *in loco* inspections, provided that prior notice is served on the target entity. The target entity is entitled to object to the inspection. The prior notice requirement has caused such inspections to be rare.

746. Seeking to preserve the element of surprise of the investigating activities, the GS may also engage in dawn raiding operations. Search and seizure warrants, however, may only be issued by the courts, and, for such purposes, the GS is required to resort to the Office of the CADE Attorney General (PFE).

747. Dawn raiding is performed by the Federal or State Civil Police, frequently in the presence of GS officers and members of the Office of the Attorney General (Prosecutors).

748. The participation of the competition authorities in a dawn raiding, however, must be authorized by a competent judicial authority and, whenever permitted shall seek: (i) to permit efficiency in the selection of the documents and papers, (ii) to ensure that the largest number of evidence on the investigated conduct is obtained and (iii) to avoid the seizure of documents and papers unrelated to the object of the investigation. Raids may only be carried out at daylight of working days.

749. The warrant enabling the dawn raiding must contain: (i) the address where the seizure is to take place (there is no requirement for the exact indication where the

67. Resolution by the sixth Chamber of the Federal Regional Court (TRF) for the first. Region in hearing Civil Appeal No. 2000.34.00.000087-1/DF, on 14 Jun. 2010, in re *Usinas Siderúrgicas de Minas Gerais – USIMINAS v. Conselho Administrativo de Defesa Econômica – CADE.*

68. *See* Motion for Clarification in Act of Concentration No. 08012.009599/2009-66, resolved on 9 Jun. 2010, filed by *Pepsico do Brasil Ltda. and Quercegen Agronegócios I Ltda.*

69. *See* Motion for Clarification in Act of Concentration No. 08012.005296/2010-16, resolved on 4 Aug. 2010, filed by *UBS AG.*

material to be seized is located), (ii) the motives and purpose of the action and (iii) that the order be issued by the competent authority. The order must permit the seizure of documents that are located in the indicated place, regardless of who shall be the owner of such documents. Usually, the investigators may seize, without limitation, inventory, objects, papers of any nature, commercial books, computers and magnetic files, and may request copies of any documents or electronic data.

750. It is the understanding of the CADE that the judicial warrant authorizing a dawn raiding is not subject to any suspensive effect. Thus, the use by the GS of the seized material is not conditional upon the final trial court resolution on the relevant precautionary action, given the CADE statutory obligation to proceed with related investigation.[70]

751. Under Law No. 12529, obstructing in any way an authorized or expressly objected inspection by the administrative tribunal, the Councillor Examiner or the GS shall subject the offender to a fine between BRL 20,000 and BRL 400,000 depending on the economic status of the obstructing party.

752. Obstructing a police dawn raiding supported by a court warrant represents a criminal offence (Article 329 of the Brazilian Penal Code – Resistance) subject to jail sentences of two months to two years or of one year to three years (if the raid fails to occur as a result of the obstruction).

III. Cooperation with Other State Institutions

753. Both in the exercise of investigating and of competition advocacy activities, the competition authorities have entered in multiple formal cooperation agreements such as:

Agreement with Government Ministries:

(a) Agreement No. 1/2008 between the Federal Government, acting through the Ministry of Justice, and the CADE, of 30 December 2008.

Agreements with Regulatory Agencies:

(a) Agreement among the SDE/SEAE and the BACEN, of 14 July 2006.
(b) Technological Interoperations Agreement among the CADE, the SEAE and the SDE, of 16 March 2007.
(c) Technical Cooperation Agreement between the CADE and the Brazilian Securities Exchange Commission (CVM), of 24 July 2008.
(d) Technical Agreement among the CADE/SDE/SEAE and the ANS, of 2 June 2009.
(e) Technical Cooperation Agreement between the CADE and the Civil Aviation National Agency (ANAC), of 19 November 2009.
(f) Agreement between the CADE and the National Department of Mineral Production (DNPM), of 7 April 2010.

70. Administrative Process No. 08012.004702/2004-77 (resolved on 9 May 2012), in re, *SDE, ex officio v. Peróxidos do Brasil Ltda. et alii.*

(g) Technical Cooperation Agreement between the CADE, the SDE and the Industrial Property National Institute (INPI), of 7 June 2010.
(h) Agreement between the CADE, the SDE, the SEAE and ANEEL, of 21 July 2010, for the Joint Acting Seeking the Prevention and Repression of Offences to the Economic Order in the Electric Field.
(i) Cooperation Agreement No. 2/2013 between the CADE and the ANVISA, of 29 January 2013.
(j) Cooperation Agreement No. 5/2013 between the CADE and the ANS, of 18 March 2013.
(k) Technical Cooperation Agreement No. 6/2013 between the CADE and the ANP, of 3 April 2013.

Agreements with Judicial-Related Entities:

(a) Cooperation Agreement No. 4/2013 between the CADE and the Federal Judges' Association (AJUFE), of 20 February 2013.

Agreement with Research and Academic Institutions:

(a) Agreement between the CADE and the Applied Economic Research Institute (IPEA), of 18 August 2010.
(b) Cooperation Agreement No. 1/2013 between the CADE and the Economic and Social Law Studies Center (CEDES), of 28 January 2013.

Agreements with Consumer Law-Related Authorities:

(a) Cooperation Agreement between the CADE and the Consumer National Secretariat (SENACON) of the Ministry of Justice, of 18 July 2012.

754. Cooperation with other State institutions is an increasing activity of the competition authorities and additional cooperation agreements are expected, with prejudice of such authorities' constant contacts and interface with virtually all regulatory agencies, principal Government departments and State criminal authorities. In the State of São Paulo, the SDE has played an important role in the creation, in 2008, of a special permanent task force in São Paulo Prosecutors Office, named Special Task Force for the Repression of Cartels and Money Laundering, and the Recovery of Assets – GEDEC. The SDE has been replaced by the GS in its interface with the GEDEC.

§3. Right of Defence

I. Content and Notification of Opening Decisions

755. Investigations may be commenced by the GS through a preparatory proceeding or through an administrative investigation or an Administrative Process.

756. Generally, preparatory proceedings seek to informally investigate facts that may or may not constitute an anticompetitive conduct, and only preliminary information or insufficient evidence is made available to the authorities. Whenever circumstantial evidence is in the possession of the authorities, but insufficient to permit a formal charge, administrative investigations are commenced. Once sufficient evidence of an anticompetitive conduct is available and a possible offender is identified, then a formal administrative process is commenced.

757. Not infrequently, however, the authorities improperly resort to *in camera* preparatory proceedings or to administrative investigations in order to proceed with investigations on a confidential basis, disregarding the parties' right of ample defence and adversary proceedings.

758. Opening decisions in connection with preparatory proceedings are internal to the GS, and no formal notification of the parties is required. Parties and third interested parties are invited to comment on facts or requested to supply information or documents at the discretion of the authorities. The authorities will not volunteer to parties any document describing the reasons for their engagement in preparatory proceedings, provided that parties (not third interested parties) are permitted to have access to the dockets and to obtain copies thereof.

759. A decision of the technical staff of the GS in charge of the preparatory proceedings of dismissing, and closing a preparatory proceeding, is appealable only to the GS.

760. In the event the authorities will determine that the facts may characterize an anticompetitive conduct, but available circumstantial evidence is insufficient for a formal charge, an administrative investigation will be opened. Although no statutory provision requires the notification of defendants of the proceedings, such notification is customary, requiring the party to comment thereon.

761. The GS shall issue a monocratic resolution as to whether the conclusions of the administrative investigation should be converted into an Administrative Process or closed, provided that the CADE administrative tribunal does have a call-back right to review the Superintendent General's decision to close an administrative investigation.

762. Preparatory proceedings are to be closed within thirty days and administrative investigations are to be closed within 180 days, extendable for additional sixty days, but such statutory terms are not mandatory and are seldom observed.

763. Should sufficient evidence of an anticompetitive conduct, in the opinion of the GS be available, it shall bring a formal charge through an Administrative Process. Such Process should commence within ten days from the closing of the prior administrative investigation. Such term, again, is not mandatory to the authorities and is frequently disregarded.

764. Once an Administrative Process is installed, the defendants will be notified by mail, receipt requested, and contain a copy of the commencement order and of the complaint, if any. The opening decision issued by the GS must contain: (a) the identification of the defendant and of the claimant, if any, (b) the description of the charge and of the facts under investigation, (c) the determination of the allegedly offended statutory provisions, (d) the order of notification of the defendant to file the response to the action within thirty days (such term may be extended by an additional ten-day term, upon request) and (e) the order to the defendant to specify the evidence that it wishes to produce and allowing the defendant to present up to three witnesses.

765. The term to respond to the charges will be doubled in case of multiple defendants represented by more than one attorney.

766. If it is not possible to serve the process personally on the defendant, it is made through official summons published in the official press (Federal Official Gazette) and in a leading local newspaper. Again, the notice will contain a copy of the complaint (if any) and of the technical opinion of the GS that supported the commencement of the Process.

767. Defendant is required to address in the response all arguments in its defence, including all documents in support of its allegations, provided that such issues may be broadly or generally addressed. All issues not addressed by defendant may be taken as a party confession of the related facts.

768. Save for confidential documents, which are accessible only to the relevant party, or to the authorities if such documents are classified, the records are public; any interested party can freely obtain copies of the records.

II. The Proceedings: Hearings, Access to File, Briefs

769. Defendants are not required to be represented by attorneys-at-law and in all cases will have full access to the dockets of the Administrative Process, save for such documents and information that the authorities deem to be confidential, seeking to protect sensitive competitive information from being made available to competitors, or classified. Confidential information can only be accessed by the party having an interest thereon, and classified information can only be accessed by the competent authorities.

770. Upon the expiration of the term for the filing of the responses to the charge, the GS will specify, in thirty business days, the evidence that it intends to produce, including witness depositions, provided that, de facto, the GS will take all other initiatives it may deem convenient or necessary to prove its case in the course of the procedures. Public authorities are required by law to render all assistance to, and to supply all information required by, the Superintendency.

771. Perusals and expertise may be made, as applicable, for the conclusion of the discovery phase, provided that such perusals and expertise are rare. Scholar and expert opinions are customarily submitted by defendants.

772. The burden of proof is by law vested unto the GS, provided, however, that de facto such burden is generally reversed and incriminating evidence, including mere circumstantial evidence, is frequently given a heavier weight in the investigating authorities' view. Presumption of innocence is widely disregarded.

773. Within up to five business days as of the conclusion of the discovery phase, the GS shall notify the respondent to present new (final) allegations, within five business days. Again, such a term is doubled whenever there are multiple defendants represented by more than one attorney-in-fact.

774. Within up to fifteen business days as of the expiration of the term set forth above, the Superintendency shall submit the records to the President of the administrative tribunal and recommend, on a reasoned report, whether the case is to be dismissed or whether an anticompetitive conduct should be affirmed.

775. The law does not provide for a term for the conclusion of the discovery phase. Historically, de facto, investigations normally take years to be concluded.

III. Final Hearing and Decision

776. Upon receiving the records, the President of the administrative tribunal shall randomly assign the case to a Councillor Examiner, who may, on a discretionary basis, require the non-binding opinion of the Office of the CADE Attorney General (PFE). Such opinion is to be given within twenty days.

777. The Councillor Examiner may, on a discretionary basis, order further investigation or actions, including to the GS. The Councillor will be permitted to complement (or to re-initiate, if deemed necessary or convenient) the discovery phase. Requests for additional information and documents and other initiatives, including the hearing of the parties, of experts and of third interested parties, and the submission of formal and information motions and expert and scholar opinions, as well as meetings with Councillors, members of the Panel of the administrative tribunal, are rather common.

778. The Councillor Examiner may also request the non-binding opinion of the Office of the Federal Attorney General (MPF), provided that the MPF has the statutory authority to, at its discretion, issue unsolicited non-binding opinions.

779. Once such supplementary discovery phase is concluded, the Councillor Examiner shall notify the defendants, enabling them to submit, within fifteen business days (again, doubled in case of multiple defendants represented by more than one attorney-in-fact), a final summation.

780. Within fifteen business days as of the receipt of the final summations, the Councillor Examiner shall call for the trial of the case by the Panel of the administrative tribunal.

781. At the Final Session, the Superintendent General, the Chief Economist, the CADE Attorney General, the complainant (if his participation is deemed convenient or of interest to the Panel of the administrative tribunal) and the defendant's attorney-in-fact, in such order, will be allowed to address the Panel and make oral submissions for fifteen minutes. The MPF, acting as *custos legis*, will also be permitted to make oral submissions for fifteen minutes after the defendant's submission. Third parties or individuals, at the request of the Councillor Examiner, may be called to the stand. Whereupon, the Councillor Examiner will cast his vote.

782. Following, the member Councillors of the administrative tribunal will debate (the defendants and their attorneys-in-fact may be called for clarifications) and vote, and a final determination will be made by simple majority. In case of a tie, the President of the administrative tribunal will decide (swing vote).

783. All CADE Resolutions are subject to judicial control and review.

Chapter 2. Voluntary Notifications and Clearance Decisions in Merger Control

§1. Preliminary Filing Obligations

I. Criteria and Thresholds

784. Pursuant to Article 88 of the Brazilian Competition Law (Law No. 12,529/11), the 'acts of economic concentration' which cumulatively meet the following thresholds shall be subject to the CADE notification requirement:[71]

(1) – at least one of the groups involved in the transaction has recorded, in the last balance sheet, gross annual sales or total turnover in Brazil, in the year preceding the transaction, equivalent or superior to BRL 750,000,000 (seven hundred and fifty million reais); and
(2) – at least one other group involved in the transaction has registered, in the last balance sheet, gross annual sales or total turnover in the country, in the year preceding the transaction, equivalent or superior to BRL 75,000,000 (seventy five million reais).

785. The Law (Article 90) defines an 'act of economic concentration' as being a transaction in which:

(1) – two or more previously independent undertakings merge;
(2) – one or more undertakings acquire, directly or indirectly, by purchase or exchange of stocks, shares, bonds or securities convertible into stocks or assets, whether tangible or intangible, by contract or by any other means or way, the control or parts of one or other undertaking;
(3) – one or more undertaking incorporate one or other companies, or
(4) – two or more companies enter into an associative contract, *consortium* or JV.

786. Neither the law nor the CADE has defined an 'associative contract', thus creating a large uncertainty as to the notification requirement in connection with collaboration agreements.

787. An important case preceding the discussions on the definition of 'associative contract' may be found in the resolution adopted by the CADE in Act of Concentration No. 08012.000182/2010-71 (resolved on 11 March 2010), involving *Monsanto do Brasil Ltda. and Iharabras S.A. Indústrias Químicas*, whereby mere supply agreements that: (a) do not require the transfer of rights in connection of competitively sensitive assets, (b) do not provide for exclusive clauses or equivalent clauses of any nature

71. Amounts adjusted by Inter-ministerial Ordinance No. 994, of 30 May 2012.

capable of restricting decision-making rights in connection with assets (products or services), (c) have a term of less than five years (considering eventual extensions), (d) contain immediate termination clauses at no cost to the interested party and (e) do not represent the negotiation of a product volume in excess of 20% of the relevant market output are not subject to the CADE notification requirement.

788. However, the matter is still unsettled, as it can be seen in Act of Concentration No. 08012.006625/2011-19 (resolved on 27 July 2011), in re. *Monsanto do Brasil Ltda. e Milênia Agrociências S.A.* which, although recognizing that the relevant supply agreement was entered on a non-exclusive basis and provided for the unilateral termination, thereof, by any of the parties at no cost, subject only to a prior notice, the CADE recognized it, merely because the parties had met the statutory turnover threshold calling for the CADE notification requirement.

789. Law No. 12529/11, however, expressly exempted from the notification requirement collaboration agreements *consortia* and JVs dedicated to public tender bids promoted by the Public Administration and to the related contracts.

790. Further, and in connection with the purchase of stock (Article 90, item II of Law No. 12529/11), CADE Resolution No. 2/2012, of 29 May 2012, ruled that the transactions are subject to the notification requirement whenever they:

I. – Result in a stock control.

II. – Do not result in the stock control but grant the purchaser the status of the largest individual stockholder of the target company or that meet any of the following *de minimis* rules:

(i) whenever the target company is not a competitor, nor operates in a vertically related market:

(1) the purchase shall grant the purchaser direct or indirect ownership of 20% or more of the capital stock or of the voting stock of the target company;
(2) the purchase is made by a purchaser, holder of 20% or more of the capital stock or of the voting stock of the target company, and the stock that is directly or indirectly purchased from a single seller, individually considered, shall represent 20% or more of the capital stock or the voting stock of the target company.

(ii) whenever the target company is a competitor or operates in a vertically related market:

(1) the purchase shall grant a direct or indirect participation of 5% or more of the capital stock or of the voting stock of the target company;
(2) the last purchase which, either individually or added to other purchases, shall result in a shareholding increase greater than or equal to 5%, should the investor already hold 5% or more of the capital stock or of the voting stock of the target company.

III. – Are made by a controlling stockholder, provided that the stockholding that is directly or indirectly acquired from a single seller, considered individually, is equal to or in excess of 20% (twenty per cent) of the capital stock or of the voting stock of the target company.

791. For the purposes of qualifying a transaction under items I and II above, the activities of the purchasing undertaking and those of the other undertakings of its economic unit are to be jointly considered.

792. For such purposes, an economic unit is defined to be (Article 4, §1, of CADE Resolution No. 2), on a cumulative basis:

(1) – the undertakings that are under common internal or external control; and
(2) – the undertakings in which any of the undertakings mentioned in item I above shall be directly or indirectly the holder of 20% or more of the capital stock or of the voting stock.

793. In the case of investment funds, the following shall be considered as members of the same economic unit, on a cumulative basis:

(1) – the funds that are under the same management;
(2) – the manager;
(3) – the quotaholders that are the direct or indirect holders of more than 20% of the quotas of at least one of the funds mentioned in item I above; and
(4) – the undertakings that are members of the fund's portfolio in which the direct or indirect participation of the fund is equal or superior to 20% of the capital stock or of the voting stock.

794. All transactions subject to notification requirements are improperly called 'acts of economic concentration', albeit in certain cases the underlying deal shall have the opposite effect, such as in the case of termination of a JV, purchase or lease of inoperative assets of a bankrupt estate, sale of minority shareholding, market entry etc.

795. In conflict with Constitutional principles of free initiative, the Brazilian Competition Law carries a presumption of illegality of mergers and acquisition, and as such is questionable as to its constitutionality in that respect. In Article 88, §5, of Law No. 12529/11, all acts of concentration yielding the elimination of competition in a substantial portion of the relevant market, or that may create or strengthen a dominant position, or result in the domination of the relevant market of goods or services are by law prohibited.

796. By reversing the constitutional principle of presumption of legality of mergers and acquisitions, the law rules that certain acts of concentration may be permitted, as long as the limits strictly necessary to achieve the following objections are observed:

(1) cumulatively or alternatively:

(a) Increase productivity or competitiveness.
(b) Improve the quality of goods or services.
(c) Encourage efficiency and technological or economic development.

(2) a relevant part of the benefits resulting from the transaction is shared with consumers.

II. Turnover Calculation

797. As mentioned, all acts of concentration, in which at least one of the economic units involved in the transaction shall have gross annual sales or total turnover equivalent or superior to BRL 750,000,000 and, cumulatively, at least one other group shall have gross annual sales or total turnover equivalent or superior to BRL 75,000,000 will be subject to the CADE notification requirement.

798. For the purpose of calculating such turnover, only the turnover obtained in Brazil shall be taken into account. The calculation of the turnover of Brazilian companies is based on the accounting turnover[72] shown in the financial statements. With respect to foreign companies, the turnover will consider the income obtained from exports to Brazil or from other funds originated from the country (e.g., payment for services rendered to Brazilian companies).[73]

799. Should such turnover be denominated in a currency other than reais, the amount thereof in a foreign denomination is to be converted into the Brazilian currency by the exchange rate in force on the last working day of the relevant fiscal year.[74] Such exchange rate methodology is not mandatory, and the parties may suggest a different criteria as long as they justify the selected methodology and period of reference.

III. Other Relevant Notions

800. Mergers and acquisitions (acts of concentration) are reviewed through a procedure called 'Administrative Process for the Analysis of Acts of Economic Concentration'.[75]

801. The review of 'acts of concentration' is carried out under a rather rigid structure-conduct-performance paradigm, whereby the market structure is deemed to be the result of market supply (control of production assets) and demand (structure of preferences) conditions.

72. Motion for Revision based on new fact No. 08700.003776/05-19, resolved on 24 May 2006, filed by TBA Informática Ltda.
73. *See* the vitamin cartel case (Administrative Process No. 08012.004599/1999-18 brought against *F. Hoffman – La Roche Ltd., Basf Aktiengesellschaft and Rhône-Poulenc* (formerly Aventis Animal Nutrition)), in which the fine was based on the turnover of the vitamins exported to Brazil.
74. *See* Motion for Clarification No. 08012.002915/2009-79, resolved on 16 Sep. 2009, filed by Penske Logistics do Brasil Ltda.
75. In Pòrtuguese: '*Processo Administrativo para Análise de Ato de Concentração Econômica*'.

802. Key elements of such analysis are: (a) determination of the relevant market and of the market structure (market shares), (b) the review of barriers to entry and entry thresholds, (c) rivalry and (d) economic efficiencies.

803. Market share is dependent on the definition of 'relevant market', both in its product and geographic dimensions.

804. Identification of the relevant market is made pursuant to the Hypothetical Monopolist Test that seeks to determine the smallest group of products and the smallest geographic area that are necessary to enable a presumed monopolist to impose a small, albeit significant and non-transitory price increase.

805. From the supply-side, the principle variables considered are, without limitation, raw materials and inputs, technology, level of unionization, legal framework and environment etc. From the demand-side, demand elasticity, substitute products, growth levels, season and cyclic characteristics are, *inter alia*, considered.

806. The market-structure analysis will then proceed by determining the number of incumbent and eventually potential players, product differentiation, and barriers to entry, cost structure, vertical integrations and product diversification.

807. In determining a market structure, it is important to have in mind the concept of economic unit. Thus, not only all those firms that operate in a given market that are controlled (internally or externally, de jure or de facto) or are under a dominant influence by another are to be considered as a single economic unit, but also those firms in which the party to the transaction has a relevant influence in the corporate or business decision-making process.[76]

808. Examples of a 'relevant influence' are:

(a) the minority shareholder that has the right to appoint members to the management of the target company does enjoy a relevant influence in the decision-making process of the latter;[77] and
(b) the participation of an investment fund in an act of concentration, that participates in the decision-making process of the target company, having an actual influence in the determination of its strategic policy and management, specially through the appointment of members to the board of directors, shall be recognized as having a relevant influence.[78]

809. Actually, the CADE has only recently become more flexible in identifying an economic unit. Indeed, in Act of Concentration No. 08012.004864/2008-39, resolved on 25 June 2008, involving *RIM 1947 Participações S.A., JRM 1953 Participações S.A. and ZRM 1955 Participações S.A.*, it was decided that even in such cases of a merely financial investment in a minority shareholding in the target company, a relevant influence was to be affirmed in connection with the new investors, to the extent that each of the shares would enjoy voting rights in the General Shareholders' Meeting.

76. *See* Act of Concentration No. 08012.004841/2010-49, resolved on 4 Aug. 2010, involving *MIH Buscapé International B.V. and Park One Holdings Inc.*
77. *See* Act of Concentration No. 08012.010626/2008-62, resolved on 4 Feb. 2009, involving *Dufer S.A. and Usinas Siderúrgicas de Minas Gerais S.A. – USIMINAS.*
78. *See* Act of Concentration No. 08012.012235/2008-81, resolved on 5 Aug. 2009, involving *Capital Mezanino Fundo de Investimento em Participações and Livraria Cultura S.A.*

Such position was subsequently reversed, shown in CADE's Resolution in Act of Concentration No. 08012.000900/2009-76, resolved on 27 May 2009, involving *Visum Sistemas Eletrônicos S/A and Governança e Gestão Participações S/A.*, whereby the Council ruled that, in connection with a transaction involving an equity investment fund, it would not be reasonable to consider the fund investors as a single economic unit, given that their primary interest is the financial result of the investments and not the operational activities of the target companies.

810. The conduct aspect of the paradigm will subsequently take into account issues such as pricing, product and advertising strategies, research and development, investments.

811. Both market structure and conduct analysis will consider the impact of taxes, subsidies, international trade rules, regulation, price-control rules whenever applicable, etc.

812. Conduct analysis is primarily interested in the determination of the probability of individual or coordinated exercise of market power, in which the presence of barriers to entry play an important role, whether such barriers are regulatory, technological or otherwise, including the presence of brand barriers or barriers resulting from idle capacity, logistics or import duties.

813. Entry thresholds in a relevant market are to be assessed based on the standards of probability (meaning, if the new sales opportunities yielding from the market growth absorb a new entrant, by the analysis of the minimum viable scale – MVS enabling a newcomer to sustainably operate in the field), timeliness (possibility of feasibility of the business in a time lower than two years) and sufficiency (based on the analysis of idle capacity and of capacity of supply of the sales opportunities created by the market growth).

814. In the presence of high barriers to entry, the conduct portion of the paradigm shall proceed to the analysis of rivalry among the incumbent players, seeking to either confirm or dismiss conjectures of probability of unilateral or coordinated exercise of market power.

815. The rivalry analysis seeks to determine if, should a firm resulting from the transaction shall unilaterally or in coordinated fashion exercise its market power, the consumers shall have means to redirect their demand to other market competitors. In this context, if, on the one hand, a high market idle capacity tend to reduce the possibility of entry by a newcomer, on the other hand, such may be a rivalry factor, given that the market players that have idle capacity tend to minimize their losses (or maximize their profits) by optimizing the use of their respective installed capacities.

816. Finally, in reviewing performance, the analysis will be dedicated to examine productive and allocative efficiencies, technical progress and full employment. Innovation does currently play a minor role in the analysis, provided that more recent CADE precedents involving dynamic markets or markets under the process of technology converge (e.g., computer and telecommunication industries) are given greater attention to innovation as a source of creation of new markets or in the change of scope of existing markets.

817. In order to be entertained by the CADE in the review process, efficiencies are to be: (a) specific to the transaction and cannot be obtained through any other manner, (b) in a period shorter than two years and (c) feasible, so as to cause the transaction to have a smaller competitive impact. They cannot be speculative or resulting in a mere pecuniary gain, and be to the benefit of the consumer, provided that, as such standard is concerned, the efficiencies are accountable only when derived from variable costs (or predominantly of variable costs) and by disregarding reductions exclusive to fixed costs.[79]

818. Generally, however, the review of economic efficiencies plays little (actually, hardly any) importance in the clearance process. Indeed, as ruled by the CADE in Act of Concentration No. 08012.007776/2008-99 (resolved on 21 July 2010), in re. *Cobb-Vantress, Inc. and Hendrix Genetics B.V.,* whenever an act of concentration yields the control over a significant market share, the CADE is not authorized to clear the transaction, even in the presence of high efficiencies yielding therefrom.

§2. Structure of Proceeding

I. Preliminary Assessment and Full Investigation

819. Generally, all 'acts of concentration' are equally assessed, regardless of their impact on the relevant market. The only exempting *de minimis* concept is related to transactions that do not yield stock control, but meet the rules set forth in Article 10 of CADE Resolution No. 2, of 29 May 2011, meaning:

(i) whenever the target company is neither competitor nor operates in a vertically related market:

(1) the purchase shall not grant the purchaser direct or indirect ownership of 20% or more of the capital stock or of the voting stock of the target company;
(2) the purchase is made by a purchaser, holder of 20% or more of the capital stock or of the voting stock of the target company, and the stock that is directly or indirectly purchased from a single seller, individually considered, shall represent less than 20% of the capital stock or the voting stock of the target company.
(ii) whenever the target company is a competitor or operates in a vertically related market:
(1) the purchase shall not grant a direct or indirect participation of 5% or more of the capital stock or of the voting stock of the target company.
(2) the last purchase which, either individually or added to other purchases, shall result in a shareholding increase lesser than 5%, should the investor already hold 5% or more of the capital stock or of the voting stock of the target company.

79. *See* CADE Resolution in Act of Concentration No. 08012.005889/2010-74 (resolved on 14 Dec. 2011, in re, *Fisher S/A Comércio, Indústria and Agricultura e Citrovita Agro Industrial Ltda.*

820. Exempting standards for associative and collaboration agreements are still under consideration by the CADE.

821. Although under the constitutional principle of free initiative, commercial transactions are to be presumed licit transactions, it is important to note that, as a matter of fact, the competition authorities tend to view all 'acts of concentration' as presumably restrictive to trade and illicit. Hence, the review procedures will generally tend to follow a rather conservative rationale.

822. Notification requires in any event the payment of a BRL 45,000 notification fee.

823. The request for approval of the acts of concentration must be addressed (preferably jointly by all parties thereto) to the CADE and must contain the extensive information and documents listed in the Annexes to CADE Resolution No. 2/11 (Annex I for complex cases and Annex II for simple cases eligible for fast-track review), in addition to the receipt of payment of the respective CADE notification fee.

824. The parties may request that confidential treatment be granted to information and/or documents, provided that such motion is made in clear form and supported by legal and economic arguments.

825. Upon the filing of the notification, the GS shall publish summons in the Federal Official Gazette, informing the market on the application and allowing third interested parties to file statements of objection within thirty days.

826. The GS shall subsequently review the notification and then either: (a) immediately clear the transaction, (b) order additional investigative actions to determine if the case is in adequate conditions for its review in the merits or if the parties are to complement the relevant application, or (c) declare the case to be a complex case and order the actions that it may deem appropriate.

827. Upon the conclusion of such supplementary phase, the GS will either: (a) unconditionally clear the transaction, or (b) file a statement of objections with the administrative tribunal, recommending the issue of a full or partial divestiture order. The applicants will be permitted to respond to, and qualified third interested parties will be permitted to comment on, the statement of objections filed by the GS within thirty days therefrom.

828. All GS resolutions clearing a given transaction are subject: (a) to third-party appeals to the administrative tribunal, and (b) to the administrative tribunal calling the case back for review. In case of clearance by the GS, the transaction can only be closed once the relevant decisions shall become an administrative res judicata.

829. In any case, upon the delivery of the dockets to the administrative tribunal, the case shall be assigned, randomly, to a Councillor Examiner, who may report to the Tribunal recommending a final determination, if he shall believe that the case is ready for trial, or order a complementary action.

830. The Councillor Examiner, at his discretion and depending on the complexity of the issues under consideration, requests the opinion of the CADE technical bodies (the Office of the CADE Attorney General – PFE – on legal matters, and the DEE on economic issues). Again, should the case involve more relevant legal and/or economic issues, the MPF, an institution unrelated to the CADE, but incumbent with the preservation of the legal institutions and the adequate enforcement of the law (*custos legis*), may also issue a non-binding opinion for the administrative tribunal considerations.

831. In any event and in short, at the end of the merger review procedures, the CADE, through its administrative tribunal will likely clear a transaction in the following cases:

(a) the transaction shall result in no control of a significant portion of the relevant market; and
(b) if the transaction shall result in a significant portion of the relevant market, but the exercise of market power is improbable.

832. In transactions involving the telecommunication industry and in those involving the banking system, clearance must also be secured at the ANATEL and the BACEN, as the case may be.

833. In light of a statement of objections by the GS or for any other reason in the course of the review process, the parties may apply for a Concentration Control Agreement[80] (ACC), seeking to amicably settle an anticipated remedy or on the terms of the statement of objections. Such a motion may be filed at any time between the date the notification is originally filed with the CADE and up to thirty days after the filing of the statement of objections by the GS. The CADE Resolution on any such motion for an ACC is discretionary.

834. At the final determination Session, the Superintendent General, the Chief Economist, the CADE Attorney General, the third interested parties (if authorized by the Panel of the administrative tribunal, at the discretion of the member Councillors) and the parties shall be permitted to present final oral submissions. Whereupon, the administrative tribunal shall rule by majority vote for the clearance of the transaction or for the issue of a full or partial divestiture order.

835. A resolution by the administrative tribunal is unappealable at the administrative level, but may always be reviewed by judicial control.

II. Time Framework

836. The notification of an act of concentration must be made prior to the closing of the underlying transaction. Reportable transactions that are closed prior to their clearance by the CADE shall be null and void, and subject the parties' offenders to a pecuniary fine between BRL 60,000 and BRL 60,000,000, and to the commencement of an Administrative Process.

837. Pending the CADE clearance, the parties must preserve the status quo of the competitive environment existing prior to the transaction between the contracting parties. For such purposes, the parties must not only maintain the existing physical structures but also refrain from transferring any assets or exercising any kind of influence of one party on the other, as well as refrain from exchanging commercially sensitive information that is not strictly necessary for the execution of the relevant binding transaction documents.

838. The maximum term for a clearance review process of an act of concentration is of 240 days from the date of notification. Such term may be extended by sixty days.

80. In Portuguese, *Acordo em Controle de Concentração.*

If the review process is not concluded within such time frame, the act of concentration shall be considered as tacitly approved.

839. Under the current Brazilian Competition Law, during the first year of its effectiveness, the average time for the review of acts of concentration was of sixty-nine days for ordinary cases and of twenty days for summary, fast-track proceedings.[81]

840. All 'acts of concentration' shall face the same procedural route for analysis, provided that transaction having a minor impact on the market may be reviewed under summary, fast-track procedures.

841. Pursuant to Article 8 of CADE Resolution No. 2/12, the following cases are eligible for summary review:

(1) – Classic and cooperative JVs: cases of association of two or more separate undertakings for the formation of a new company under common control, that exclusively seeks to participate in a market the products/services of which are not horizontally or vertically related.

(2) – Consolidation of control: the acquisition of stockholding by the controlling shareholder whenever the share that is directly or indirectly acquired from single seller, considered individually, shall be equal to or superior to 20% of the capital stock or the voting stock.

(3) – Replacement of market player: cases where the purchaser or its economic unit did not participate, prior to the transaction, in the relevant market, or in markets that are vertically related, or in other markets in which the target company or its economic unit operated.

(4) – Low market-share participation with horizontal concentration: cases in which the transaction shall yield a share in the relevant market that is provenly lower than 20%, in the Superintendency General opinion, leaving no doubts as to the irrelevance of the transaction from a competitive point of view.

(5) – Low market-share participation with vertical integration: cases when the purchaser or its economic unit shall provenly not own a market share superior to 20% in the vertically integrated market shares, prior to the transaction.

(6) – Other cases: cases when, albeit not covered by the preceding hypothesis, are considered simple enough, in the opinion of the GS, so that they do not deserve a deeper analysis.

842. The adoption of a fast-track procedure does not require the party to formally apply for it, provided, however, that such adoption is not a matter of right of the interested parties, but exclusive to the discretion of the Superintendent. Further, a decision by the Superintendent to adopt summary proceedings shall not preclude him from cancelling their original decision and reverting to ordinary proceedings, at any time.

843. In short, simple cases may be ultimately heard by the Superintendent General in a time frame of approximately one month, while cases of a moderate complexity may be heard within three months, while complex cases may take up to the maximum statutory term.

---

81. For more information *see* http://www.cade.gov.br/upload/Balan%C3%A7o%201%20ano%20nova%20lei%20%28consolidado%29.pdf.

III. Right of Defence

844. Parties to 'acts of concentration' enjoy full rights of defence and shall be at all times permitted to supply information and documents and to directly debate their case before the competition authorities, both formally and informally.

845. Third interested parties, both consenting and objecting to the transactions, are also allowed to have full access to the records (save for confidential, market-sensitive information and documents, and for classified information) and to participate in the review process, virtually with the same rights of the applicants.

846. Should the CADE issue a full or a partial divestiture order, the adversely affected parties shall have the right to resort to full judicial control and review.

§3. Clearance and Conditional Clearance

I. Conditions and Undertakings

A. Content

847. In reviewing an act of concentration, upon the conclusion of all procedural phases of the analysis, the CADE administrative tribunal will assess the net effect of the transaction to the market and the consumers.

848. As a consequence, the administrative tribunal may determine to unconditionally approve the act of concentration, reject it or partially approve it, in which case it shall impose structural or behavioural conditions to the clearance of the transaction and the effectiveness thereof.

849. In general terms, the administrative tribunal will clear a transaction should it:

(1) yield no control of a significant portion of the market;
(2) if yielding a control of a significant portion of the market, evidence that the exercise of market power after the merger will be improbable;
(3) if the chances of the exercise of market power after the merger fail to be improbable, the net effect of the transaction shall be positive.

850. In statutory language (Article 88, §6, of Law No. 12529/11), the acts of concentration may be cleared, as long as the limits that are strictly necessary to achieve their purpose are observed, whenever:

(1) on a cumulative or alternative basis, they shall:

   (a) increase productivity or competitiveness;
   (b) improve the quality of goods and services; or
   (c) enable efficiency and the economic or technological development.

(2) a relevant portion of the benefits resulting from the act of concentration shall be passed on to the consumers.

851. Should a partial divestiture order be issued as a condition to the clearance of the transaction, the administrative tribunal is bound to require from the applicant certain undertakings seeking to mitigate the eventual harmful impact of the act of concentration on the affected relevant market, which undertakings may include:

(1) the sale of assets or a group of assets that constitute an entrepreneurial activity;
(2) a company spin-off;
(3) the sale of a stock control;
(4) the accounting or legal splitting of activities;
(5) the compulsory licensing of intellectual property rights; or
(6) any other action or remedies as necessary to eliminate the harmful impacts on the economic order.

852. Structural remedies are the preference of the CADE, given the difficulties and costs related to the monitoring of behavioural remedies, which are considered less effective than the former.

853. Structural remedies usually seek to eliminate barriers to entry or excessive market power. Principal remedies are: (a) the sale of a company or a part of it, and (b) the sale of a brand or production line. Such remedies may be complete (the sale of a business unit, ensuring the buyer to have all of the conditions necessary to operate it in an autonomous and effective manner) or partial (the sale of patents, know-how and technology, ensuring that the buyer shall be in the possession of all assets and assistance to preserve their exploitation).

854. Behavioural remedies may entail: (a) the sharing of distribution networks, (b) the suspension or termination of exclusivity arrangements, (c) the temporary supply of goods and services to specified clients or competitors, (d) the prohibition to enter into requirement contracts etc. Although a remedy in the past,[82] the CADE will not interfere in product pricing, as it refuses to be considered a price-control agency.

855. Remedies may be 'surgical' (affecting a specific aspect of the competitive concern) or 'business-guided' (affecting an entire business unit), provided that, in any event, such remedies are to be considered feasible, objective and limited by their purpose of achieving efficiencies and preserving the levels of competition in the marketplace.

856. The purpose of structural remedies is, on an *ex ante* perspective, to create conditions for the consolidation of a competitive environment or by simply reducing the impact of the negative effects on competition inherent to market concentrations. In other words, structural remedies seek to eliminate barriers and market power.

82. *See* Act of Concentration No. 26/95 (resolved on 19 Dec. 1995), involving *Albarus S.A. Indústria e Comércio and Rockwell do Brasil S.A.* in which the CADE cleared a virtual monopoly (in excess of 90% of market share) in the declining 'Salisbury' axle market, in exchange, *inter alia*, of Albarus progressively reducing average prices between 1997 and 2000, between 0.8% and 4.6% in the OEM market and between 4.5% and 21.3% in the aftermarket, and undertaking to meet all of the market's demand between 1996 and 2000.

857. Examples of structural remedies are the sale of a company, the partial alienation of a company asset, such as trademarks, plants, production lines.

858. Whenever the remedy shall involve the sale of company assets, the CADE divestiture order may require a full or a partial remedy. In the case of a full remedy, the order shall contemplate the sale of all of the business in a specific field to a buyer capable thereby of operating such business, thereafter, in a fully independent manner. Partial remedies may entail the sale of only a part of the affected business, such as the assignment of patent rights, the transfer of know-how or of technology, provided that the assignee or purchaser, thereof, shall be in the possession of all assets and assistance capable of preserving its presence in the marketplace.

859. In the case of sale of assets it is usually sought, furthermore, that the sale be made within the shortest time frame possible and, as much as possible to purchasers that are, or may become, actual competitors of the seller.

860. Simply to clarify such standards, a few examples of such remedies are the following.

861. In Act of Concentration No. 08012.007419/2004-31 where the company *Engemix S.A.* purchased concrete-disposal assets from competing *Holcim S.A.,* the CADE determined that the transaction resulted in a significant market concentration in the cities of Blumenau and Brusque and neighbouring cities, all in the State of Santa Catarina; in the cities of Curitiba and neighbouring cities, and of Foz do Iguaçu, all in the State of Paraná.

862. In determining the negative impact of the transaction in such cities, the CADE ordered the sale by Engemix of the assets purchased from Holcim in Blumenau – SC, Curitiba – PR and Foz do Iguaçu – PR, within ninety days from the publication of its decision in the Federal Official Gazette, subject to full divestiture of the transaction and the payment of a daily fine equal to 100 Fiscal Reference Unit (UFIR) – approximately BRL 2,000.

863. Another benchmark case relates to the full divestiture order issued by the CADE involving the chocolate manufacturers Nestlé and Garoto. This decision is currently being contested in the Brazilian Courts.

864. In the CADE decision, it was ordered that the business be sold to a third interested party approved by the CADE having a market share not exceeding 20%, but capable of preserving the use of the Garoto brand in the market.

865. While structural remedies have a correctional purpose, seeking to eliminate the structural conditions yielding from the transaction that grant dominance to a newly formed undertaking and restore the pre-existing competitive environment, behavioural remedies have more of a compensatory nature and envisage ensuring the effectiveness of alleged efficiencies and their sharing with consumers.

866. Due to the lesser monitoring difficulties and costs, however, structural remedies are preferred to behavioural remedies, which are, nevertheless, adopted independently or in conjunction with structural remedies.

867. The principal behavioural remedies are: opening of exclusive distribution channels to competitors, termination of exclusivity arrangements, temporary supply of goods or services to competing concerns, obligation not to enter into certain types of agreements, such as requirement contracts. The CADE is not a price-control agency.

Thus, price-adjustment restrictions or the granting of discounts, although remedies adopted in the past, are no longer considered.

868. For example, in Act of Concentration No. 08012.000497/00-01, resolved on 19 November 2003, involving *Serrana S/A* and *Nevada Woods Sociedad Anónima*, related to the merger of leading fertilizer companies, the CADE considered ordering the parties to ensure the sale of raw materials to a pool of small- and medium-size mixers and access by such pool to volume discounts under a formula to be established.

B. Timing

869. Article 92 of Law No. 12529/11, which intended to allow negotiations with the GS in connection with prospective undertakings to enable the clearance of acts of concentrations, was vetoed by the President of the Republic. Such veto, however, does not prevent applicants from informally discussing with the GS or with the member Councillors of the administrative tribunal, the terms of an ACC to be approved by the latter.

870. Although subject to negotiations with the GS or with the Councillor Examiner, ACCs must be approved by the administrative tribunal.

871. Compliance with the administrative tribunal partial divestiture order or with the terms of the ACC may vary on a case-by-case basis, but may generally vary between thirty days to five years for structural remedies, and to permanent conduct in case of behavioural remedies.

872. While examining the GS or a third interested party statement of objection or pending a call-back by the Councillor Examiner of the GS decision to clear a transaction, the latter may authorize, upon the applicant's motion, thereto, taking into account the specific circumstances, the precarious and provisional closing of the transaction, by imposing on the parties such conditions that shall preserve the reversibility of the act of concentration.

873. The CADE Resolutions are not appealable at the administrative level, but are subject to review before the Judiciary.

§4. Relations with Other Merger Control Authorities

I. Other Authorities Within the Local Jurisdiction

874. The CADE frequently interfaces with other authorities (especially regulatory authorities) in the course of review of an 'act of concentration'. Regulatory agencies in most cases are required by law to cooperate with the CADE on their matters of expertise, and are often consulted:

(a) Formal cooperation agreements have been signed by the competition authorities, such as with the BACEN, the Securities Exchange Commission (CVM), the ANS, the Civil Aviation National Agency (ANAC), the DNPM, the INPI, the Sanitary

Vigilance National Agency (ANVISA), the ANEEL, the ANP, the IPEA, the Consumer National Secretariat (SENACON) and the CEDES.

875. By law, however, the review of 'acts of concentration' affecting the telecommunications industry is initially the jurisdiction of the ANATEL, which will issue its technical non-binding opinion.

876. There is also a large debate as to whether the CADE has authority to review mergers and acquisitions involving financial institutions. Exclusive jurisdiction is claimed by the BACEN and the matter is currently under discussion in the Judiciary. The CADE is of the opinion that the BACEN has jurisdiction on regulatory matters, while competition issues are under its own. In any event, both institutions cooperate with each other in the review of related transactions.

II. International Coordination

877. Although an active participant in the international scenario, participant of multiple international fora, such as the ICN, the OCDE and the Mercosul, and despite having signed various international cooperation agreements (with Russia, Argentina, US, Portugal, Chile, Canada, the European Community, China and Peru), international cooperation between foreign authorities and Brazilian competition authorities is somewhat limited in connection with the review of 'acts of concentration'.

878. Conference calls between the CADE (Examiner Fernando Furlan) and members of the US Federal Trade Commission to discuss the global 'Act of Concentration' involving *Owens Corning and Saint Gobain* (Act of Concentration No. 08012.001885/2007-14) were, however, reported.

879. The foregoing notwithstanding, the CADE frequently comments resolutions by authorities of the European Commission and the Federal Trade Commission in its own resolutions, but mostly as an illustration of Comparative Law. Such information, however, is only occasionally taken as a rationale for a CADE final determination, but always in support of the CADE Resolution (if not the subject of dissenting). Resorting to resolutions by the European Commission have become recurrent in the past few years, to the detriment of the opinions of the US Federal Trade Commission.

Chapter 3. Challenging of the Administrative Decision

§1. Competent Courts

880. Under the Brazilian Federal Constitution (Article 5, item XXXV), no administrative act is immune from judicial review; all CADE Resolutions may be reviewed and annulled by the courts.

881. The competition authorities tend to consider themselves immune or superior to the Judiciary and to due process of law rules.

882. In Administrative Process No. 08012.009088/99-48, involving *Conselho Regional de Farmácia do Distrito Federal v. Merck Sharp & Dhome Farmacêutica Ltda. et al.*, the Office of the CADE Attorney General (Opinion No. 291/2007, dated 25 May 2007, footnote No. 32, expressly stated that:[83]

> I agree that the individual (constitutional) guarantees not always are perfectly consistent with the enforcement of competition (…) (free translation).

883. By the same token, in Preliminary Investigation No. 08012.002673/2007-51, involving *Associação Nacional de Fabricantes de Autopeças – ANFAPE v. Volkswagen do Brasil Indústria de Veículos Ltda., Fiat Automóveis S.A and Ford Motor Company Ltda.*, the CADE, in light of court decisions granting car manufacturers the right to prevent independent aftermarket auto-part manufacturers from counterfeiting products protected by industrial property rights, ruled that the Council is an independent body of the Public Administration and, as such, not bound by judicial resolutions handed in cases in which the CADE was not a party.

884. It is hard to believe, however, that such unconstitutional interpretation would be upheld in the Judiciary. Therefore and frequently, annulment actions are brought by the adversely affected party before the Federal Courts in Brasilia (where the CADE is located).

885. Appeals of trial court resolutions are initially heard by the TRF, also in Brasília, and subsequently by the STJ (whenever the appeal addresses an issue of violation of Federal Law) and by the STF, the highest judicial instance in Brazil (whenever the appeal addresses an issue of violation of the Brazilian Federal Constitution), as the case may be.

83. 'Registre-se que não existe aqui contradição com as ponderações do voto vista condutor da decisão do CADE (fls. 6583/6586). *Concorda-se que as garantias individuais nem sempre se coadunam perfeitamente com o enforcement da defesa da concorrência*, razão pela qual restou caracterizada a responsabilidade das pessoas jurídicas face à participação dos agentes, conforme as lições de João Castro e Souza colacionadas. Contudo, entende-se que isso não implica afirmar que a responsabilidade será avaliada em grupo' (emphasis added to translated excerpt).

§2. Time Limits

886. Although prolonged statutes of limitation apply (twenty years), the time for challenging a CADE decision shall greatly depend on the term granted by it for the adversely affected parties to comply.

887. Consequently, the most frequent initial move is the filing by the adversely affected party of a writ of mandamus or of a motion for injunctive relief seeking the suspension of the effects of the adverse CADE decision. *Fumus boni iuris* and *periculum in mora* are the statutory essential requirements to succeed in obtaining a favourable resolution on such interim measures.

888. In case the CADE initiates an enforcement action, such suspensive effect can only be obtained with the placement of a bond with the competent court, as collateral for compliance with the CADE Resolution.

889. Considering that annulment actions are ordinary procedures that enable (at the discretion of the first instance judge) full review of the administrative review procedures, including the re-opening of the discovery phase, and that a first instance resolution is appealable, judicial review procedures may eventually prove to be quite prolonged (not infrequently two to five years, but sometimes ten).

§3. Scope of Judicial Review

890. It is controversial whether the Judiciary may review the case entirely (including by reinstating the discovery phase) or if it is restricted to the review of formal issues of legality.

891. Under the law, the Judiciary has full authority to review the CADE Resolution entirely (both in form and substance), but, in fact, many judges attempt to preserve the authority of the CADE (i.e., give deference to CADE's decision without scrutinizing its merits) and restrict their analysis to formal issues of legality only. First instance resolutions are appealable at the Higher Appellate Courts, where the CADE has somewhat less influence.

892. The Brazilian Judiciary has relatively little experience in handling competition matters, provided that such learning process is in obvious progress.

Selected Bibliography

Brazil. CADE. Brazilian Federal Constitution, www.planalto.gov.br/ccivil_03/constituicao/constitui%C3%A7ao.htm, 30 July 2010.
Brazil. CADE. Brazilian Penal Procedures Code, www.planalto.gov.br/ccivil/decreto-lei/del2848.htm, 30 July 2010.
Brazil. CADE. Brazilian Civil Procedures Code, http://www.planalto.gov.br/ccivil_03/_ato2015-2018/2015/lei/l13105.htm.
Brazil. CADE. Law No. 8137, of 27 December 1990, www.planalto.gov.br/ccivil/leis/L8,137.htm, 30 July 2010.
Brazil. CADE. Federal General Counsel (AGU) Issued Opinion No. GM-20 AGU/LA 01/2001 (as ratified by Opinion No. 02/2009/MP/CGU/AGU), www.planalto.gov.br, 22 March 2011.
Brazil. CADE. SDE/SEAE. Joint Ordinance No. 50/2001, www.seae.fazenda.gov.br/central_documentos/legislacao, 30 July 2010.
Brazil. CADE. SEAE. Ordinance No. 70/2002, www.seae.fazenda.gov.br/central_documentos/legislacao, 30 July 2010.
Brazil. CADE. SDE. Ordinance No. 51, of 3 July 2009. Guidelines for the Analysis of Charges in Connection with Possible Anticompetitive Offences in Public Tender Bids, http://portal.mj.gov.br/sde/main.asp?View={57C0533B-D1E4-4A0E-B83A-092D0F273F44}, 30 July 2010.
Brazil. CADE. Guidelines on Competition Compliance Programs, http://www.cade.gov.br/acesso-a-informacao/publicacoes-institucionais/guias_do_Cade/guia-compliance-versao-oficial.pdf.
Brazil. CADE. Guidelines on CADE´s Antitrust Leniency Program, http://www.cade.gov.br/acesso-a-informacao/publicacoes-institucionais/guias_do_Cade/guia-programa-de-leniencia-antitruste-do-cade-versao-preliminar-1.pdf.
Brazil. CADE. Guidelines on Cease and Desist Agreement for Cartel Cases, http://www.cade.gov.br/acesso-a-informacao/publicacoes-institucionais/guias_do_Cade/guia-tcc-versao-atual.pdf.
Brazil. CADE. Guidelines on Gun Jumping, http://www.cade.gov.br/acesso-a-informacao/publicacoes-institucionais/guias_do_Cade/guia-gun-jumping-versao-final-3.pdf.
Brazil. CADE. Guidelines for the Review of Horizontal Acts of Concentration, http://www.cade.gov.br/acesso-a-informacao/publicacoes-institucionais/guias_do_Cade/guia-para-analise-de-atos-de-concentracao-horizontal.pdf.
Brazil. CADE (Administrative Council for Economic Defense)
Brazil. Superior Court of Justice (STJ)

Cases Reference Table

Act of Concentration No. 0026/1995 (resolved on 19 December 1995). Parties: *Albarus S.A. Indústria e Comércio and Rockwell do Brasil S/A.*

Act of Concentration No. 08012.005243/1998-76 (resolved on 21 October 1998). Parties: *Remy Holding do Brasil Ltda. and Irmãos Zen S/A.*

Act of Concentration No. 08012.005846/1999-12 (resolved on 29 March 2000). Parties: *Companhia Cervejaria Brahma, Companhia Antarctica Paulista Indústria Brasileira de Bebidas e Conexos and others.*

Acts of Concentration No. 08012.002315/1999-50 and 08012.004117/1999-67 (both resolved on 22 November 2000). Parties: *Brasil-Álcool S.A, Coopersucar Armazéns Gerais S/A, Bolsa Brasileira de Álcool Ltda., Cocal-Comércio, Indústria Canaã Açúcar e Álcool Ltda. et alii.*

Act of Concentration No. 08012.001031/2000-69 (resolved on 22 November 2000). Parties: *Refrigerantes Minas Gerais Ltda. and CCSI – Indústria de Refrigerantes Ltda.*

Act of Concentration No. 08012.006897/2001-47 (resolved on 12 March 2003). Parties: *Libra Terminal Rio S/A and Multi-Rio Operações Portuárias S/A.*

Act of Concentration No. 08012.004771/2001-38 (resolved on 5 November 2003). Parties: *Vega Engenharia Ambiental S/A and Koleta Ambiental S/A.*

Act of Concentration No. 08012.001697/2002-89 (resolved on 4 February 2004). Parties: *Nestlé Brasil Ltda. and Chocolates Garoto S/A.*

Act of Concentration No. 08012.000497/2000-01 (resolved on 4 February 2004). Parties: *Serrana de Participações S/A and Nevada Woods Sociedad Anonima.*

Act of Concentration No. 08012.000002/2001-61 (resolved on 12 May 2004). Parties: *Tapon Corona Metal Plástico Ltda., Metalúrgica Cearense S/A, Indústrias Reunidas Renda S/A, Cia. De Rolhas Metálicas das Américas S/A, Aro S/A Exportação, Importação, indústria e Comércio and Amorim Pinto e Cia Ltda.*

Act of Concentration No. 08012.000001/2001-16 (resolved on 16 June 2004). Parties: *General Motors Corporation, Ford Motor Company, Renault S/A, DaimlerCrysler AG and Oracle do Brasil Sistemas Ltda.*

Act of Concentration No. 08012.003218/2004-21 (resolved on 11 August 2004). Parties: *TPG Partners IV L.P., T3 Partners II L.P. and Isola AG.*

Act of Concentration No. 08012.003632/2001-97 (resolved on 29 September 2004). Parties: *Sadia S/A, Cargill Agrícola S/A and Danone S/A.*

Act of Concentration No. 08012.002172/2004-22 (resolved on 15 June 2005). Parties: *Braco S/A, Companhia de Bebida das Américas (AmBev) and Interbrew N.V. S.A.*

Act of Concentration No. 08012.010195/2004-19 (resolved on 8 August 2007). Parties: *Suzano Bahia Sul Papel e Celulose S/A and Ripasa S/A Papel e Celulose.*

Act of Concentration No. 08012.010192/2004-77 (resolved on 8 August 2007). Parties: *Votorantim Celulose e Papel S/A and Ripasa S/A Papel e Celulose.*

Act of Concentration No. 08012.001230/2007-43 (resolved on 21 November 2007). Parties: *Embu S/A Engenharia e Comércio, Embu Empreendimentos Ltda., CCB – Cimpor Cimentos do Brasil Ltda.*

Act of Concentration No. 08012.010081/2007-11 (resolved on 12 December 2007). Parties: *Banco Santander Central Hispano S/A, Fortis N.V, Fortis S.A./N.V, The Royal Bank Of Scotland Plc.*

Act of Concentration No. 08012.009419/2004-31 (resolved on 19 March 2008). Parties: *Engemix S.A. and Holcim (Brasil) S.A.*

Selected Bibliography

Act of Concentration No. 08012.004864/2008-39 (resolved on 25 June 2008). Parties: *RIM 1947 Participações S.A., JRM 1953 Participações S.A. and ZRM 1955 Participações S.A.*

Act of Concentration No. 08012.002620/2008-11 (resolved on 25 June 2008). Parties: *TF Indústria e Comércio de Modas Ltda., Triton e Fórum Publicidade Ltda., A.M.C. Têxtil Ltda., T F Licenciamento de Marcas Ltda.*

Act of Concentration No. 08012.001885/2007-11 (resolved on 23 July 2008). Parties: *Owens Corning and Compagnie de Saint-Gobain.*

Act of Concentration No. 08012.006556/2008-48 (resolved on 27 August 2008). Parties: *Monsanto do Brasil Ltda. and Syngenta Seeds Ltda.*

Act of Concentration No. 08012.011196/2005-53 (resolved in 17 December 2008). Parties: *White Martins Gases Industriais Ltda. and Air Liquide Brasil Ltda.*

Act of Concentration No. 08012.010626/2008-62 (resolved in 4 February 2009). Parties: *Dufer S.A. and Usinas Siderúrgicas de Minas Gerais S.A. (USIMINAS).*

Act of Concentration No. 08012.008939/2008-51 (resolved on 4 March 2009). Parties: *Votorantim Cimentos Brasil Ltda. and Pavimentadora e Construtora Vicente Matheus Ltda.*

Act of Concentration No. 08012.000900/2009-76 (resolved on 27 May 2009). Parties: *Visum Sistemas Eletrônicos S/A and Governança e Gestão Participações S/A.*

Act of Concentration No. 08012.001560/2009-09 (resolved on 29 April 2009). Parties: *Monsanto do Brasil Ltda. and Wehrtec-Tecnologia Agrícola Ltda.*

Act of Concentration No. 08012.011642/2008-72 (resolved on 27 May 2009). Parties: *American Safety Razor do Brasil Ltda., ASR Exportação, Importação, Comércio e Indústria de Produtos de Barbear Ltda. and Hypermarcas S/A.*

Act of Concentration No. 08012.000637/2009-15 (resolved on 17 June 2009). Parties: *Companhia de Cimento Ribeirão Grande and CJ Mineração Ltda.*

Act of Concentration No. 08012.001383/2007-91 (resolved on 17 June 2009). Parties: *Recofarma Indústria do Amazonas Ltda. and Leão Junior S.A.*

Act of Concentration No. 08012.000238/2009-54 (resolved on 17 June 2009). Parties: *Recofarma Indústria do Amazonas Ltda., Coca-Cola Indústrias Ltda. and Spaipa S.A. – Indústria Brasileira de Bebidas.*

Act of Concentration No. 08012.012235/2008-82 (resolved on 5 August 2009). Parties: *Capital Mezanino Fundo de Investimento em Participações and Livraria Cultura S.A.*

Act of Concentration No. 08012.007963/2009-53 (resolved on 11 November 2009). Parties: *Monsanto do Brasil Ltda. and Basf S/A.*

Act of Concentration No. 08012.010109/2009-74 (resolved on 17 March 2010). Parties: *Cosan S.A. Indústria e Comércio, Crystalsev Comércio e Representação Ltda., TEAS Terminal Exportador de Álcool de Santos S.A. and Plinio Nastari Consultoria e Participações Ltda.*

Act of Concentration No. 08012.000182/2010-71 (resolved on 17 March 2010). Parties: *Monsanto do Brasil Ltda. and Iharabras S/A Indústrias Químicas.*

Act of Concentration No. 08012.003189/2009-10 (resolved on 19 May 2010). Parties: *Sanofi-Aventis Farmacêutica Ltda. and Medley S.A. Indústria Farmacêutica.*

Act of Concentration No. 08012.009986/2008-11 (resolved on 9 June 2010). Parties: *BESC S.A. Crédito Imobiliário, Banco do Estado de Santa Catarina S.A. and Banco do Brasil S.A.*

Act of Concentration No. 08012.011505/2008-38 (resolved on 17 June 2010). Parties: *Banco do Estado do Piauí S.A. and Banco do Brasil S.A.*

Act of Concentration No. 08012.000797/2010-06 (resolved on 7 July 2010). Parties: *Bayer S.A. and CVR Plant Breeding Ltda.*

Act of Concentration No. 08012.007776/2008-99 (resolved on 21 July 2010). Parties: *Cobb-Vantress, Inc. and Hendrix Genetics B.V.*

Act of Concentration No. 08012.007776/2008-99 (resolved on 21 July 2010). Parties: *Cobb-Vantress, Inc.* and *Hendrix Genetics B.V.*

Act of Concentration No. 08012.011736/2008-41 (resolved on 4 August 2010). Parties: *Banco Nossa Caixa S.A. (BNC) and Banco do Brasil S.A. (BB).*

Act of Concentration No. 08012.006343/2010-31 (resolved on 22 September 2010). Parties: *Basf S.A. and Meiji Seika Kaisha, LTD.*

Acts of Concentration Nos 08012.005789/2008-23 and 53500.012477/2008 both resolved on 20 October 2010). Parties: *Telemar Norte Leste S/A, Brasil Telecom S/A, Invitel S.A. and Banco de Investimentos Credit Suisse (Brasil) S.A.*

Act of Concentration No. 08012.004907/2010-09 (resolved on 15 December 2010). Parties: *CPLPAR Holding S.A., CPA Trading S.A. and Cattalini Terminais Marítimos Ltda.*

Act of Concentration No. 08012.010473/2009-34 (resolved on 23 April 2013). Parties: *Companhia Brasileira de Distribuição and Casa Bahia Comercial Ltda.*

Act of Concentration No. 08012.001205/2010-65 (resolved on 23 February 2011). Parties: *Braskem S.A., Petróleo Brasileiro S.A., Petrobras Química and Quattor Participações S.A.*

Act of Concentration No. 08011.000416/2011-61 (resolved on 23 March 2011). Parties: *Totvs S/A and Gens Tecnologia e Informática Ltda.*

Act of Concentration No. 08012.008810/2009-23 (resolved on 29 June 2011). Parties: *Sony Corporation, Koninklijke Philips Electronics N.V., Panasonic Corporation, Hitachi Consumer Electronics Co. Ltd., Samsung Electronics Co. Ltd. and Cyberlink Corp.*

Act of Concentration No. 08012.004423/2009-18 (resolved on 13 July 2011). Parties: *Perdigão S.A. and Sadia S.A.*

Act of Concentration No. 08012.004423/2009-18 (resolved on 13 July 2011). Parties: *Perdigão S.A. and Sadia S.A.*

Act of Concentration No. 08012.006735/2011-81 (resolved on 10 August 2011). Parties: *Bayer S.A. and Soytech Seeds Pesquisa em Soja Ltda.*

Act of Concentration No. 08012.006625/2011-19 (resolved on 27 July 2011). Parties: *Monsanto do Brasil Ltda. and Milênia Agrociências S.A.*

Act of Concentration No. 08012.004238/2010-62 (resolved on 9 November 2011). Parties: *São Cristóvão Administração e Participações Ltda.* and *Empresa Auto Ônibus Manoel Rodrigues S.A.*

Act of Concentration No. 08012.005889/2010-74 (resolved on 14 December 2011). Parties: *Fisher S/A Comércio, Indústria and Agricultura* and *Citrovita Agro Industrial Ltda.*

Act of Concentration No. 08012.009537/2011-79 (resolved on 8 February 2012). Parties: *Boston Medical Device, Inc. and ConvaTec Inc.*

Selected Bibliography

Act of Concentration No. 08012.012129/2011-02 (resolved on 14 March 2012). Parties: *Astic ED Participações S.A. and Instituição Educacional São Miguel Paulista S/S Ltda.*

Act of Concentration No. 08012.009361/2011-55 (resolved on 14 March 2012). Parties: *Bayer S.A. and Metropolitana Incorporações e Locação de Bens Ltda.*

Act of Concentration No. 08012.012722/2010-60 (resolved on 11 April 2012). Parties: *Copersucar S.A, Cosan S.A. Indústria e Comércio, Uniduto Logística S.A., Camargo Corrêa Óleo e Gás S.A., Odebrecht Transporte Participações S.A. and Petróleo Brasileiro S.A. – Petrobras.*

Act of Concentration No. 08012.001818/2012-64 (resolved on 9 May 2012). Parties: *EMDAPI — Empresa de Destinação Adequada de Pneumáticos Inservíveis Ltda., Goodyear do Brasil Produtos de Borracha Ltda, Pirelli Pneus Ltda, Bridgestone do Brasil Indústria e Comércio Ltda, Sociedade Michelin de Participações Industria e Comercio Ltda, and Continental do Brasil Produtos Automotivos Ltda.*

Acts of Concentration Nos 08012.001875/2010-81, 08012.001879/2010-60, 08012.002018/2010-07 and 08012.002259/2012-18 (resolved on 18 July 2012). Parties: *Votorantim Cimentos S.A., Camargo Corrêa S.A., Companhia Nacional de Cimento Portland, Cimpor – Cimentos de Portugal SGPS, S.A and CCB – Cimpor Cimentos do Brasil Ltda.*

Acts of Concentration Nos 08012.002018/2010-07 and 08012.001875/2010-81, (both resolved on 4 July 2012). Parties: *Carmargo Correa S/A, Votorantim Cimentos S.A., Cimpor – Cimentos de Portugal GSPS and Cimpor Cimentos do Brasil Ltda.*

Act of Concentration No. 08700.00398/2012-90 (resolved on 30 January 2013). Parties: *Unimed Franca - Sociedade Cooperativa de Serviços Médicos e Hospitalares S.A. and Hospital Regional de Franca.*

Act of Concentration No. 08012.006121/2012-80 (resolved on 30 January 2013). Parties: *Biolab Sanus Farmacêutica Ltda. Cristália Produtos Químicos Farmacêuticos ltda., Eurofarma Laboratórios S/A and Libbs Farmacêutica Ltda.*

Act of Concentration No. 08700.003356/2014-84 (resolved on 4 July 2014). Parties: *Copersucar S.A.* and *Cargill Agrícola S.A.*

Act of Concentration No. 08700.003748/2014-92 (resolved on 20 August 2014) (Dispatch No. 991 of the Superintendent-General of the CADE that approved the Opinion No. 262 of the Superintendency-General). Parties: *Bionovis S.A. - Companhia Brasileira de Biotecnologia Farmacêutica, Ares Trading AS* and *Merck KGaA.*

Act of Concentration No. 08700.005924/2014-20 (resolved on 25 August 2014) (Dispatch No. 1005 of the Superintendent-General of the CADE that approved Opinion No. 268 of the Superintendency-General). Parties: *Paraná Equipamentos S.A.* and *Caterpillar Global Mining LLC.*

Act of Concentration No. 08700.004963/2016-72 (resolved on 15 July 2016) (Dispatch No. 847 of the Superintendent-General of the CADE that approved Opinion No. 173/CGAA5/SGA1/SG pf the Superintendency-General). Parties: *Monsanto do Brasil Ltda.* and *DuPont do Brasil S.A.*

Administrative Process No. 0053/1992. Parties: *Office of the Public Attorney in the State of Sergipe v. Associação dos Hospitais do Estado de Sergipe.*

Administrative Process No. 0148/1992 (resolved on 22 October 1997). Parties: *Sindicato das indústrias de Panificação e Confeitarias do Estado de São Paulo and Associação*

das Indústrias de Panificação e Confeitaria de São Paulo v. Indústrias Alimentícias Gerais (IAG – Kibon).
Administrative Process No. 08012.005769/1998-92 (resolved on 19 January 2000). Parties: *SDE, ex officio, v. Sindicato dos Condutores Autônomos de Veículos Rodoviários de Brasília (SINDICAVIR/DF).*
Administrative Process No. 08012.000172/1998-42 (resolved on 26 March 2003). Parties: *Power-Tech Teleinformática Ltda. v. Matel Tecnologia de Informática Ltda. (Matec).*
Administrative Process No. 08000.024581/1994-77 (resolved on 3 March 2004). Parties: *Department of Economic Protection and Defence (DPDE) v. Sindicato do Comércio Varejista de Derivados de Petróleo do Distrito Federal (SINPETRO/DF), Rede Gasol (Grupo Cascão) and Rede Igrejinha.*
Administrative Process No. 08000.022487/1997-81 (resolved on 14 July 2004). Parties: *Messer Griesheim do Brasil Ltda. and Oxitec Indústria e Comércio Ltda. v. White Martins S/A. and Hospital de Clínicas da Universidade Federal do Paraná (UFPR).*
Administrative Process No. 08012.005459/2002-42 (resolved on 8 December 2004). Parties: *Attorney's Office in Bauru/SP v. Unimed de Jaú – Cooperativa de Trabalho Médico.*
Administrative Process No. 08012.008064/1997-82 (resolved on 19 January 2005). Parties: *Associação dos Concessionários Consumidores de Jazigos do Cemitério do Morumby v. Comunidade Religiosa João XXIII.*
Administrative Process No. 08012.008064/1997-82 (resolved on 19 January 2005). Parties: *Associação dos Concessionários Consumidores de Jazigos do Cemitério do Morumby v. Comunidade Religiosa João XXIII.*
Administrative Process No. 08000.016489/1997-21 (resolved on 11 May 2005). Parties: *Antônio Carlos de Moura Campos v. Ficsatur Agência de Turismo Ltda., Kamel Turismo and Chamonix Operadora de Turismo Ltda.*
Administrative Process No. 53500.001821/2002 (resolved on 14 September 2005). Parties: *Empresa Brasileira de Telecomunicações S/A (EMBRATEL) and Intelig Telecomunicações Ltda. (INTELIG) v. Telecomunicações de São Paulo S.A. (TELESP).*
Administrative Process No. 53500.001823/2002 (resolved on 14 September 2005). Parties: *Empresa Brasileira de Telecomunicações S/A (EMBRATEL) and Intelig Telecomunicações Ltda. (INTELIG) v. Telemar Norte/Leste S/A.*
Administrative Process No. 08012.009088/1999-48 (resolved on 13 October 2005). Parties: *Federal District Pharmacies Regional Council (CRF/DF) v. Abbott Laboratórios do Brasil Ltda., Akzo Nobel Ltda – Divisão Organon, Bayer S/A, Boeringher Ingelheim do Brasil Química e Farmacêutica Ltda., Bristol-Myers Squibb Brasil S/A, BYK Química Farmacêutica Ltda., Centeon Farmacêutica Ltda., Eli Lilly do Brasil Ltda., Eurofarma Laboratórios Ltda., Glaxo Wellcome S/A, Hoeschst Marion Roussel S/A, Indústria Química e Farmacêutica Schering Plough S/A, Janssen-Cilag Farmacêutica Ltda., Laboratórios Biosintética Ltda., Laboratórios Whyeth-Whitehall Ltda., Merck Sharp & Dohme Farmacêutica Ltda., Produtos Roché Química e Farmacêutica S/A, Sanofi Winthrop Farmacêutica Ltda., Schering do Brasil Química e Farmacêutica Ltda., SEARLE do Brasil Ltda.*

Selected Bibliography

Administrative Processes Nos 08000.022826/1995-11 and 08000.001430/1997-75 (both resolved on 30 August 2006). Parties: *Fortrade Fibras Sintéticas Ltda. v. Nitrocarbono S/A.*

Administrative Process No. 08000.024919/1995-62 (resolved on 30 August 2006). Parties: *Associação dos Produtores e Distribuidores de Insumos Reprográficos (APRODIR) v. Xerox do Brasil S/A.*

Administrative Process No. 08012.006274/2000-93 (resolved on 6 December 2006). Parties: *Vidraçaria Estrela – Klaier Indústria e Comércio Ltda. v. Companhia Vidraçaria Santa Marina and Blindex Vidros de Segurança Ltda.*

Administrative Process No. 08012.003048/2001-31 (resolved on 27 February 2007). Parties: *Associação NeoTV, 614 TVC S/A and others v. Globosat Programadora Ltda. and Globo Comunicações e Participações S/A.*

Administrative Process No. 08012.009312/1998-39 (resolved on 18 April 2007). Parties: *Cooperativa Regional dos Produtores Rurais de Pará de Minas Ltda. (COOPARÁ) v. Cooperativa Central dos Produtores Rurais de Minas Gerais Ltda. (CCPR).*

Administrative Process No. 08012.004599/1999-18 (resolved on 11 April 2007). Parties: *SDE, ex officio and Secretariat of Economic Monitoring (SEAE) v. La Roche Ltd., Basf Aktiengesellschaft, Aventis Animal Nutrition do Brasil Ltda. and F. Hoffmann – La Roche Ltd.*

Administrative Process No. 08012.001826/2003-10 (resolved on 19 September 2007). Parties: *SDE, ex officio v. Associação das Empresas de Vigilância do Rio Grande do Sul – ASSEVIRGS and others.*

Administrative Process No. 08012.000283/2006-66 (resolved on 17 April 2008). Parties: *SDE, ex officio v. Aro Mineração Ltda., Sociedade Mineradora Arroio dos Ratos – SOMAR and Comprove-Consultoria e Perícia Contábil Cível S/C.*

Administrative Process No. 08012.003805/2004-10 (resolved on 22 July 2009). Parties: *Primo Schincariol Indústria de Cervejas e Refrigerantes S/A v. Companhia de Bebidas das Americas (AmBev).*

Administrative Process No. 08012.004363/2000-89 (resolved on 28 October 2009). Parties: *CADE v. Companhia de Bebidas das Américas – AmBev.*

Administrative Process No. 08012.009888/2003-70 (resolved on 1 September 2010). Parties: *SDE, ex officio v. AGA S.A., Air Liquide Brasil Ltda., Air Products Brasil Ltda., White Martins Gases Industriais Ltda., White Martins Ltda., Indústria Brasileira de Gases Ltda., Newton de Oliveira, Walter Pilão, Vitor de Andrade Perez, Moacyr de Almeida, José Antônio Bortoleto de Campos, Hélio de Franceschi Junior, Gilberto Gallo, Carlos Alberto Cerezine.*

Administrative Process No. 08012.004283/2000-40 (resolved on 15 December 2010). Parties: *Comissão de Defesa do Consumidor, Meio Ambiente e Minorias da Câmara de Deputados v. Box 3 Vídeo e Publicidade Ltda. and Léo Produções e Publicidade Ltda.*

Administrative Process No. 08012.004702/2004-77 (resolved on 9 May 2012). Parties: *SDE, ex officio, v. Peróxidos do Brasil Ltda., Solvay do Brasil Ltda., Nicolas Makay Júnior, Carlos Alberto Tieghi, Paulo Francisco Trévia Schirch, Luiz Leonardo da Silva Filho, Gibran João Tarantino, Sérgio Afonso Zini, Roberto Nascimento da Silva, Degussa Aktiengesellschaft, Degussa Brasil Ltda., Weber Ferreira Porto, Dirk Egon*

Regett, Marcelo Ronald Schaalmann, Roberto de Barcellar Blanco, Sidnei Inácio Cestari, Werner Karl Ross, Hans Willmann, Wilfried Eul and *Karl-Erhard Müller.*
Administrative Process No. 08012.006439/2009-65 (resolved on 23 May 2012). Parties: *Associação Brasileira de Bebidas – ABRABE and Cervejaria Kaiser S.A. v. Companhia de Bebidas das Américas – AmBev.*
Administrative Process No. 08012.002474/2008-24 (resolved on 10 January 2013). Parties: *Associação dos Fabricantes de Refrigerantes do Brasil (Afrebras), Cervejaria Imperial, Associação Brasileira de Bebidas (Abrabe) and Cervejaria Kaiser Brasil S/A. v. Companhia de Bebidas das Américas (AmBev).*
Administrative Process No. 08012.001772/2009-88 (resolved on 10 December 2013). Parties: *SDE, ex officio v. Associação Brasileira da Indústria de Chocolates, Cacau, Amendoim, Balas e Derivados (Abicab) and others.*
Administrative Process No. 08012.004365/2010-66 (resolved on 28 January 2014). Parties: *Ministério Público do Estado de Santa Catarina v. Farmácia Frei Rogério, Farmácia Aparecida, Farmácia Atual, Farmácia Graciosa, Farmácia Moderna, Farmácia Santa Bárbara, Farmácia São João, Farmácia Sul Brasil and Farmácia Vital.*
Administrative Process No. 08012.008554/2008-93 (resolved on 11 February 2014). Parties: *Cervejaria Kaiser Brasil S/A v. Companhia de Bebidas das Américas (AmBev).*
Administrative Proceeding No. 08000.009354/97-82 (resolved on 20 August 2014). Parties: *SDE, ex officio, v. AgipLiquigás do Brasil S.A. et alii.*
Administrative Process No. 08012.009885/2009-21 (resolved on 20 April 2015). Parties: *Companhia de Saneamento Básico do Estado de São Paulo (SABESP) v. Saenge Engenharia de Saneamento e Edificações Ltda., Ônix Construções S.A. (Concic Construções Especiais S.A.), Luiz Arnaldo Pereira Mayer, Marcos Assumpção Pacheco de Medeiros; Antônio Silva de Góes, João Antônio da Silva Saramago, Paulo Bie and Marcus Perdiz da Silva.*
Administrative Process No. 08012.009462/2006-69 (resolved on 25 August 2015). Parties: *Mattel do Brasil Ltda. v. ABRINQ – Associação Brasileira dos Fabricantes de Brinquedos and Synésio Batista da Costa.*
Administrative Process No. 08012.009264/2002-71 (resolved on 20 October 2015). Parties: *SEAE v. GSL Carbon Aktiengesllchaft Showadenco Carbon, Carbides/Graphites Group, Mitsubishi Corporation, Tokai carbon and Ucar internacional.*
Administrative Process No. 08012.012081/2007-48, (resolved on 18 November 2015). Parties: *CADE v. Shopping Eldorado, Shopping Higienópolis, Shopping Jardim Sul, Morumbi Shopping and Shopping Vila-Lobos.*
Administrative Process No. 08012.003321/2004-71 (resolved on 19 April 2016). Parties: *SDE, ex officio v. Baxter AG, Immuno Produtos Biológicos, Octapharma Ag and others.*
Administrative Process No. 08012.011980/2008-12 (ongoing process), in re. *SDE ex officio v. Chunghwa Picture Tubes Ltd. et alii.*
Administrative Process No. 08012.002414/2009-92 (ongoing process). Parties: *SDE, ex officio v. Chunghwa Picture Tubes Ltd., Samsung SDI Co. Ltd., Royal Philips Electronics N.V., Philips do Brasil Ltda., LG Electronics, Inc., LG Electronics da Amazônia Ltda., LG Electronics de São Paulo Ltda., LP Displays International Ltd., LP Displays Amazônia Ltda., Technicolor S.A. (Thomson S.A.), ARV Representações*

Ltda, MT Picture Display Co. Ltd. (Matsushita Toshiba Picture Display Co. Ltd.), Toshiba Corporation, Thai CRT Company Limited, Orion Electric Corporation Ltd., Leo Mink, José Jorge Duaik, Joel Garbi, João Gordo, Roberto Ribeiro, Joon Yong Park, Seong Dae Lim, Jeong Il Son, Yang Sheng Ren, Shih-Ming Chen, Cheng Yuan Lin, Airton Rodrigues Veras, Yasukawa, Tomori, Nishimura, Montri, Kyung Hoon Choi and others.

Administrative Process No. 08012.010338/2009-99 (ongoing process). Parties: *SDE, ex officio v. Chunghwa Picture Tubes Ltd., Samsung SDI Co. Ltd., Royal Philips Electronics N.V., LG Electronics, Inc., LP Displays International Ltd., MT Picture Display Co. Ltd. (Matsushita Toshiba Picture Display Co. Ltd.), Orion Electric Corporation Ltd., Cheng Yuan Lin, Wen Jun Cheng and others.*

Administrative Process No. 08012.005255/2010-11 (ongoing process). Parties: *SDE, ex officio v. Elpida Memory Inc., Hitachi Ltd., Hynix Semiconductor, Inc.; Infineon Technologies, AG; Micron Technology, Inc.; Mitsubishi Electric Corp.; Nanya Technology Corporation; NEC Corporation; Samsung Electronics Company, Ltd.; Samsung Semiconductor, Inc.; Toshiba Corporation; Sun Woo Lee; Yeongho Kang; Young Woo Lee; Il Ung Kim; Thomas Quinn, Young Hwan Park,; T. Rudd Corwin; Heinrich Florian; Günter Hefner; Peter Schaefer; Dae Soo Kim; Chae Kyun Chung; Kun Chul Suh; Choon Yub Choi; Alfred P. Censullo; and D. James Sogas.*

Administrative Process No. 08012.002608/2007-26 (ongoing process). Parties: *Cervejaria Kaiser Brasil S/A v. Companhia de Bebidas das Américas (AmBev) and Cervejarias Reunidas Skol Caracu S/A.*

Administrative Process No. 08012.000291/2004-41 (ongoing process). Parties: *Agência Nacional de Energia Elétrica (ANEEL) v. Conservo Brasília Empresa de Segurança Ltda. and others.*

Administrative Process No. 08012.012740/2007-56 (ongoing process). Parties: *Ministério Público Federal – Procuradoria da República no Rio Grande do Sul v. Administradora Gaúcha de Shopping Centres S/C Ltda. (Shopping Iguatemi) and others.*

Administrative Process No. 08012.004674/2006-50 (ongoing process). Parties: *Senator Eduardo Matarazzo Suplicy v. ABIEF – Associação Brasileira de Embalagens Flexíveis and others.*

Motion for Clarification No. 08700.003200/2006-32 on Act of Concentration No. 08012.005539/2004-60 (resolved on 22 November 2006). Parties: *Petrobrás Distribuidora S/A and Agip do Brasil S/A.*

Motion for Clearance No. 0020/1997 (resolved on 22 October 1997). Consultants: *Ferrero do Brasil Indústria Doceira and Alimentar Ltda.*

Motion for Clarification in Act of Concentration No. 08012.002915/2009-79 (resolved on 16 September 2009). Parties: *Penske Logistics do Brasil Ltda. and ABX Logistics – Air & Sea Worldwide NV/S.A.*

Motion for Clarification in Act of Concentration No. 08012.009599/2009-66 (resolved on 9 June 2010). Parties: *Pepsico do Brasil Ltda. and Quercegen Agronegócios I Ltda.*

Motion for Clarification in Act of Concentration No. 08012.005296/2010-16 (resolved on 4 August 2010). Parties: *UBS AG and Link Holding Financeira S.A.*

Motion for Revision based on new fact No. 08700.003776/05-19 in Administrativa Process No. 08012.005296/2010-16 (resolved on 24 May 2006). Parties: *SDE, ex officio v. TBA Informática Ltda. and Microsoft Infomática Ltda.*

Motion for Settlement No. 08700.001151/2012-41 (resolved on 25 April 2012). Parties: *Telemar Norte Leste S/A, Telemar Internet Ltda., Brasil Telecom S/A* and *BRT Serviços de Internet S/A.*, Administrative Process No. 08012.001099/1999-71 (resolved in 23 May 2012). Parties: *Steel Placas Indústria e Comércio Ltda. v. Comepla Indústria e Comércio, Reprinco Indústria e Comércio Ltda,* and *Queiroz & Souza Comércio de Placas Automotivas Ltda.*

Motion for Settlement No. 08700.006078/2014-66 (resolved on 6 August 2014). Parties: *Hipercard Banco Múltiplo S.A. and Bompreço Bahia Supermercados Ltda.*

Preliminary Investigation No. 08012.006744/1997-16 (resolved on 10 November 1999). Parties: *ABRADES – Associação Brasileira de Distribuidores Exclusivos de Sorvetes v. Kibon S.A. – Indústrias Alimentícias and Kraft Suchard Brasil S/A.*

Preliminary Investigation No. 08012.009264/2003-5 (resolved on 6 April 2005). Parties: *Siderúrgica Oriente Ltda. and Massa Falida da Companhia Metalúrgica do Espírito Santo v. Companhia Vale do Rio Doce (CVRD).*

Preliminary Investigation No. 08012.006717/2000-46 (resolved on 26 July 2006). Parties: *Labo Cine do Brasil Ltda. v. Eastman Kodak Company – Latin American Region.*

Preliminary Investigation No. 08000.019594/1997-12 (resolved on 30 August 2006). Parties: *Interlar – Hidráulica e Materiais para Construção Ltda. v. Indústria de Fundição Tupy Ltda.*

Preliminary Investigation No. 53500.004242/2004 (resolved on 17 January 2007). Parties: *Telemar Norte Leste S/A v. Telesp Celular S.A ('Vivo')* et al.

Preliminary Investigation No. 53500.005669/2002 (resolved on 11 July 2007). Parties: *Empresa Brasileira de Telecomunicações S.A. (EMBRATEL) v. Brasil Telecom S.A.*

Preliminary Investigation No. 08012.003882/1999-13 (resolved on 10 October 2007). Parties: *SWC – Prestadora de Serviços em Taxímetros v. Fumaça Instrumentos de Precisão Ltda. and Silmar Eletrônica e Mecânica de Precisão Ltda.*

Preliminary Investigation No. 08012.000387/2000-03 (resolved on 12 December 2007). Parties: *ABRANET – Associação Brasileira de Acesso, Serviços e Informações de Provedores de Internet v. Telecomunicações de São Paulo S/A (Telefonica), Terra Livre/ZAZ – Ces Interpatent Ltda., Unibanco – União de Bancos Brasileiros S.A., Banco Brasileiro de Descontos S/A – Bradesco and Internet Grátis – IG (Vladisvostok Comercial Ltda.).*

Preliminary Investigation No. 08012.003380/1999-57 (resolved on 16 January 2008). Parties: *Regional Council of Pharmacy of the State of Sao Paulo (CRF/SP) v. UNIMED Intrafederativa – Federação do Nordeste Paulista et alii.*

Preliminary Investigation No. 08012.007897/2005-98 (resolved on 23 July 2008). Parties: *Refinaria de Petróleo de Manguinhos S.A. and Refinaria de Petróleo Ipiranga S.A v. Petróleo Brasileiro S.A. (Petrobrás).*

Preliminary Investigation No. 08012.005052/2001-34 (resolved on 23 July 2008). Parties: *SDE, ex officio, v. Fundação Ruben Berta, Transbrasil S/A Linhas Aéreas, Amadeus Global Travel Distribution S/A, Amadeus Brasil Ltda. and Varig S/A.*

Selected Bibliography

Preliminary Investigation No. 08012.006637/2005-03 (resolved on 3 September 2008). Parties: *Regional Pharmacy Council of Minas Gerais v. Unimed Minas/ Federação Interfederativa das Cooperativas de Trabalho Médico do Estado de Minas Gerais.*

Preliminary Investigation No. 08012.005307/2002-40 (resolved on 26 November 2008). Parties: *Amadeus Global Travel Distribution S.A and Amadeus Brasil Ltda. v. Sabre International Inc.*

Preliminary Investigation No. 08012.007692/1999-11 (resolved on 17 December 2008) Parties: *Auto Posto Esmeraldas Ltda. v. Esso Brasileira de Petróleo Ltda.*

Preliminary Investigation No. 08012.009696/2008-78 (resolved on 10 December 2008). Parties: *Associação Brasileira dos Provedores de Acesso, Serviços e Informações da Rede Internet (ABRANET) v. Telecomunicações de São Paulo S.A. (TELESP).*

Preliminary Investigation No. 08012.006111/2003-53 (resolved on 4 February 2009). Parties: *Agência Reguladora de Serviços Públicos do Rio Grande do Norte (ASERP) v. Companhia Energética do Rio Grande do Norte (COSERN) and Neoenergia S.A.*

Preliminary Investigation No. 08012.005181/2006-37 (resolved on 29 April 2009). Parties: *Videolar S.A. v. Koninklijke Philips Electronics N.V.*

Preliminary Investigation No. 08012.006899/2003-06 (resolved on 22 July 2009). Parties: *Instituto Radiológico Bento Gonçalves Ltda. v. Sociedade Dr Bartholomeu Tacchini.*

Preliminary Investigations Nos 08012.006835/2003-05 and 08012.004062/2005-86 (both resolved on 28 October 2009). Parties: *SDE, ex officio v. ASA Indústria e Comércio Ltda., Associação Brasileira das Indústrias de Produtos de Limpeza e Afins – ABIPLA, Blue Chemical do Brasil Indústria e Comércio de Detergentes Ltda., Ceras Johnson Ltda., Procter & Gamble Industrial e Comercial Ltda., Química Amparo Ltda., Quinvale Industrial Ltda., Reckit & Colman Indústria Ltda., REVEL S.A. Indústria e Comércio, SAVON – Indústria, Comércio, Importação e Exportação Ltda. and Unilever Brasil Ltda.*

Preliminary Investigation No. 08012.005994/2004-65 (resolved on 11 November 2009). Parties: *Leopoldo Ubiratan Carreiro Pagotto v. Sindicato das Empresas de Artes Fotográficas no Estado de São Paulo.*

Preliminary Investigation No. 08012.009914/2006-11 (resolved on 25 November 2009). Parties: *Pneus Hauer Brasil Ltda. v. Federal Union.*

Preliminary Investigation No. 08012.008443/2007-04 (resolved on 16 December 2009). Parties: *Attorney General's Office v. Adidas Brasil Ltda., ASICS Tiger do Brasil Indústria e Comércio Ltda., Nike do Brasil Comércio e Participações Ltda., Puma Sports Ltda., São Paulo Alpargatas S.A. (Rainha, Topper e Distribuidor Mizuno), Vulcabrás do Nordeste S.A (Olympikus).*

Preliminary Investigation No. 08012.001952/2008-89 (resolved on 20 January 2010). Parties: *Dry Color Especialidades Químicas Ltda. v. Colormatrix América do Sul Ltda.*

Preliminary Investigation No. 08012.008845/2006-10 (resolved on 3 March 2010). Parties: *CADE v. Companhia Ultragás S.A., Copagaz Distribuidora de Gás Ltda., Liquigás Distribuidora S.A., Nacional Gás Butano Distribuidora Ltda. and SHV Gás Brasil Ltda.*

Preliminary Investigation No. 08012.006274/2009-21 (resolved on 7 April 2010). Parties: *Roberto Marinho Paredes v. Companhia de Bebidas das Americas (AmBev).*

Preliminary Investigation No. 08012.001366/2009-15 (resolved on 9 June 2010). Parties: *Federal Prosecutor – Attorney's Office in Minas Gerais v. TAM Linhas Aéreas S.A. and Gol Linhas Aéreas S.A.*

Preliminary Investigation No. 08012.003762/2005-53 (resolved on 9 June 2010). Parties: *Mérito Assessoria & Consultoria Empresarial Ltda. (Med Life Saúde) v. Sociedade Matonense de Benemerência (Hospital Carlos Fernando Malzoni).*

Preliminary Investigation No. 08012.007704/2004-18 (resolved on 7 July 2010). Parties: *Antônio Luís Guimarães de Álvares Otero v. Qualix Serviços Ambientais Ltda., CAVO Serviços e Meio Ambiente S/A, CBPO Engenharia Ltda., Cliba Ltda., Consita Ltda., Construban Engenharia e Construções Ltda., Construtora Gomes Lourenço Ltda., Construtora Oas Ltda., Construtora Queiroz Galvão S/A, Delta Construções, Fernando José Morais Fisher, H. Guedes Engenharia Ltda., Heleno & Fonseca Construtécnica S/A José Eduardo da Costa Freitas, Leão Ltda., Limpebras Engenharia Ambiental Ltda., LOT Operações Técnicas Ltda., Luiz Claudio Ferreira Leão, Marcelo Franzine, MB Engenharia e Meio Ambiente S/C Ltda., Múcio de Castro Maia, SPL Construtora e Pavimentadora Ltda., Stemag Engenharia e Construções Ltda., Vagner Roberto Monari, Vega Engenharia Ambiental S/A, Villanova Engenharia e Desenvolvimento Ambiental S/A, Wilney Marcio Barquete.*

Preliminary Investigation No. 08012.003648/1998-05 (resolved on 18 August 2010). Parties: *Figueroa Campos Indústria e Comércio Ltda. v. White Martins S/A.*

Preliminary Investigation No. 08012.002673/2007-51 (resolved on 15 December 2010). Parties: *Associação Nacional dos Fabricantes de Autopeças (ANFAPE) v. Volkswagen do Brasil Indústria de Veículos Automotores Ltda., Fiat Automóveis S.A. and Ford Motor Company Brasil Ltda.*

Preliminary Investigation No. 08012.011463/2007-54 (resolved on 19 January 2011) Parties: *Prontomed Sociedade Simples v. Santa Casa de Arcos.*

Preliminary Investigation No. 08012.006978/2005-71 (resolved on 19 January 2011). Parties: *CADE v. Câmara do Livro do DF.*

Preliminary Investigation No. 08012.101986/2006-01 (resolved on 1 March 2011). Parties: SDE, *ex-officio, v. Cooperativa Central dos Produtores Rurais de MG – CCPR.*

Preliminary Investigation No. 08700.004336/2007-41 (resolved on 18 May 2011). Parties: *Tribunal Regional do Trabalho da 1ª Região v. ThyssenKrup Elevadores S/A.*

Preliminary Investigation No. 08012.000204/2001-11 (resolved on 4 May 2011) Parties: *Labnew Indústria e Comércio Ltda.v. Becton, Dickinson Indústrias Cirúrgicas Ltda.,*

Preliminary Investigation No. 08012.000204/2001-11 (resolved on 4 May 2011) Parties: *Labnew Indústria e Comércio Ltda.v. Becton, Dickinson Indústrias Cirúrgicas Ltda.,*

Preliminary Investigation No. 08012.002417/2008-45 (resolved on 13 July 2011). Parties: *Redisbel — Redenção Distribuidora de Bebidas Ltda. v. Companhia de Bebidas da América – AMBEV.*

Preliminary Investigation No. 08012.002856/2008-58 (resolved on 27 July 2011). Parties: *Procuradoria Geral da República v. Juntas Comerciais dos Estados e do Distrito Federal.*

Preliminary Investigation No. 08012.001743/2002-40 (resolved on 27 July 2011). Parties: *João Carlos Ferreira da Silva v. Editora Globo, Editora Nova Era, Editora Civilização Brasileira, Editora Record, Editora Moderna e Salamandra, Editora Ltda., Editora Renovar, Editora Saraiva, Editora Rocco, Editora Revista dos Tribunais,*

Selected Bibliography

Editora Nova Fronteira, Editora Lúmen Júris, LTC Editora, Editora Guanabara Koogan, Editora Forense, Editora Cortez, Editora Atlas et alii.

Preliminary Investigation No. 08012.004308/2005-10 (resolved on 13 July 2011). Parties: *Ministério Público do Estado do Rio de Janeiro v. Informix do Brasil Comércio e Serviços Ltda.*

Preliminary Investigation No. 08700.000558/2008-75 (resolved on 13 July 2011). Parties: *RIOURBE — Empresa Municipal de Urbanização v. Ortosíntese Indústria e Comércio Ltda.*

Preliminary Investigation No. 08012.001022/2008-25 (resolved on 25 January 2012), in re. *Sindicato da Indústria da Extração do Sal no Estado do Rio Grande do Norte – SIESAL* and *Federação das Indústrias do Estado do Rio Grande do Norte – FIERN v. Sociedad Anóonima Empresa Marítima – Empremar S/A.*

Preliminary Investigation No. 08012.012495/2007-77 (resolved on 30 January 2013) in re. *Sindicato dos Cultivadores de Cana-de-Açúcar do Estado de Pernambuco v. ANP.*

Preliminary Investigation No. 08012.006307/1999-73 (resolved on 23 February). Parties: *CADE v. Sindicato de Produtores de Castanha de Caju – SINCAJU.*

Writ of mandamus – Mandado de Segurança No. 2002.34.00.033475-0/DF (Resp 664189 at STF) (ongoing process). Parties: *Bradesco S.A. and Banco de Crédito Nacional S/A (BCN) v. CADE.*

BRAZIL. 28th Civil Circuit of Belo Horizonte, Minas Gerais

Class Action No. 00.24 09709934-5 (ongoing process). Parties: *Associação de Hospitais de Minas Gerais (AHMG) v. White Martins Gases Industriais Ltda., Air Liquide Brasil Ltda., AGA S/A, Air Products Brasil Ltda. and Indústria Brasileira de Gases Ltda. (IBG).*

BRAZIL. Federal Circuit

Class Action No. 0029912-22.2001.403.6100 (2001.61.00.029912-6) (resolved on 16 May 2010). Parties: *Ministério Público Federal v. Abbott Laboratórios do Brasil Ltda. et alii.* Judge of the 14th. Civil Trial Court in São Paulo, Alternate Judge, Cláudia Rinaldi Fernandes, resolved (trial court level) in 16 June 2010.

Ordinary Annulment Action No. 2008.34.00.011433-3 (ongoing process). Parties: *Dow Agrosciences Industrial Ltda. and Monsanto Company v. CADE.*

Ordinary Civil Actions Nos 2007.34.00.043978-7 and others. Parties: *Abbott Laboratórios do Brasil Ltda. et alii v. CADE.* Resolved (trial court level) on 9 December 2011, at the 4th Federal Court of the Federal District (Judge Itagiba Catta Preta Neto). Ongoing process at the appeal level at TRF).

Selected Bibliography

Index

The numbers here refer to paragraph numbers.

Abuse of dominance, 96, 196–204, 443, 504, 505, 687

Cartels, 63, 103, 106, 188–191, 258, 274, 319, 325, 329–379, 732
Civil enforcement, 304–317
Complaints, 320, 733–736
Concentrations, 100–101, 120, 158, 165, 169, 178, 193, 205, 206, 253, 387, 400, 425, 524, 582–726, 819, 823, 836, 838, 844, 847, 848, 850
Concerted practices, 185–192
Conglomerate mergers, 676–705
Cooperation agreements, 61, 62, 395–421, 582, 753, 874, 877

Damages, 258, 305, 307–312, 315
De minimis, 92–94, 194, 211, 790, 819
Discrimination, 359, 509–528, 573
Dominant Position, 75, 99, 105, 153–184, 203–205, 240, 251, 423, 443, 448, 457, 469, 487, 492, 497, 505, 507, 512, 525, 536, 626, 686, 727, 795

Excessive/unfair pricing, 506–508
Exclusive dealing, 203, 441–450
Exclusive distributorship, 433–440

Failing firm defence, 644, 698
Franchising, 465–473

Group boycotts, 370–374

Horizontal agreements, 332–421
Horizontal mergers, 590–651

Information exchange, 380–394
Intellectual Property licensing, 481–502
Interim measures, 301–303, 313–317, 887
Investigating and search powers, 744–752

Judicial review, 880, 890–892
Joint ventures, 126, 213–221, 389, 390, 392, 413, 414, 449, 582, 587, 669, 706–726, 841

Know-how and trade secret licensing, 474–502

Leniency, 255–269

Market/client allocation, 361–365
Market power, 109, 130, 138, 153–184, 203, 354, 435, 436, 455, 463, 508, 562, 616–624, 626, 627, 629, 634, 647, 654, 657, 726, 812, 815, 853
Merger control *see* Concentrations

Patent licensing, 481–502
Per se prohibitions, 109–116
Predation, 529–546
Price fixing, 335, 346–360, 352–354, 358, 359, 375, 466
Price squeeze, 573–581
Production/Innovation limitation, 345, 366–369

Rebates, 383, 555–561
Refusal to deal, 562–572
Relevant market, 72, 93, 96, 97, 101, 105, 120, 137–152, 153, 154, 156, 158, 159, 189, 203, 205, 251, 332, 337, 370, 443, 458, 459, 472, 475, 492, 503, 536, 538, 539, 553, 590, 606–608, 610, 611, 620,

621, 625, 636, 648, 650, 655, 656, 696, 706, 716, 719, 787, 795, 802–804, 813, 819, 831, 841, 851Requests for information, 288, 737–743
Right of defence, 755–783, 844–846

Selective distribution, 451–464
Settlement Agreements, 270–277
State-owned enterprises, 88–91
Sensible effect, 92–94
Statement of objections, 685, 704, 827, 833, 872

Trademark licensing, 481–502
Tying, 547–554

Undertakings, 96–99, 503–581, 847–873

Vertical agreements, 422–502

Made in the USA
Monee, IL
16 September 2026

63296745R00111